CW01668814

The Sp

PLACE

An anthology of travel writings

compiled by Malcolm Venter

Oxford
Cape Town
1992

OXFORD UNIVERSITY PRESS

Walton Street, Oxford OX2 6DP, United Kingdom

Oxford New York Toronto
Delhi Bombay Calcutta Madras Karachi
Petaling Jaya Singapore Hong Kong Tokyo
Nairobi Dar es Salaam Cape Town
Melbourne Auckland

and associated companies in
Berlin Ibadan

THE SPIRIT OF PLACE
ISBN 0 19 570719 2
First published 1992

Publisher's Note:
In this anthology, foreign words and phrases appearing in bold are listed in the glossary at the back of the book.

© Oxford University Press 1992

OXFORD is a trademark of Oxford University Press

All rights reserved. No part of this publication may be reproduced, stored in a retrieval system, or transmitted in any form or by any means, electronic, mechanical, photocopying, recording or otherwise, without the prior written permission of the copyright owner.

Cover photography by Juan Espi

Published by Oxford University Press Southern Africa, Harrington House, Barrack Street, Cape Town, 8001, South Africa

Set in 9½ on 12 pt Garamond by Theiner Typesetting (Pty) Ltd
Reproduction by Theiner Typesetting (Pty) Ltd
Printed and bound by Clyson Printers

"...we are all travellers in what John Bunyan calls the wilderness of this world..."

Robert Louis Stevenson

"...all experience is an arch wherethro'
Gleams that untravell'd world, whose margin fades
Forever and ever when I move."

Tennyson *Ulysses*

CONTENTS

PREFACE

The Spirit of Place is an anthology of stories, extracts and letters which capture different writers' feelings about places that have a special meaning for them. The pieces are autobiographical, and the descriptions of each place will certainly inspire the reader to travel widely - in spirit, if not in body.

The selection of writings is as different as the places covered in the anthology. Many of the authors are South African, others write from all corners of the earth. Some of the pieces are thought-provoking, possibly even polemic, while others are intended mainly to entertain. Genres differ - there are explanatory or descriptive extracts from larger pieces, journal entries, letters, and short stories. Some pieces are serious in tone, others comic, or whimsical. Settings include southern Africa, Egypt, Europe, North America, India and Greece.

The anthology therefore presents the reader with a wide variety of styles, perspectives and experiences, and should serve as a useful introduction to various authors of note.

Each piece is prefaced with an introductory note on the author, intended to give the reader some idea of who the author is, and why he or she has been included in this anthology. Background information has also been included. A comprehensive glossary at the back of the book provides additional information on foreign words and phrases.

Bon voyage!

Malcolm Venter
Durbanville
March 1992

• INNOCENTS ABROAD •

Herman Charles Bosman (1905–1951)

Herman Charles Bosman was born in Kuilsriver, near Cape Town, and later went to the Transvaal, where he qualified as a teacher. In 1926, the year in which he took up his first teaching post in the Marico District, he was sentenced to death for shooting his step-brother. His sentence was subsequently commuted to life sentence. He was released after four years, whereupon he returned to Johannesburg.

Bosman's short stories are the subject of most of his fame: Roy Campbell once described them as 'the best that ever came out of South Africa'. According to the editors of The Companion to South African English Literature, *'any anthology of South African short stories that excludes the work of this prolific writer would not be judged complete'.*

Bosman travelled abroad on a number of occasions, and here expresses some of his beliefs about travel. The extract is from **A Cask of Jerepigo,** *which was first published by Human and Rousseau.*

A singular circumstance with regard to my own life, that I have observed in the course of the years, is that when I have been passing through a fairly lengthy period of mental strain, so that I find myself to be badly in need of a change, then I discover that it is the people around me who are making arrangements to go on extended vacations. Not me, of course. Oh, no. And another queer thing, too, that I have noticed, is that when I am in this condition in which I sigh for a change of scene, for a little while to bask pleasantly in the sun, then through some inexplicable linking together of coincidence the reading matter that I accumulate over a week-end all deals with people on holiday. This week-end, for instance, I find myself with Mark Twain's *The Innocents Abroad*, Jerome K. Jerome's *Three Men on the Bummel* and an Afrikaans translation of Silvio Pellico's *Ten Years in Prison.* Three delightfully escapist volumes, each having as theme the recording of a brief time of recess from the daily grind.

I am reading these books, of course. And I find them very interesting, of course – even after (in the case of *The Innocent Abroad*) the eleventh reading. But all the time, at the back of my mind, I am conscious of the existence of certain wicked, envious thoughts. Mark Twain, Jerome K. Jerome and Silvio Pellico had all the luck, I feel: they had, all three of them, each in a different way, been furnished on a generous scale with facilities for taking it easy.

At the present moment there are I just don't know how many people of my acquaintance who are proceeding abroad on a variety of earnest quests – relating, in the main, to the establishment of commercial ties or the pursuit of knowledge. Only a small minority make the candid admission that they are going overseas – to England or Europe, mostly – because there are certain features associated with foreign travel that are not altogether disagreeable.

A little while ago I had occasion to take leave, in Johannesburg, of a young lady with literary interests who was shortly embarking for England to study further. The passenger-list of every boat sailing from Cape Town to Southampton contains a liberal sprinkling of the names of South Africans of both sexes in this category. Sometimes it is more than a sprinkling, so that the list has got a peculiarly mottled sort of appearance that, for all its oddity, is not altogether unpleasing to the eye.

Anyway, this young lady in question, with literary interests, who was to make one of the boat-load of passengers sailing from Cape Town to Southampton on that particular week, informed me, in as casual a way as you please, that she was going to the United Kingdom.

My, I thought. There was something for you, now. Not like it was in the old days, when we used to board a boat for just plain England. No, she was proceeding to the whole of the United Kingdom. Meaning England and Scotland together, I reflected, through the Union of the Crowns, not to mention the legislative incorporation of England and Scotland in 1707. Naturally, I was impressed. A journey covering 6 000 miles of geographical distance could, I know, present certain vexatious aspects at times. But here was this young lady so utterly heedless of her personal safety as to be preparing to travel through a pretty solemn space of history as well. I only hoped that she would be cautioned in advance about that dangerous corner near the turn of the seventeenth century. It would be too bad if she got beheaded, or something, through accidental involvement in a religious or dynastic issue that could not have any deep significance for her.

I even wondered if that was, perhaps, why she had said 'United Kingdom' in such reverential tones. With such devout gravity. Almost as though she had said 'Kingdom Come.'

Afterwards, however, when the young lady had left, it struck me that she might have said that she was going to the United Kingdom – all of it, like that and not just England, or London – merely so as to be on the safe side, in case the Union Castle liner went off its course and, instead of Southampton, docked in the Stronsay Firth, Orkney Islands, in the shoals among the Scotch mists, with the skipper none the wiser.

Yet, during all this time, while the young lady with literary interests who was going abroad was talking, there was something that I felt I had to tell her. But I never got so far, of course. For one thing, she was talking so fast about what she believed the United Kingdom to be like (this being her first visit there), that I couldn't get in more than a couple of words now and again, edgeways. For another thing, it is no use trying to teach people with literary interests anything.

Nevertheless, if I could have got in a complete sentence, and if I thought that that young lady would pay any attention to what I had to communicate, then I would have tried to give her some sort of idea as to how far the United Kingdom really is removed from South Africa. I would have tried to make it clear to her as to why it is only in the English language that the expression, 'keeping one's distance', has got currency. I mean, if you talk to a person in England, and he's at all well-bred, he'll keep you at a proper distance. And when two well-bred people (I am not talking about loafers, now), converse in the southern part of the United Kingdom (I am saying nothing about the northern part, now), each one keeping the other at a proper distance, then the space between them is considerably more than just the 6 000 miles separating Table Bay from Southampton Water.

What I am seeking to infer is that when one arrives in Southampton, having accomplished the voyage from Cape Town, one is not of necessity brought any nearer to the United Kingdom (southern part).

Some time later I realised that I was just being jealous of this girl because she was going abroad under conditions that were novel to me. Everything connected with her departure seemed to me so unorthodox. For instance, she wasn't afraid to let anybody know where she was going. And then, she spent a long time in saying good-bye to people. And she was leaving South Africa because she wished to go elsewhere, and not because she had to get out of South Africa – quick. Furthermore, she would arrive in London, eventually, because that was where she wanted to be – and not just through the circumstance of there not having been a ship for Australia when she went to make enquiries at the Cape Town docks, at night.

I can see now that what I resented was the unconventional way in which this young lady set about her trip overseas. She even left a forwarding address. The next thing, I felt, that she would do when she got to London, would be to go and visit Westminster Abbey and the Tower and the Tate Gallery and the National Gallery and the Victoria and Albert Museum, and get mistaken ideas about culture, instead of walking about in the sleet, battling for a living, with cardboard in her shoes.

But how do we know that this young lady's way of doing things, unorthodox though it appears, may not perhaps be the right way? When one is in Paris, for instance, should one not perhaps go and visit the Louvre and Notre Dame and the Madeleine? I wonder ...

Maybe, next time I'm around there, I just will go and give those places the once-over.

• WHY NOT STAY AT HOME? •

Aldous Huxley (1894–1963)

Aldous Huxley, novelist and essayist, was born in England but later moved to California. He obtained a degree in English in Oxford and then moved into the world of writing. In the years that he lived in Italy, he wrote the sceptical and witty novels associated with his name, the most famous of which is **Brave New World**. *During that period he also published several books of essays.*

The essay which follows first appeared in an anthology entitled **Along the Road**, *published by Chatto and Windus.*

Some people travel on business, some in search of health. But it is neither the sickly nor the men of affairs who fill the Grand Hotels and the pockets of their proprietors. It is those who travel 'for pleasure' as the phrase goes. What **Epicurus**, who never travelled except when he was banished, sought in his own garden, our tourists seek abroad. And do they find their happiness? Those who frequent the places where they resort must often find this question, with a tentative answer in the negative fairly forced upon them. For tourists are, in the main, a very gloomy-looking tribe. I have seen much brighter faces at a funeral than in the Piazza of St. Mark's. Only when they can band together and pretend, for a brief, precarious hour, that they are at home, do the majority of tourists look really happy. One wonders why they come abroad.

The fact is that very few travellers really like travelling. If they go to the trouble and expense of travelling, it is not so much from curiosity, for fun, or because they like to see things beautiful and strange, as out of a kind of snobbery. People travel for the same reason as they collect works of art: because the best people do it. To have been to certain spots on the earth's surface is socially correct; and having been there, one is superior to those who have not. Moreover, travelling gives one something to talk about when one gets home. The subjects of conversation are not so numerous that one can neglect an opportunity of adding to one's store.

To justify this snobbery, a series of myths has gradually been elaborated. The places which it is socially smart to have visited are aureoled with glamour, till they are made to appear, for those who have not been there, like so many fabled Babylons or Baghdads. Those who have travelled have a personal interest in cultivating and disseminating these fables. For if Paris and Monte Carlo are really so marvellous as it is generally supposed, by the inhabitants of Bradford or Milwaukee, of Tomsk and Bergen, that they are – why, then, the merit of the travellers who have actually visited these places is the greater, and their superiority over the stay-at-home the more enormous. It is for this reason (and because they pay the hotel proprietors and the steamship companies) that the fables are studiously kept alive.

Few things are more pathetic than the spectacle of inexperienced travellers, brought up on these myths, desperately doing their best to make external reality square with fable. It is for the sake of the myths and, less consciously, in the name of snobbery that they left their homes; to admit disappointment in the reality would be to admit their own foolishness in having believed the fables and would detract from their merit in having undertaken the pilgrimage. Out of the hundreds of thousands of Anglo-Saxons who frequent the night-clubs and dancing-saloons of Paris, there are a good many, no doubt, who genuinely like that sort of thing. But there are also very many who do not. In their hearts, secretly, they are bored and a little disgusted. But they have been brought up to believe in a fabulous 'Gay Paree', where everything is deliriously exciting and where alone it is possible to see what is technically known as Life. Conscientiously, therefore, they strive, when they come to Paris, to be gay. Night after night the dance halls and the bordellos are thronged by serious young compatriots of Emerson and Matthew Arnold, earnestly engaged in trying to see life, neither very steadily nor whole, through the ever thickening mists of Heidsieck and Roederer.

Still more courageously determined are their female companions; for they, mostly (unless they are extremely 'modern'), have not the Roederer to assist them in finding Paris gay. The saddest sight I ever saw was in a Montmartre *boite* at about five o'clock of an autumn morning. At a table in a corner of the hall sat three young American girls, quite unattended, adventurously seeing life by themselves. In front of them, on the table, stood the regulation bottles of champagne; but for preference – perhaps on principle – they were sipping lemonade. The jazz band played on monotonously; the tired drummer nodded over his drums, the saxophonist yawned into his saxophone. In couples, in staggering groups, the guests departed. But grimly, indomitably, in spite of their fatigue, in spite of the boredom which so clearly expressed itself on their charming and ingenuous faces, the three young girls sat on. They were still there when I left at sunrise. What stories, I reflected, they would tell when they got home again! And how envious they would make their untravelled friends. 'Paris is just wonderful ...'

To the Parisians, the fable brings in several hundred milliards of good money. They give it a generous publicity; business is business. But if I were the manager of a Montmartre dancing-saloon, I think I should tell my waiters to act their gay parts with a little more conviction. 'My men,' I should say to them, 'you ought to look as though you believed in the fable out of which we make our living. Smile, be merry. Your present expression, which is a mingling of weariness, disgusted contempt for your clients and cynical rapacity, is not inspiring. One day the clients might be sober enough to notice it. And where should we be then?'

But Paris and Monte Carlo are not the only resorts of pilgrimage. There are also Rome and Florence. There are picture galleries, churches and ruins as well as shops and casinos. And the snobbery which decrees that one must like Art – or, to be more accurate, that one should have visited the places where Art is to be seen – is almost as tyrannous as that which bids one visit the places where one can see Life.

All of us are more or less interested in Life – even in that rather smelly slice of it that is to be found in Montmartre. But a taste for Art – or at any rate the sort of art that is found in galleries and churches – is by no means universal. Hence the case of the poor tourists who, from motives of snobbery, visit Rome and Florence, is even more pathetic than the case of those who repair for the same reasons to Paris and Monte Carlo. Tourists 'doing' a church wear a mask of dutiful interest; but what lassitude, what utter weariness of spirit looks out, too often, at their eyes! And the weariness is felt, within, still more acutely because, precisely, of the necessity of simulating this rapt attentiveness, of even going hypocritically into raptures over the things that are starred in the **Baedeker**. There come moments when flesh and blood can stand the strain no longer. **Philistinism** absolutely refuses to pay the tribute it owes to taste. Exasperated and defiant, the tourist swears that he won't so much as put his nose inside another church, preferring to spend his days in the lounge of the hotel, reading the continental *Daily Mail.*

•

We call such people travellers because they do not stay at home. But they are not genuine travellers, not travellers born. For they travel, not for travelling's sake, but for convention's. They set out, nourished on fables and fantastical hopes, to return, whether they avow it or not, disappointed. Their interest in the real and actual being insufficiently lively, they hanker after mythology, and the facts, however curious, beautiful and varied, are a disillusionment. It is only the society of their fellow-tourists, with whom they conspire, every now and then, to make a little oasis of home in the foreign wilderness, coupled with the consciousness of a social duty done, that keeps them even moderately cheerful in the face of the depressing facts of travel.

• SPAIN REVISITED •

Laurie Lee (1914–)

Laurie Lee was born in Gloucester in England. At the age of thirteen he walked to London, then travelled on foot through Spain, where he was trapped for a while by the outbreak of the Civil War. In **A Rose for Winter** *Lee describes his return to southern Spain after an absence of fifteen years. This extract is from the beginning of the book and describes the city of Algeciras.*

One critic, C V Wedgewood, writes that in **A Rose for Winter** *'Laurie Lee has the poet's assurance and originality in the use of words. He also has the artist's eye. His writing ... flames with colour .... This is a book warmly recommended to all who enjoy strong and lively writing with the warmth, colour, drama and humour of the south.' Kingsley Amis, the famed writer of* Lucky Jim, *expresses a very different opinion of Lee's style of travel writing in a review appended on page 217.*

A brilliant November morning with a sky of diamond blue above the bay and the red flowers of a long summer still glowing darkly on the Rock. The intense blackness of the lampless night has rolled away to reveal, incandescent on the northern horizon, the country we had come to seek. It crouched before us in a great ring of lion-coloured mountains, raw, sleeping and savage. There were the scarred and crumpled valleys, the sharp peaks wreathed in their dusty fires, and below them the white towns piled high on their little hills and the empty roads running crimson along the faces of the cliffs. Already, across the water, one heard, or fancied one heard, the sobbing of asses, the cries and salty voices cutting through the thin gold air. And from a steep hillside rose a column of smoke, cool as marble, pungent as pine, which hung like a signal over the landscape, obscure, imperative and motionless.

So we left Gibraltar to its trim English streets, to its Genoese money-changers, Maltese tobacconists, Hindu silk-merchants and crook-boned Cockney soldiers, and we went down to the quay and gathered our bags and boarded the ferry for Spain.

The ferry flew the Spanish flag, had paddle-wheels, and was old, black-funnelled and squat as a duck. It was the type one might have seen, a hundred years ago, running missionaries up the Congo, loaded with whips and bibles. But today, being Saturday, it was packed to the rails with smugglers. As we moved across the oil-blue waters, innocent in the naked sun, they disposed their Gibraltar loot about them. Strapped to their limbs, under their clothes, went cigarettes, soap, sweets, tinned milk, coffee, corned beef and jars of jam. Then the port of Algeciras drew near, and fishermen cried to us from their boats, and we bounced off a yacht, bumped heavily against the quay, and tied up in a tangle, and landed.

The acid-yellow stones, the quay littered with straw and palms, the green-cloaked policemen carrying pistols, the lax and amiable formalities of passports and customs; then we stood free at last upon the ground, surrounded by Spain and the smell of fish-boxes. I turned then and spoke, after many years, my first words of Spanish, to a porter, and we understood each other. We bargained, our baggage was loaded on to a hand-cart, and we entered the town.

And here was the scene so long remembered: the bright facades still crumbling in the sun; the beggars crowding the quaysides, picking up heads of fish; the vivid shapely girls with hair shining like pitch; the tiny, delicate-stepping donkeys; and the barefoot children scrambling around our legs. Here were the black signs charcoaled starkly on the walls: '*Pension La Africana*',[1] '*Vinos y Comestibles*',[2] '*España Libre*',[3] '*Amor! Amor!*'[4] Here were the bars and the talking men, the smell of sweet cognac and old dry sherries. A clear cold air, churches and oranges, and a lean-faced generation moving against white walls in sharp silhouettes of scarlet and black. It did not take more than five minutes to wipe out fifteen years and to return me whole to this thorn-cruel, threadbare world, sombre with dead and dying Christs, brassy with glittering Virgins.

We took a room in a hotel which stood close to the harbour's edge, high above the masts of the fishing boats. It was called 'The Queen of the Sea', and its walls were faced with the wave-blue tiles of Seville. Its dining-room was a **patio** of pillars standing under a green-glass roof, and its green furniture was hand-painted with roses, hunting dogs and bulls. The proprietor

---

1 *Pension La Africana – The African Inn*
2 *Vinos y Comestibles – Wine and groceries*
3 *España Libre – Free Spain*
4 *Amor! Amor! – Love! Love!*

was a swarthy Moor, morose, fatnecked, with a Farouk-like paunch. He spent his days chewing cold fat pork and playing glum games with the cash register. Ramon, the manager, who was quiet and courtly, had a long dark face of extreme nobility and torment. The rest of the staff included six chambermaids, four waiters, three kitchen-maids, two washer women, a clerk, a cook, a page-boy, a night-watchman and a turnkey. Yet this hotel was one of the cheapest in the town.

We soon settled in and the place served us well. It was an active, busy inn. The rooms were full of coughs, groans, cries and laughter; the stairways full of the songs of chambermaids, and the beds full of fleas – the progenitors of long exhausted dreams. But the food was plentiful. Our first meal, served at half-past two that afternoon, offered us olives, sardines, shell-fish, prawns, a large dish of rice served with meat and saffron, flan and fruit, and a bottle of wine fetched in for a shilling.

After such a meal, drenched in the green, brutish, stimulating oils of the hills, there was nothing one could do. So we climbed to our room overlooking the bay and lay in a lethargy till five o'clock while the girls in the sewing-room above sat singing the languorous songs of their villages.

At five o'clock there was a new awakening. The cafe tables on the pavement below began to fill up with the customers of the evening. Waiters ran to and fro with prawns and **manzanilla**. Minstrels struck up on guitars and mandolines. There also arrived an army of touts and merchants – shoeblacks, newsboys, lottery-ticket sellers, gypsies with charms, boys with combs and postcards, women with baskets of cakes and sweets. Among the throbbing chords of the musicians arose their high-pitched cries: *'Ay, carne membrillo!'*,[5] *'Ay, dulces buenas!'*,[6] *'Limpia! Limpia!'*,[7] *'Africa d'hoy!'*.[8] It was time to be up and about.

Night in the town. The shops still glow. One walks through thick crowds which the day's end has called forth into the streets, a multitude which flows down the hill towards the harbour, giving off, as it goes, a remorseless pebbly chatter like the drag of a stream in flood. Here, during the late hours before the evening meal, the whole town passes before one. Here, in the

---

5 *Ay, carne membrillo! – We have quince jam!*

6 *Ay, dulces buenas! – We also have jams!*

7 *Limpia! Limpia! – Clean! Clean!*

8 *Africa d'hoy! – Africa Today!*

dim patches of light thrown forth from the doors of wine-shops, one sees the great eyes of the girls, formal as Persian paintings, and brick-red mouths and bodies loose as dancers'. And the young men, wickedly handsome, with thick greased hair and curling moustaches, each face a gypsy's warning, each jacket slung like a cape over the swaggering shoulder.

These boys were made for quartered hose, for Toledo swords and quick flashing brawls of honour. But today their claws are clipped and rhetoric their only weapon.

At this time, too, pass all the other characters of the Spanish streets: the dark veiled women hurrying home from the priest; the Civil Guard whom nobody greets; gold-skinned sailors and strutting carters; goat-faced ruffians down from the hills; and old men with the hollow eyes of hermits, their skin stretched thin on chill ascetic bones. Then come the merry, dirt-grained beggar children, aping the professional whine but giggling helplessly behind it; and the cripples crawling on hands and knees; the curious idiots waltzing and singing in long tattered cloaks; and the ghostly blind, with their lottery tickets, stalking obliviously through the crowds, calling their numbers like mystic incantations, their white eyes fixed on the empty sky.

So the first night in Spain wore itself out. For hours I watched and wandered, feeling the hot ground under my feet, hearing again the broken lazy dialect of Andalusia, and seeing in the faces around me the dark, unconquered countenances of the Moors. At twopence a glass I drank white wine, sharp and strong as the cheese of a goat. Then I walked back down to the harbour, mazed and unsteady, and the lights of Gibraltar poured out of the sky like a heap of diamonds on the flat dark sea.

It was late now and the harbour was deserted. Cafe chairs were piled up on the pavements and a watchman slept on the stones. All was dim light and shadows and a lapping of invisible water. Suddenly, from a dark doorway, a figure appeared and blocked my path, a young man with fierce slit-eyes and a crumbling pock-marked face. Stealthily he rolled up the sleeves of his American flying-jacket and I saw that his naked arms were strapped to the elbows with watches.

'You wan' good Swiss?' he said hurriedly. 'You wan' Parkair Fifty-one? Come on, fella. Cost you nothin'. Is very cheap. Is ***contrabando***'.

I paused to take him in. Meanwhile, he kept edging away, looking quickly to right and to left, like a wild animal at a water-hole, too nervous to drink.

Ah, contrabando. Sweet fruit of Algeciras. I dodged behind him and slipped into my hotel. I was back indeed, and there was a loud ticking in my ears.

• LILAC IN THE RAIN •

J B Priestley (1894–1984)

J B Priestley, son of a Yorkshire schoolmaster, started his literary career as a critic in London after service in World War One and a period at Cambridge University. He turned to novel-writing and scored a great success in 1929 with **Good Companions**. *He also wrote a number of dramas and literary biographies.*

This essay, which describes his visit to the romantic German town of Heidelberg, was originally published in an anthology titled **Self Selected Essays**.

When we went out, after our first lunch in Heidelberg, the gentle drizzle suddenly became a downpour, so we took refuge in a motor-coach that promised to spend the next hour or so wandering round the town. The only other passengers were four sad American women. In a few minutes the guide arrived, first to salute us and then to beam upon us. He was a spectacled, long-haired fellow in the inevitable peaked cap, and he looked like an unsuccessful student of metaphysics. His English was fluent but fantastic, and appeared to have been learned entirely from books. It sounded more foreign than German itself. Listening to him, you could never quite believe that this guide was a serious, real person and not an actor playing a foreigner in an old-fashioned farce. No sooner had the motor-coach started than he began bombarding us with queer syllables. 'Aboaf, vere you see now, zet eez 'Oly 'Ill, ven ze Chairman Beoples vairst begin.' This is how he opened his performance, and the American women, who – poor things – had been conducted and guided out of their senses, looked at him and at the Holy Hill in dumb despair.

When, after the Day of Judgment, the earth is remade and all the things that have disillusioned us are hurled into the fiery pit, Heidelberg, I trust, will remain as it is now and have its place in that smaller world. Heidelberg is dead right. The moment I set eyes on it, a little bell rang in my mind. It is what I have always imagined an old German town would be. When they sing about a town in the **lieder**, they mean a place like Heidelberg. It is the right lovable mixture of the beautiful, the heavy grotesque, and the absurd. That vast, dark, strawberry-coloured ruin, the Castle, could not have been better devised. At one minute, when the mists blow across it like smoke from a cauldron and the wooded hills above are conjured into remote mountains, it is at once elfish and grim, a **Nibelungen** fastness, set to the thunder of Wagnerian trombones. The next minute, however, when the mist has vanished before the sun and there is a lovely blue beyond the tender green of the first above, the place wears the look of an operetta back-cloth, is electoral, eighteenth-century, charming and ridiculous, and could be introduced with propriety into that piece by old Johann Strauss we saw last night at the Stadt Theatre. The town is as perfectly German, as say, Wells or Oxford is English.

When you remember the sentimentality of the German, the further sentimentality of nearly all graduates, and the loveliness of Heidelberg in spring, it must, you will agree, be a terrific business for an old Heidelbergian to revisit the place. This morning I saw an old gentleman totter towards his waiting car, and he was wearing one of those fantastic hats of the students' unions. He must have been nearly bursting. What a town to be goldenly young and foolish in! Even I, who had never been in the town before, felt like an old Heidelbergian. I could have gone about the enchanted streets crying over my lost youth. It is not the situation of the place that works the magic, though its situation is almost miraculous; it is not the river, the Castle, the woods above, not the old buildings near the Rathaus and the Kornmarkt, though no doubt all these play their part; it is the blossom and the atmosphere. Here is a town smiling out of a garden in a wood. The chestnuts are bright with pink or white candles; the hawthorns are all in flower; the magnolia and laburnum are neighbours down every street; the villas of the professors are overhung with wistaria; and everywhere the rain is sweetening the lilac. I do not know what Heidelberg is like at any other season, but now it is a place filled with wet lilac. The Neckar winds smoothly between its steep, green hills; the mists, like puffs from a giant's cigarette, swirl about the red castle hanging above the town; and there, between them, are the little streets of wet lilac. I hope that among these students with the comic hats, which they are for ever raising, there are some poets, some good old-fashioned rhymesters, so that the purple and white blossom shall not go unsung. Let them raise their hats to the rain-drenched lilac.

I nearly burned my passport and my boats this morning. We had sauntered along the Leopoldstrasse, which is entirely filled with bright little shops, the greenest of green leaves, and this multitude of blossom, and as we walked along, the rain shrank to a few glittering drops. We returned down and found ourselves in a little street just behind the Stadt Theatre. A few people were hanging about, and they were listening to a good round baritone voice that was singing a jovial air and being excellently accompanied by a piano. It came, this voice, from the upper window of a villa, an oldish, slightly dilapidated but altogether delightful villa that had the spring itself blossoming in its courtyard. The jovial voice came rolling out above the shining leaves and the blossom. Obviously it belonged to a member of the Stadt Theatre troupe, who was practising next week's operetta. There is nothing in all this, I admit; and yet, for a moment, there was everything in it. I said to myself: I will stay here for ever, for this is the town I have dreamt about when I have awakened to find myself miserable in my own world; I will wander along the Philosophen Weg across the Neckar and watch the mists above the Castle; I will eat my share of ragout of calf and fillet of swine's flesh at the Ritter and drink my Niersteiner and Goldberg at the Silver Harp; I will sleep in a bed that has everything on top, and will, if necessary, wear a comic hat and peer through spectacles at Gothic newspapers; and no doubt many pleasant things will be ***verboten***; but here, in this enchanting town of mists and wet lilac and learning and operetta, I will stay. Probably I would have been bored in a fortnight; but nevertheless it was a great moment, and I believe I shall remain in spirit an old Heidelbergian.

The people are unusually pleasant, smiling, and attentive, but of course they do not live up to their town. Indeed, to be brutally frank, they are a plain lot and might have been plucked out of the streets and offices of Dusseldorf or Essen. This will not do. Germany ought to look to this. These people ought to have a picturesque, slightly fantastic air, with a suggestion of the romantic 1830s about it, something of the poetical-philosophical-mysterious-handsome-stranger-with-cloak-and-staff line of business. These streets should be filled with beautiful, tender maidens ready at any moment to go into a decline, and with men whose minds are fixed on Truth, Beauty, Goodness, Love, Tobacco, Drink, and nothing else. The place ought to have a Jean Paul Richter and early Carlyle flavour. The Eternal Yea – whatever that is – ought to be easily obtainable in the town. The place itself has this atmosphere, but not the citizens, who are making an all too successful attempt to look like all the other Germans. Only the students, magnificent and happy in their yellow, green and scarlet hats, keep it up.

I do not know what *drang* is on in Germany now. The famous ***Drang nach Osten*** came to an unpleasant conclusion a few years ago, and if anything has taken its place, I do not know what it is. But I suggest – with all the usual apologies of the ignorant and interfering outsider – a new one, a *Drang nach Heidelberg* that is, ***nach*** misty castles and rococo mansions and little steamers setting out pompously for nowhere and small towns where everybody knows the chief tenor and metaphysicians lost in the fumes of tobacco from huge untidy packets and solemn little societies with coloured hats and tender songs in the moonlight and sausage and beer and fireworks and waltz tunes in the woods. It can't be done, I suppose, for now there must be world politics and rationalisation of industry and stunts in Persia and commercial campaigns in South America, together with large motor-cars and too much electricity and new buildings that look as if they were designed in Mars for a race of ambitious ants. The radio resounds through a host of steel and concrete electrified flats. This is a Germany one can respect. But give me the Germany I can smile at and love, with the Stadt baritone trolling above the wet lilac.

• THE CAMARGUE •

Roy Campbell (1901–1957)

Born in Durban, Roy Campbell spent most of his life overseas, living first in England, then Spain and finally Portugal, where he died in a motor accident in 1957.

In his early years in South Africa, he and William Plomer edited the literary magazine Voorslag *which was controversial in its time because it challenged many of the complacencies of white South Africans. He has published numerous poems, of which* The Serf, The Zulu Girl, Autumn *and* Horses on the Camargue *are probably the best-known.*

This extract is taken from his second autobiography, **Light on a Dark Horse**, *which was published in 1951.*

You can tell almost the moment you get into Provence by the pines and the rocks, the olives, almonds, vines, cypresses and poplars to which the elms and oaks give place. By far the best way to enter Provence is by the ancient highway of her great and noble river, on one of the barges coming down from Lyons. This famous highway was the main trade route of Western Europe until the invention of the railways put it comparatively out of use, and reduced its traffic by about ninety per cent.

On my second visit to Provence I came down from Lyons on a barge, having got a job from the patron of a couple of barges. On our way down to Marseilles one of our barges came to grief, between Arles and Fos, and, while the patron was waiting for a tug, he offered to release me, if I liked, as he might be held up for a day or so. Seeing I was bound for the very parts we were passing through, and he had shipped another hand at Arles, he kindly let me off on the towpath and I decided to go to Saint Louis du Rhone. The patron at first was against letting me go because of the danger from cattle and wild stallions, but I prevailed.

The mistral was loose that day, clashing the reeds and tearing at the tamarisks. The Alpilles were sparkling like dark blue crystals through the heavenly bluish-white air that shimmers over the Crau to the north-east. The voice of the mistral is more full of legends and myths than that of any other wind that blows in any other part of the world. I have never heard it blowing on the Crau or the Camargue without remembering those wonderful lines of Milton -

And airy tongues that syllable men's names
By sands and shores and desert wildernesses.

Where the Camargue crosses the border of Provence into the Languedoc it is known as the Sauvage. The people who live there are mostly cowboys, fishermen and fowlers. Since half the country consists of water and reeds, everybody leads an amphibious life. I've seen punts tied to the first-floor window like life-boats, ready for when the family change floors. The only reason why the people haven't got webbed feet is because they've got bow-legs instead, from trying to keep their feet out of the water – by living half the year in their stirrups, and the other half squatting in punts.

All round you can see hundreds of wild horses and cattle grazing together in mixed groups like the zebras and wildebeest do in Africa. They're not tame animals gone wild. They're wild animals in the same sense as African zebras and buffaloes are wild animals. They've been there since prehistoric times, with the beavers and wild boars that you still find there. The cowboys sort them out from time to time, but otherwise nobody molests them.

When I landed from the barge I wanted to hike to the sea. I soon repented. I saw a house which *seemed* very near and I started to walk to it. On the way there I scared part of a big flock of flamingos. They spread out all their red wings together, and it looked like a sort of super-sunrise in broad daylight. The house looked quite near. But it took me half the day to get there. It was deserted except for the women-folk; and they sent me packing. I heard afterwards that they mistook me for a runaway crook: and they had some nasty-looking dogs. So I spent the night in the swamps with bulls bellowing all round and I was almost eaten alive by mosquitoes. The wild boars, foxes, beavers, and ferrets also made noises all round me.

Next day I struck off inland and came to another house, a big one with stables and barns. They seemed to expect me, or anyone else who turned up. There was a big crowd there, and people were doling out wine and bread. The crowd had turned up from miles around as spectators and volunteers in a big rodeo that was being held. The branding was finished and they were coursing bulls and having games, to wind up the show with a flourish. One of the games was very pretty. I remember a sort of mixture of rugby and polo played on horseback with a bunch of flowers for a ball.

They had an arena made of carts tied together with a wall on one side, and when I got there they'd just let out a three-year-old bull with rather wide horns. It was an open competition without any rules. This was lucky for me as I hadn't learned the local game. So I just sat on the barricade and let the bull pass me about four times till he got used to me and took no more notice of me. Then I took a flying jump and came down with a ju-jitsu lock on his horns like we do from horseback in the Dominions. Another fellow, Leon Raoux of Istres, jumped down and swung it by the tail. It came over very nicely and we sat on its head and took off the prize from between its horns. That was the first bull I ever turned by hand. The last time I turned the big bull at Istres, Raoux also had it by the tail.

When they found I was a cattleman, the people of the house, the Raouxes, gave me a fine time. Some neighbours of theirs, the Ferauds, took me away to another house and let me stay and work with them for a long time. One of the brothers Feraud was for many years mayor of Fos sur Mer. I have often been back there since, and liked it better each time. I've even got to love the rather dismal scenery of waving reeds and tamarisks.

• TRAVELS WITH A • DONKEY

Robert Louis Stevenson (1850–1894)

Robert Louis Stevenson was born in Edinburgh. He entered Edinburgh University in 1867 and studied engineering, but soon abandoned this for law and was admitted to the bar in 1875. An infection of the lungs caused him to undertake frequent journeys in search of healthier climes: one such journey in France he described in the book **Travels with a Donkey in the Cervennes**.

He is probably best known for his children's books, especially **Kidnapped** *and* **Treasure Island**, *but he wrote many other novels, including the famous* **Dr Jekyll and Mr Hyde**. *This extract is taken from* **Travels with a Donkey**, *published in 1879.*

The bell of Monastier was just striking nine as I got quit of these preliminary troubles and descended the hill through the common. As long as I was within sight of the windows, a secret shame and the fear of some laughable defeat withheld me from tampering with Modestine. She tripped along upon her four small hoofs with a sober daintiness of gait; from time to time she shook her ears or her tail; and she looked so small under the bundle that my mind misgave me. We got across the ford without difficulty – there was no doubt about the matter, she was docility itself – and once on the other bank, where the road begins to mount through pine-woods, I took in my right hand the unhallowed staff, and with a quaking spirit applied it to the donkey. Modestine brisked up her pace for perhaps three steps, and then relapsed into her former **minuet.** Another application had the same effect, and so with the third. I am worthy the name of an Englishman, and it goes against my conscience to lay my hand rudely on a female. I desisted, and looked her all over from head to foot; the poor brute's knees were trembling and her breathing was distressed; it was plain that she could go no faster on a hill. God forbid, thought I, that I should brutalise this innocent creature; let her go at her own pace, and let me patiently follow.

In the meantime there came up behind us a tall peasant, perhaps forty years of age, of an ironical snuffy countenance, and arrayed in the green tail-coat of the country. He overtook us hand over hand, and stopped to consider our pitiful advance.

'Your donkey,' says he, 'is very old?'

I told him, I believed not.

Then, he supposed, we had come far.

I told him, we had but newly left Monastier.

'*Et vous marchez comme ca!*'[1] cried he; and, throwing back his head, he laughed long and heartily. I watched him, half prepared to feel offended, until he had satisfied his mirth; and then, 'You must have no pity on these animals,' said he; and, plucking a switch out of a thicket, he began to lace Modestine about the sternworks, uttering a cry. The rogue pricked up her ears and broke into a good round pace, which she kept up without flagging, and without exhibiting the least symptom of distress, as long as the peasant kept beside us. Her former panting and shaking had been, I regret to say, a piece of comedy.

My ***deus ex machina***, before he left me, supplied some excellent, if inhumane, advice; presented me with the switch, which he declared she would feel more tenderly than my cane; and finally taught me the true cry or masonic word of donkey-drivers, 'Proot!' All the time, he regarded me with a comical, incredulous air, which was embarrassing to confront; and smiled over my donkey-driving, as I might have smiled over his orthography, or his green tail-coat. But is was not my turn for the moment.

I was proud of my new lore, and thought I had learned the art to perfection. And certainly Modestine did wonders for the rest of the forenoon, and I had a breathing space to look about me. It was Sabbath; the mountain-fields were all vacant in the sunshine; and as we came down through St. Martin de Frugeres, the church was crowded to the door, there were people kneeling without upon the steps, and the sound of the priest's chanting came forth out of the dim interior. It gave me a home feeling on the spot; for I am a countryman of the Sabbath, so to speak, and all Sabbath observances, like a Scottish accent, strike in me mixed feelings, grateful and the reverse. It is only a traveller, hurrying by like a person from another planet, who can rightly enjoy the peace and beauty of the great ascetic feast. The sight of the resting country does his spirit good. There is something better than music in the wide unusual silence; and it disposes him to amiable

1 *Et vous marchez comme ça! – And you walk like this!*

thoughts, like the sound of a little river or the warmth of sunlight.

In this pleasant humour I came down the hill to where Goudet stands in a green end of a valley, with Chateau Beaufort opposite upon a rocky steep, and the stream, as clear as crystal, lying in a deep pool between them. Above and below, you may hear it wimpling over the stones, an amiable stripling of a river, which it seems absurd to call the Loire. On all sides, Goudet is shut in by mountains; rocky footpaths, practicable at best for donkeys, join it to the outer world of France; and the men and women drink and swear, in their green corner, or look up at the snow-clad peaks in winter from the threshold of their homes, in an isolation, you would think, like that of Homer's Cyclops. But it is not so; the postman reaches Goudet with the letterbag; the aspiring youth of Goudet are within a day's walk of the railway at Le Puy; and here in the inn you may find an engraved portrait of the host's nephew, Regis Senac, 'Professor of Fencing and Champion of the two America's,' a distinction gained by him, along with the sum of five hundred dollars, at Tammany Hall, New York, on the 10th April, 1876.

I hurried over my mid-day meal, and was early forth again. But, alas, as we climbed the interminable hill upon the other side, 'Proot!' seemed to have lost its virtue. I prooted like a lion, I prooted mellifluously like a sucking-dove; but Modestine would be neither softened nor intimidated. She held doggedly to her pace; nothing but a blow would move her, and that only for a second. I must follow at her heels, incessantly belabouring. A moment's pause in this ignoble toil, and she relapsed into her own private gait. I think I never heard of anyone in as mean a situation. I must reach the lake of Bouchet, where I meant to camp, before sundown, and, to have even a hope of this, I must instantly maltreat this uncomplaining animal. The sound of my own blows sickened me. Once, when I looked at her, she had a faint resemblance to a lady of my acquaintance who formerly loaded me with kindness; and this increased my horror of my cruelty.

To make matters worse, we encountered another donkey, ranging at will upon the roadside; and this other donkey chanced to be a gentleman. He and Modestine met nickering for joy, and I had to separate the pair and beat down their young romance with a renewed and feverish **bastinado.** If the other donkey had had the heart of a male under his hide, he would have fallen upon me tooth and hoof; and this was a kind of consolation – he was plainly unworthy of Modestine's affection. But the incident saddened me, as did everything that spoke of my donkey's sex.

It was blazing hot up the valley, windless, with vehement sun upon my shoulders; and I had to labour so consistently with my stick that the sweat ran into my eyes. Every five minutes, too, the pack, the basket, and the pilot-coat would take an ugly slew to one side or the other; and I had to stop Modestine, just when I got her to a tolerable pace of about two miles an hour, to tug, push, shoulder, and readjust the load. And at last, in the village of Ussel, saddle and all, the whole **hypothec** turned round and grovelled in the dust below the donkey's belly. She, none better pleased, incontinently drew up and seemed to smile; and a party of one man, two women, and two children came up, and, standing round me in a half-circle, encouraged her by their example.

I had the devil's own trouble to get the thing righted; and the instant I had done so, without hesitation, it toppled and fell down upon the other side. Judge if I was hot! And yet not a hand was offered to assist me. The man, indeed, told me I ought to have a package of a different shape. I suggested, if he knew nothing better to the point in my predicament, he might hold his tongue. And the good-natured dog agreed with me smilingly. It was the most despicable fix. I must plainly content myself with the pack for Modestine, and take the following items for my own share of the portage: a cane, a quart flask, a pilot-jacket heavily weighted in the pockets, two pounds of black bread, and an open basket full of meats and bottles. I believe I may say I am not devoid of greatness of soul; for I did not recoil from this infamous burden. I disposed it, Heaven knows how, so as to be mildly portable, and then proceeded to steer Modestine through the village. She tried, as was indeed her invariable habit, to enter every house and every courtyard in the whole length; and, encumbered as I was, without a hand to help myself, no words can render an idea of my difficulties. A priest, with six or seven others, was examining a church in process of repair, and he and his acolytes laughed loudly as they saw my plight. I remembered having laughed myself when I had seen good men struggling with adversity in the person of a jackass, and the recollection filled me with penitence. That was in my old light days, before this trouble came upon me. God knows at least that I shall never laugh again, thought I. But oh, what a cruel thing is a farce to those engaged in it!

A little out of the village, Modestine, filled with the demon, set her heart upon a by-road, and positively refused to leave it. I dropped all my bundles, and, I am ashamed to say, struck the poor sinner twice across the face. It was pitiful to see her lift her head with shut eyes, as if waiting for another blow. I came very near crying; but I did a wiser thing than that, and sat squarely down by the roadside to consider my situation under the cheerful influence of tobacco and a nip of brandy. Modestine, in the meanwhile, munched some black bread with a contrite hypocritical air. It was plain that I must make a sacrifice to the gods of shipwreck. I threw away the empty bottle destined to carry milk; I threw away my own white bread, and, disdaining to act by general average, kept the black bread for Modestine;

lastly, I threw away the cold leg of mutton and the egg-whisk, although this last was dear to my heart. Thus I found room for everything in the basket, and even stowed the boating-coat on the top. By means of an end of cord I slung it under one arm; and although the cord cut my shoulder, and the jacket hung almost to the ground, it was with a heart greatly lightened that I set forth again.

I had now an arm free to thrash Modestine, and cruelly I chastised her. If I were to reach the lakeside before dark, she must bestir her little shanks to some tune. Already the sun had gone down into a windy-looking mist; and although there were still a few streaks of gold far off to the east on the hills and the black fir-woods, all was cold and grey about our onward path. An infinity of little country by-roads led hither and thither among the fields. It was the most pointless labyrinth. I could see my destination overhead, or rather the peak that dominates it; but choose as I pleased, the roads always ended by turning away from it, and sneaking back towards the valley, or northward along the margin of the hills. The failing light, the waning colour, the naked, unhomely, stony country through which I was travelling, threw me into some despondency. I promise you, the stick was not idle; I think every decent step that Modestine took must have cost me at least two emphatic blows. There was not another sound in the neighbourhood but that of my unwearying bastinado.

Suddenly, in the midst of my toils, the load once more bit the dust, and, as by enchantment, all the cords were simultaneously loosened, and the road scattered with my dear possessions. The packing was to begin again from the beginning; and as I had to invent a new and better system, I do not doubt but I lost half an hour. It began to be dusk in earnest as I reached a wilderness of turf and stones. It had the air of being a road which should lead everywhere at the same time; and I was falling into something not unlike despair when I saw two figures stalking towards me over the stones. They walked one behind the other like tramps, but their pace was remarkable. The son led the way, a tall, ill-made, sombre, Scottish-looking man; the mother followed, all in her Sunday's best, with an elegantly embroidered ribbon to her cap, and a new felt hat atop, and proffering, as she strode along with kilted petticoats, a string of obscene and blasphemous oaths.

I hailed the son, and asked him my direction. He pointed loosely west and north-west, muttered an inaudible comment, and, without slackening his pace for an instant, stalked on, as he was going, right athwart my path. The mother followed without so much as raising her head. I shouted and shouted after them, but they continued to scale the hillside, and turned a deaf ear to my outcries. At last, leaving Modestine by herself, I was constrained to run after them, hailing the while. They stopped as I drew near, the mother still cursing; and I could see she was a handsome, motherly, respectable-looking woman. The son once more answered me roughly and inaudibly, and was for setting out again. But this time I simply collared the mother, who was nearest me, and, apologising for my violence, declared that I could not let them go until they had put me on my road. They were neither of them offended – rather mollified than otherwise; told me I had only to follow them; and then the mother asked me what I wanted by the lake at such an hour. I replied, in the Scottish manner, by inquiring if she had far to go herself. She told me, with another oath, that she had an hour and a half's road before her. And then, without salutation, the pair strode forward again up the hillside in the gathering dusk.

I returned for Modestine, pushed her briskly forward, and, after a sharp ascent of twenty minutes, reached the edge of a plateau. The view, looking back on my day's journey, was both wild and sad. Mount Mézenc and the peaks beyond St. Julien stood out in trenchant gloom against a cold glitter in the east; and the intervening field of hills had fallen together into one broad wash of shadow, except here and there the outline of a wooded sugar-loaf in black, here and there a white irregular patch to represent a cultivated farm, and here and there a blot where the Loire, the Gazeille, or the Laussonne wandered in a gorge.

Soon we were on a high-road, and surprise seized on my mind as I beheld a village of some magnitude close at hand; for I had been told that the neighbourhood of the lake was uninhabited except by trout. The road smoked in the twilight with children driving home cattle from the fields; and a pair of mounted stride-legged women, hat and cap and all, dashed past me at a hammering trot from the canton where they had been to church and market. I asked one of the children where I was. At Bouchet St. Nicolas, he told me. Thither, about a mile south of my destination, and on the other side of a respectable summit, had these confused roads and treacherous peasantry conducted me. My shoulder was cut, so that it hurt sharply; my arm ached liked toothache from perpetual beating; I gave up the lake and my design to camp, and asked for the ***auberge*.**

•

From Bleymard after dinner, although it was already late, I set out to scale a portion of the Lozere. An ill-marked stony drove-road guided me forward; and I met nearly half-a-dozen bullock-carts descending from the woods, each laden with a whole pine-tree for the winters' firing. At the top of the woods, which do not climb very high upon this cold ridge, I struck leftward by a path among the pines, until I hit on a dell of green turf, where a streamlet made a little spout over some stones to serve me for a water-tap. 'In a more sacred or sequestered bower ... nor nymph nor faunus haunted.' The trees were not old, but they grew thickly round the glade: there was no outlook, except north-eastward upon distant hill-tops, or straight upward to the sky; and the encampment felt secure and private like a room. By the time I had made my arrangements and fed Modestine, the day was already beginning to decline. I buckled myself to the knees into my sack and made a hearty meal; and as soon as the sun went down, I pulled my cap over my eyes and fell asleep.

Night is a dead monotonous period under a roof; but in the open world it passes lightly, with its stars and dews and perfumes, and the hours are marked by changes in the face of Nature. What seems a kind of temporal death to people choked between walls and curtains, is only a light and living slumber to the man who sleeps afield. All night long he can hear Nature breathing deeply and freely; even as she takes her rest, she turns and smiles; and there is one stirring hour unknown to those who dwell in houses, when a wakeful influence goes abroad over the sleeping hemisphere, and all the outdoor world are on their feet. It is then that the cock first crows, not this time to announce the dawn, but like a cheerful watchman speeding the course of night. Cattle awake on the meadows; sheep break their fast on dewy hillsides, and change to a new lair among the ferns; and houseless men, who have laid down with the fowls, open their dim eyes and behold the beauty of the night.

At what inaudible summons, at what gentle touch of Nature, are all these sleepers thus recalled in the same hour to life? Do the stars rain down an influence, or do we share some thrill of mother earth below our resting bodies? Even shepherds and old country-folk, who are the deepest read in these arcana, have not a guess as to the means or purpose of this nightly resurrection. Towards two in the morning they declare the thing takes place; and neither know nor inquire further. And at least it is a pleasant incident. We are disturbed in our slumber only, like the luxurious Montaigne, 'that we may the better and more sensibly relish it.' We have a moment to look upon the stars. And there is a special pleasure for some minds in the reflection that we share the impulse with all outdoor creatures in our neighbourhood, that we have escaped out of the Bastille of civilisation, and are become, for the time being, a mere kindly animal and a sheep of Nature's flock.

When that hour came to me among the pines, I wakened thirsty. My tin was standing by me half full of water. I emptied it at a draught; and feeling broad awake after this internal cold aspersion, sat upright to make a cigarette. The stars were clear, coloured, and jewel-like, but not frosty. A faint silvery vapour stood for the Milky Way. All around me the black fir-points stood upright and stock-still. By the whiteness of the pack-saddle, I could see Modestine walking round and round at the length of her tether; I could hear her steadily munching at the sward; but there was not another sound, save the indescribable quiet talk of the runnel over the stones. I lay lazily smoking and studying the colour of the sky, as we call the void of space, from where it showed a reddish grey behind the pines to where it showed a glossy blue-black between the stars. As if to be more like a pedlar, I wear a silver ring. This I could see faintly shining as I raised or lowered the cigarette; and at each whiff the inside of my hand was illuminated, and became for a second the highest light in the landscape.

A faint wind, more like a moving coolness than a stream of air, passed down the glade from time to time; so that even in my great chamber the air was being renewed all night long. I thought with horror of the inn at Chasserades and the congregated nightcaps; with horror of the nocturnal prowesses of clerks and students, of hot theatres and pass-keys and close rooms. I have not often enjoyed a more serene possession of myself, nor felt more independent of material aids. The outer world, from which we cower into our houses, seemed after all a gentle habitable place; and night after night a man's bed, it seemed, was laid and waiting for him in the fields, where God keeps an open house. I thought I had rediscovered one of those truths which are revealed to savages and hid from political economists: at the least, I had discovered a new pleasure for myself. And yet even while I was exulting in my solitude I became aware of a strange lack. I wished a companion to lie near me in the starlight, silent and not moving, but ever within touch. For there is a fellowship more quiet even than solitude, and which, rightly understood, is solitude made perfect. And to live out of doors with the woman a man loves is of all lives the most complete and free.

As I thus lay, between content and longing, a faint noise stole towards me through the pines. I thought, at first, it was the crowing of cocks or the barking of dogs at some very distant farm; but steadily and gradually it took articulate shape in my ears, until I became aware that a passenger was going by upon the high-road in the valley, and singing loudly as he went. There was more of good-will than grace in his performance; but he trolled with ample lungs; and the sound of his voice took hold upon the hillside and set the air shaking in the leafy glens. I have heard people passing by night in sleeping cities; some of them sang; one, I remember, played loudly on the bagpipes. I heave heard the rattle of a cart or carriage spring up suddenly after hours of stillness, and pass, for some minutes, within the range of my hearing as I lay abed. There is a romance about all who are abroad in the black hours, and with something of a thrill we try to guess their business. But here the romance was double: first, this glad passenger, lit internally with wine, who sent up his voice in music through the night; and then I, on the other hand, buckled into my sack, and smoking alone in the pinewoods between four and five thousand feet towards the stars.

When I awoke again (Sunday, 29th September), many of the stars had disappeared; only the stronger companions of the night still burned visibly overhead; and away towards the east I saw a faint haze of light upon the horizon, such as had been the Milky Way when I was last awake. Day was at hand. I lit my lantern, and by its glowworm light put on my boots and gaiters; then I broke up some bread for Modestine, filled my can at the water-tap, and lit my spirit-lamp to boil myself some chocolate. The blue darkness lay long in the glade where I had so sweetly slumbered; but soon there was a broad streak of orange melting into gold along the mountain-tops of Vivarais. A solemn glee possessed my mind at this gradual and lovely coming in of day. I heard the runnel with delight; I looked round me for something beautiful and unexpected; but the still black pinetrees, the hollow glade, the munching ass, remained unchanged in figure. Nothing had altered but the light, and that, indeed, shed over all a spirit of life and of breathing peace, and moved me to a strange exhilaration.

• THE BALLAD OF A STRANGE TOWN •

G K Chesterton (1874–1936)

Gilbert Keith Chesterton was born in London in fashionable Kensington. He was educated at St Paul's School where, although he did not distinguish himself as a scholar, he did reveal a budding literary talent in the school magazine. He later became a much-celebrated writer of novels, short stories, poetry and essays, and was a noted literary critic, lecturer and broadcaster. During the 1920s he visited various countries in Europe, of which he wrote a number of pieces on travel.

This extract is from **Tremendous Trifles**, *which was published in 1909.*

My friend and I, in fooling about Flanders, fell into a fixed affection for the town of Mechlin or Malines. Our rest there was so restful that we almost felt it as a home, and hardly strayed out of it.

We sat day after day in the market-place, under little trees growing in wooden tubs, and looked up at the noble converging lines of the Cathedral tower, from which the three riders from Ghent, in the poem, heard the bell which told them they were not too late. But we took as much pleasure in the people, in the little boys with open, flat Flemish faces and fur collars round their necks, making them look like burgomasters; or the women, whose prim, oval faces, hair strained tightly off the temples, and mouths at once hard, meek, and humorous, exactly reproduced the late medieval faces in Memling and Van Eyck.

But one afternoon, as it happened, my friend rose from under his little tree, and, pointing to a sort of toy train that was puffing smoke in one corner of the clear square, suggested that we should go by it. We got into the little train, which was meant really to take the peasants and their vegetables to and fro from their fields beyond the town, and the official came round to give us tickets. We asked him what place we should get to if we paid fivepence. The Belgians are not a romantic people, and he asked us (with a lamentable mixture of Flemish coarseness and French rationalism) where we wanted to go.

We explained that we wanted to go to fairyland, and the only question was whether we could get there for fivepence. At last, after a great deal of international misunderstanding (for he spoke French in the Flemish and we in the English manner), he told us that fivepence would take us to a place which I have never seen written down, but which when spoken sounded like the word 'Waterloo' pronounced by an intoxicated patriot; I think it was Waerlowe. We clasped our hands and said it was the place that we had been seeking from boyhood, and when we had got there we descended with promptitude.

For a moment I had a horrible fear that it really was the field of Waterloo; but I was comforted by remembering that it was in quite a different part of Belgium. It was a cross-roads, with one cottage at the corner, a perspective of tall trees like Hobbema's 'Avenue', and beyond only the infinite flat chessboard of the little fields. It was the scene of peace and prosperity; but I must confess that my friend's first action was to ask the man when there would be another train back to Mechlin. The man stated that there would be a train back in exactly one hour. We walked up the avenue, and when we were nearly half an hour's walk away it began to rain.

We arrived back at the cross-roads sodden and dripping, and, finding the train waiting, climbed into it with some relief. The officer on this train could speak nothing but Flemish, but he understood the name of Mechlin, and indicated that when we came to Mechlin Station he would put us down, which, after the right interval of time, he did.

We got down, under a steady downpour, evidently on the edge of Mechlin, though the features could not easily be recognized through the grey screen of the rain. I do not generally agree with those who find rain depressing. A shower-bath is not depressing; it is rather startling. And if it is exciting when a man throws a pail of water over you, why should it not also be exciting when the gods throw many pails? But on this soaking afternoon, whether it was the dull sky-line of the Netherlands or the fact that we were returning home without any adventure, I really did think things a trifle dreary. As soon as we could creep under the shelter of a street we turned into a little café kept by one woman. She was incredibly old, and she spoke no French. There we drank black coffee and what was called 'cognac fine'. 'Cognac fine' were the only two French words used in the establishment, and they were not true. At least, the fineness (perhaps by its very ethereal delicacy) escaped me. After a little my friend who was more restless than I, got up and went out, to see if the rain had stopped and if we could at once stroll back to our hotel by the station. I sat finishing my coffee in a colourless mood, and listening to the unremitting rain.

Suddenly the door burst open, and my friend appeared, transfigured and frantic.

'Get up!' he cried, waving his hands wildly. 'Get up! We're in the wrong town! We're not in Mechlin at all. Mechlin is ten miles, twenty miles off – God knows what! We're somewhere near Antwerp.'

'What!' I cried, leaping from my seat, and sending the furniture flying. 'Then all is well, after all! Poetry only hid her face for an instant behind a cloud. Positively for a moment I was feeling depressed because we were in the right town. But if we are in the wrong town – why, we have our adventure after all! If we are in the wrong town, we are in the right place.'

I rushed out into the rain, and my friend followed me somewhat more grimly. We discovered we were in a town called Lierre, which seemed to consist chiefly of bankrupt pastrycooks who sold lemonade.

'This is the peak of our whole poetic progress!' I cried enthusiastically. 'We must do something, something sacramental and commemorative! We cannot sacrifice an ox, and it would be a bore to build a temple. Let us write a poem.'

With but slight encouragement, I took out an old envelope and one of those pencils that turn bright violet in water. There was plenty of water about, and the violet ran down the paper, symbolising the rich purple of that romantic hour. I began, choosing the form of an old French ballade; it is the easiest because it is the most restricted –

Can Man to Mount Olympus rise,
And fancy Primrose Hill the scene?
Can a man walk in Paradise
And think he is in Turnham Green?

And could I take you for Malines,
Not knowing the nobler thing you were?
O Pearl of all the plain, and queen,
The lovely city of Lierre.

Through memory's mist in glimmering guise
Shall shine your streets of sloppy sheen,
And wet shall grow my dreaming eyes,
To think how wet my boots have been.
Now if I die or shoot a Dean –

Here I broke off to ask my friend whether he thought it expressed a more wild calamity to shoot a Dean or to be a Dean. But he only turned up his coat collar, and I felt that for him the muse had folded her wings. I re-wrote –

Now if I die a Rural Dean,
Or rob a bank I do not care,
Or turn a Tory. I have seen
The lovely city of Lierre.

'The next line,' I resumed, warming to it; but my friend interrupted me.

'The next line,' he said somewhat harshly, 'will be a railway line. We can get back to Mechlin from here, I find, though we have to change twice. I dare say I should think this jolly romantic but for the weather. Adventure is the champagne of life, but I prefer my champagne and my adventures dry. Here is the station.'

We did not speak again until we had left Lierre, in its sacred cloud of rain, and were coming to Mechlin, under a clearer sky, that even made one think of stars. Then I leant forward and said to my friend in a low voice –

'I have found out everything. We have come to the wrong star.'

He stared his query, and I went on eagerly: 'That is what makes life at once so splendid and so strange. We are in the wrong world. When I thought that was the right town, it bored me; when I knew it was wrong, I was happy. So the false optimism, the modern happiness, tires us because it tells us we fit into this world. The true happiness is that we don't fit. We come from somewhere else. We have lost our way.'

He silently nodded, staring out of the window, but whether I had impressed or only fatigued him I could not tell. 'This,' I added, 'is suggested in the last verse of a fine poem you have grossly neglected –

'Happy is he and more than wise
Who sees with wondering eyes and clean
This world through all the grey disguise
Of sleep and custom in between.
Yes; we may pass the heavenly screen,
But shall we know when we are there?
Who know not what these dead stones mean,
The lovely city of Lierre.'

Here the train stopped abruptly. And from Mechlin church steeple we heard the half-chime: and Joris broke silence with 'No bally ***hors d'oeuvres*** for me: I shall get on to something solid at once.'

L'Envoy

Prince, wide your Empire spreads, I ween,
Yet happier is that moistened Mayor,
Who drinks her cognac far from fine,
The lovely city of Lierre.

• PARIS •

Ernest Hemingway (1898–1961)

Ernest Hemingway was an American short story writer and novelist. He began his writing career as a cub reporter on the Kansas City Star. *In 1921 he went to France, where he worked as a foreign correspondent for the* Toronto Star *and subsequently settled in Paris.*

His most well-known works include the novels **A Farewell to Arms** *and* **For Whom the Bell Tolls** *and his long short story* **The Old Man and the Sea.** *Economy of style and skilful characterisation are the hallmarks of his craft, and in 1954 he was awarded the Nobel Prize for Literature.*

Then there was the bad weather. It would come in one day when the fall was over. We would have to shut the windows in the night against the rain and the cold wind would strip the leaves from the trees in the place Contrescarpe. The leaves lay sodden in the rain and the wind drove the rain against the big green autobus at the terminal and the Café des Amateurs was crowded and the windows misted over from the heat and the smoke inside. It was a sad, evilly run cafe where the drunkards of the quarter crowded together and I kept away from it because of the smell of dirty bodies and the smell of sour drunkenness. The men and women who frequented the Amateurs stayed drunk all the time, or all of the time they could afford it; mostly on wine which they bought by the half-litre or litre. Many strangely named aperitifs were advertised, but few people could afford them except as a foundation to build their wine drunks on.

All of the sadness of the city came suddenly with the first cold rains of winter, and there were no more tops to the high white houses as you walked but only the wet blackness of the street and the closed doors of the small shops, the herb sellers, the stationery and the newspaper shops, the midwife – second class – and the hotel where Verlaine had died, where I had a room on the top floor where I worked.

It was either six or eight flights up to the top floor and it was very cold and I knew how much it would cost for a bundle of small twigs, three wire-wrapped packets of short, half-pencil-length pieces of split pine to catch fire from the twigs, and then the bundle of half-dried lengths of hard wood that I must buy to make a fire that would warm the room. So I went to the far side of the street to look up at the roof in the rain and see if any chimneys were going, and how the smoke blew. There was no smoke, and I thought about how the chimney could be cold and might not draw and of the room possibly filling with smoke, and the fuel wasted, and the money gone with it, and I walked on in the rain. I walked down past the Lycee Henri Quatre and the ancient church of St-Etienne-du-Mont and the wind-swept Place du Pantheon and cut in for shelter to the right and finally came out on the lee side of the boulevard St-Michel and worked on down it past the Cluny and the boulevard St-Germain until I came to a good cafe that I knew on the place St-Michel.

It was a pleasant cafe, warm and clean and friendly, and I hung up my old waterproof on the coat rack to dry and put my worn and weathered felt hat on the rack above the bench and ordered a ***café au lait***. The waiter brought it and I took out a notebook from the pocket of the coat and a pencil and started to write. I was writing about up in Michigan and since it was a wild, cold, blowing day it was that sort of day in the story. I had already seen the end of fall come through boyhood, youth and young manhood, and in one place you could write about it better than in another. That was called transplanting yourself, I thought, and it could be as necessary with people as with other sorts of growing things. But in the story the boys were drinking and this made me thirsty and I ordered a rum St James. This tasted wonderful on the cold day and I kept on writing, feeling very well and feeling the good Martinique rum warm me all through my body and spirit.

A girl came in the cafe and sat by herself at a table near the window. She was very pretty with a face fresh as a newly minted coin if they minted coins in smooth flesh with rain-freshened skin, and her hair was black as a crow's wing and cut sharply and diagonally across her cheek.

I looked at her and she disturbed me and made me very excited. I wished I could put her in the story, or anywhere, but she had placed herself so she could watch the street and the entry and I knew she was waiting for someone. So I went on writing.

The story was writing itself and I was having a hard time keeping up with it. I ordered another rum St James and I watched the girl whenever I looked up, or when I sharpened the pencil with a pencil-sharpener with the shavings curling into the saucer under my drink.

I've seen you, beauty, and you belong to me now, whoever you are waiting for and if I never see you again, I thought. You belong to me and all Paris belongs to me and I belong to this notebook and this pencil.

Then I went back to writing and I entered far into the story and was lost in it. I was writing it now and it was not writing itself and I did not look up nor know anything about the time nor think where I was nor order any more rum St James. I was tired of rum St James without thinking about it. Then the story was finished and I was very tired. I read the last paragraph and then I looked up and looked for the girl and she had gone. I hope she's gone with a good man, I thought. But I felt sad.

I closed up the story in the notebook and put it in my inside pocket and I asked the waiter for a dozen *portugaises* and a half-carafe of the dry white wine they had there. After writing a story I was always empty and both sad and happy, as though I had made love, and I was sure this was a very good story although I would not know truly how good until I read it over the next day.

As I ate the oysters with their strong taste of the sea and their faint metallic taste that the cold white wine washed away, leaving only the sea taste and the succulent texture, and as I drank their cold liquid from each shell and washed it down with the crisp taste of the wine, I lost the empty feeling and began to be happy and to make plans.

Now that the bad weather had come, we could leave Paris for a while for a place where this rain would be snow coming down through the pines and covering the road and the high hillsides and at an altitude where we would hear it creak as we walked home at night. Below Les Avants there was a chalet where the **pensione** was wonderful and where we would be together and have our books and at night be warm in bed with the windows open and the stars bright. That was where we could go. Travelling third class on the train was not expensive. The pension cost very little more than we spent in Paris.

I would give up the room in the hotel where I wrote and there was only the rent of 74 rue du Cardinal Lemoine which was nominal. I had written journalism for Toronto and the cheques for that were due. I could write that anywhere under any circumstances and we had money to make the trip.

Maybe away from Paris I could write about Paris as in Paris I could write about Michigan. I did not know it was too early for that because I did not know Paris well enough. But that was how it worked out eventually. Anyway we would go if my wife wanted to, and I finished the oysters and the wine and paid my score in the cafe and made it the shortest way back up the Montagne Ste-Geneviève through the rain, that was now only local weather and not something that changed your life, to the flat at the top of the hill.

'I think it would be wonderful, Tatie,' my wife said. She had a gently modelled face and her eyes and her smile lighted up at decisions as though they were rich presents. 'When should we leave?'

'Whenever you want.'

'Oh, I want to right away. Didn't you know?'

'Maybe it will be fine and clear when we come back. It can be very fine when it is clear and cold.'

'I'm sure it will be,' she said. 'Weren't you good to think of going, too.'

•

When we came back to Paris it was clear and cold and lovely. The city had accommodated itself to winter, there was good wood for sale at the wood and coal place across our street, and there were braziers outside of many of the good cafes so that you could keep warm on the terraces. We burned *boulets* which were moulded, egg-shaped lumps of coal dust, on the wood fire, and on the streets the winter light was beautiful. Now you were accustomed to see the bare trees against the sky and you walked on the fresh-washed gravel paths through the Luxembourg gardens in the clear sharp wind. The trees were sculpture without their leaves when you were reconciled up them, and the winter winds blew across the surface of the ponds and the fountains blew in the bright light. All the distances were short now since we had been in the mountains.

Because of the change in altitude I did not notice the grade of the hills except with pleasure, and the climb up to the top floor of the hotel where I worked, in a room that looked across all the roofs and the chimneys of the high hill of the quarter, was a pleasure.

The fireplace drew well in the room and it was warm and pleasant to work. I brought mandarins and roasted chestnuts to the room in paper packets and peeled and ate the small tangerine-like oranges and threw their skins and spat their seeds in the fire when I ate them and roasted chestnuts when I was hungry. I was always hungry with the walking and the cold and the working. Up in the room I had a bottle of **kirsch** that we had bought back from the mountains and I took a drink of kirsch when I would get towards the end of a story or towards the end of the day's work. When I was through working for the day I put away the notebook, or the paper, in the drawer of the table and put any mandarins that were left in my pocket. They would freeze if they were left in the room at night.

It was wonderful to walk down the long flights of stairs knowing that I'd had good luck working. I always worked until I had something done and I always stopped when I knew what was going to happen next. That way I could be sure of going on the next day. But sometimes when I was starting a new story and I could not get it going, I would sit in front of the fire and squeeze the peel of the little oranges into the edge of the flame and watch the sputter of blue that they made.

I would stand and look out over the roofs of Paris and think, 'Do not worry. You have always written before and you will write now. All you have to do is write one true sentence. Write the truest sentence that you know.' So finally I would write one true sentence, and then go on from there. It was easy then because there was always one true sentence that I knew or had seen or had heard someone say. If I started to write elaborately, or like someone introducing or presenting something, I found that I could cut that scroll-work or ornament out and throw it away and start with the first true simple declarative sentence I had written. Up in that room I decided that I would write one story about each thing that I knew about. I was trying to do this all the time I was writing, and it was good and severe discipline.

It was in that room too that I learned not to think about anything that I was writing from the time I stopped writing until I started again the next day. That way my subconscious would be working on it and at the same time I would be listening to other people and noticing everything. I hoped; and I would read so that I would not think about my work and make myself impotent to do it. Going down the stairs when I had worked well – and that needed luck as well as discipline – was a wonderful feeling and I was free then to walk anywhere in Paris.

• ON TWO CITIES •

G K Chesterton (1874–1936)

This piece by Gilbert Keith Chesterton is on London and Paris, and was originally published in a collection of essays titled **All Things Considered,** *in 1924.*[1]

A little while ago I fell out of England into the town of Paris. If a man fell out of the moon into the town of Paris he would know that it was the capital of a great nation. If, however, he fell (perhaps off some other side of the moon) so as to hit the city of London, he would not know so well that it was the capital of a great nation; at any rate, he would not know that the nation was as great as it is. This would be so even on the assumption that the man from the moon could not read our alphabet, as presumably he could not, unless elementary education in that planet has gone to rather unsuspected lengths. But it is true that a great part of the distinctive quality which separates Paris from London may be even seen in the names. Real democrats always insist that England is an aristocratic country. Real aristocrats always insist (for some mysterious reason) that it is a democratic country. But if any one has any real doubt about the matter let him consider simply the names of the streets. Nearly all the streets out of the Strand, for instance, are named after the first name, second name, third name, fourth, fifth, and sixth names of some particular noble family; after their relations, connections, or places of residence – Arundel Street, Norfolk Street, Villiers Street, Bedford Street, Southampton Street, and any number of others. The names are varied, so as to introduce the same family under all sorts of different surnames. Thus we have Arundel Street and also Norfolk Street; thus we have Buckingham Street and also Villiers Street. To say that this is not aristocracy is simply intellectual impudence. I am an ordinary citizen, and my name is Gilbert Keith Chesterton; and I confess that if I found three

---

1 *The life of G K Chesterton is introduced on page 37.*

streets in a row in the Strand, the first called Gilbert Street, the second Keith Street, and the third Chesterton Street, I should consider that I had become a somewhat more important person in the commonwealth than was altogether good for its health. If Frenchmen ran London (which God forbid!), they would think it quite as ludicrous that those streets should be named after the Duke of Buckingham as that they should be named after me. They are streets out of one of the main thoroughfares of London. If French methods were adopted, one of them would be called Shakespeare Street, another Cromwell Street, another Wordsworth Street; there would be statues of each of these persons at the end of each of these streets, and any streets left over would be named after the date on which the Reform Bill was passed or the Penny Postage established.

Suppose a man tried to find people in London by the names of the places. It would make a fine farce, illustrating our illogicality. Our hero, having once realized that Buckingham Street was named after the Buckingham family, would naturally walk into Buckingham Palace in search of the Duke of Buckingham. To his astonishment he would meet somebody quiet different. His simple lunar logic would lead him to suppose that if he wanted the Duke of Marlborough (which seems unlikely) he would find him at Marlborough House. He would find the Prince of Wales. When at last he understood that the Marlboroughs live at Blenheim, named after the great Marlborough's victory, he would, no doubt, go there. But he would again find himself in error if, acting upon this principle, he tried to find the Duke of Wellington, and told the cabman to drive to Waterloo. I wonder that no one has written a wild romance about the adventures of such an alien, seeking the great English aristocrats, and only guided by the names; looking for the Duke of Bedford in the town of that name, seeking for some trace of the Duke of Norfolk in Norfolk. He might sail for Wellington in New Zealand to find the ancient seat of the Wellingtons. The last scene might show him trying to learn Welsh in order to converse with the Prince of Wales.

But even if the imaginary traveller knew no alphabet of this earth at all, I think it would still be possible to suppose him seeing a difference between London and Paris, and, upon the whole, the real difference. He would not be able to read the words 'Quai Voltaire', but he would see the sneering statue and the hard, straight roads; without having heard of Voltaire he would understand that the city was Voltairean. He would not know that Fleet Street was named after the Fleet Prison. But the same national spirit which kept the Fleet Prison closed and narrow still keeps Fleet Street closed and narrow. Or, if you will, you may call Fleet Street cosy, and the Fleet Prison cosy. I think I could be more comfortable in the Fleet Prison, in an

English way of comfort, than just under the statue of Voltaire. I think that the man from the moon would know France without knowing French; I think that he would know England without having heard the word. For in the last resort all men talk by signs. To talk by statues is to talk by signs; to talk by cities is to talk by signs. Pillars, palaces, cathedrals, temples, pyramids, are an enormous dumb alphabet: as if some giant held up his fingers of stone. The most important things at the last are always said by signs, even if, like the Cross on St. Paul's, they are signs in heaven. If men do not understand signs, they will never understand words.

For my part, I should be inclined to suggest that the chief object of education should be to restore simplicity. If you like to put it so, the chief object of education is not to learn things; nay, the chief object of education is to unlearn things. The chief object of education is to unlearn all the weariness and wickedness of the world and to get back into that state of exhilaration we all instinctively celebrate when we write by preference of children and of boys. If I were an examiner appointed to examine all examiners (which does not at present appear probable), I would not only ask the teachers how much knowledge they had imparted; I would ask them how much splendid and scornful ignorance they had erected, like some royal tower in arms. But, in any case, I would insist that people should have so much simplicity as would enable them to see things suddenly and to see things as they are. I do not care so much whether they can read the names over the shops. I do care very much whether they can read the shops. I do not feel deeply troubled as to whether they can tell where London is on the map so long as they can tell where Brixton is on the way home. I do not even mind whether they can put two and two together in the mathematical sense; I am content if they can put two and two together in the metaphorical sense. But all this longer statement of an obvious view comes back to the metaphor I have employed. I do not care a dump whether they know the alphabet, so long as they know the dumb alphabet.

Unfortunately, I have noticed in many aspects of our popular education that this is not done at all. One teaches our London children to see London with abrupt and simple eyes. And London is far more difficult to see properly than any other place. London is a riddle. Paris is an explanation. The education of the Parisian child is something corresponding to the clear avenues and the exact squares of Paris. When the Parisian boy has done learning about the French reason and the Roman order he can go out and see the thing repeated in the shapes of many shining public places, in the angles of many streets. But when the English boy goes out, after learning about a vague progress and idealism, he cannot see it anywhere. He cannot see anything anywhere, except Sapolio and the *Daily Mail.* We must either alter London to suit the ideals of our education, or else alter our education to suit the great beauty of London.

• DULL LONDON •

D H Lawrence (1885–1930)

David Herbert Lawrence was born into a mining family in England in 1885. In 1919 he and his wife left England and travelled for a number of years. They settled for a while in New Mexico, returning to Europe in 1929. The following year he died of tuberculosis.

Regarded as one of the great English novelists of the century, D H Lawrence wrote much poetry and many short stories, and published a number of essays.

The essay following was written in 1928, and published by Heinemann in a collection of essays by Lawrence titled **Selected Essays.**

It begins the moment you set foot ashore, the moment you step off the boat's gangway. The heart suddenly, yet vaguely, sinks. It is no lurch of fear. Quite the contrary. It is as if the life-urge failed, and the heart dimly sank. You trail past the benevolent policeman and the inoffensive passport officials, through the fussy and somehow foolish customs – we don't *really* think it matters if somebody smuggles in two pairs of false-silk stockings – and we get into the poky but inoffensive train, with poky but utterly inoffensive people, and we have a cup of inoffensive tea from a nice inoffensive boy, and we run through small, poky but nice and inoffensive country, till we are landed in the big but unexciting station of Victoria, when an inoffensive porter puts us into an inoffensive taxi and we are driven through the crowded yet strangely dull streets of London to the cosy yet strangely poky and dull place where we are going to stay. And the first half-hour in London, after some years abroad, is really a plunge of misery. The strange, the grey and uncanny, almost deathly sense of *dulness* is overwhelming. Of course, you get over it after a while, and admit that you exaggerated. You get into the rhythm of London again, and you tell yourself that it is *not* dull. And yet you are haunted, all the time, sleeping or waking, with the uncanny feeling: It is dull! It is all dull! This life here is one vast complex of dulness! I am dull! I am being dulled! My spirit is being dulled! My life is dulling down to London dulness.

This is the nightmare that haunts you the first few weeks of London. No doubt if you stay longer you get over it, and find London as thrilling as Paris or Rome or New York. But the climate is against me. I cannot stay long enough. With pinched and wondering gaze, the morning of departure, I look out of the taxi upon the strange dulness of London's arousing; a sort of death; and hope and life only return when I get my seat in the boat-train, and hear all the Good-byes! Good-bye! Good-bye! Thank God to say Good-bye!

Now to feel like this about one's native land is terrible. I am sure I am exceptional, or at least an exaggerated case. Yet it seems to me most of my fellow-countrymen have the pinched, slightly pathetic look in their faces, the vague, wondering realization: It is dull! It is always essentially dull! My life is dull!

Of course, England is the easiest country in the world, easy, easy and nice. Everybody is nice, and everybody is easy. The English people on the whole are surely the *nicest* people in the world, and everybody makes everything so easy for everybody else, that there is almost nothing to resist at all. But this very easiness and this very niceness become at last a nightmare. It is as if the whole air were impregnated with chloroform or some other pervasive anaesthetic, that makes everything easy and nice, and takes the edge off everything, whether nice or nasty. As you inhale the drug of easiness and niceness, your vitality begins to sink. Perhaps not your physical vitality, but something else: the vivid flame of your individual life. England can afford to be so free and individual because no individual flame of life is sharp and vivid. It is just mildly warm and safe. You couldn't burn your fingers at it. Nice, safe, easy: the whole ideal. And yet under all the easiness, is a gnawing uneasiness, as in a drug-taker.

It used not to be so. Twenty years ago London was to me thrilling, thrilling, thrilling, the vast and roaring heart of all adventure. It was not only the heart of the world, it was the heart of the world's living adventure. How wonderful the Strand, the Bank, Charing Cross at night, Hyde Park in the morning!

True, I am now twenty years older. Yet I have not lost my sense of adventure. But now all the adventure seems to me crushed out of London. The traffic is too heavy! It used to be going somewhere, on an adventure. Now it only rolls massively and overwhelmingly, going nowhere, only dully and enormously *going*. There is no adventure at the end of the buses' journey. The bus lapses into an inertia of dulness, then dully starts again. The traffic of London used to roar with the mystery of man's adventure on the seas of life, like a vast sea-shell, murmuring a thrilling, half-comprehensible story. Now it booms like monotonous, far-off guns, in a monotony of crushing something, crushing the earth, crushing out life, crushing everything dead.

And what does one do, in London? I, not having a job to attend to, lounge round and gaze in bleak wonder on the ceaseless dulness. Or I have luncheons and dinners with friends, and talk. Now my deepest private dread of London is my dread of this talk. I spend most of my days abroad, saying little, or with a bit of chatter and a silence again. But in London I feel like a spider whose thread has been caught by somebody, and is being drawn out of him, so he must spin, spin, spin, and all to no purpose. He is not even spinning his own web, for his own reasons.

So it is in London, at luncheon, dinner, or tea. I don't want to talk. I don't mean to talk. Yet the talk is drawn out of me, endlessly. And the others talk, endlessly also. It is ceaseless, it is intoxicating, it is the only real occupation of us who do not jazz. And it is purely futile. It is quite as bad as ever the Russians were: talk for talk's sake, without the very faintest intention of a result in action. Utter inaction and storms of talk. That again is London to me. And the sense of abject futility in it all only deepens the sense of abject dulness, so all there is to do is to go away.

• SO THIS IS LONDON •

Herman Charles Bosman (1905–1951)

A short while after his release from prison, Herman Charles Bosman travelled to Britain, and in this journalistic essay describes his visit to London in 1934. It was published in the **Uncollected Essays** *collection which appeared a while after his death.*[1]

What a South African first notices, when he comes to London, is the immense age of everything around him. Ancient marbles, scarred by centuries, and cold and silent tombs, and relics of dead kings.

You pass down Whitehall towards Victoria Street, and your path is strewn with vanished glories. Everywhere you are reminded of crumbled crowns, of forlorn majesties and lost splendours, of sceptres dropped from jewelled hands that have long lain in dust.

Then, when you have been suitably impressed by the hushed solemnity of the past, you discover that in London there is something older than her monuments, something more venerable than her tombs. I refer to the assortment of jokes that are classified generally as Cockney wit. These jokes be old indeed, my friends. Here – ah, here – is age.

The popular newspapers devote a great deal of prominence to this 'good-enough-for-Bert-Thomas-to-illustrate' type of funny story. But I find, after two years of earnest application, that the points of these jokes still elude me. Perhaps it will all just dawn on me, one day, suddenly.

Until that happens, however, I shall remain humble in the presence of Cockney humour. I shall go on feeling that I am missing something.

Talking of humour brings me, naturally to Hyde Park. It was here, one night, that I came across a man who told me the funniest Afrikaans story I had ever heard. It was about a predikant and the district drunkard.

---

1 *The writing of Herman Charles Bosman is introduced on page 9.*

Afterwards, I thought much about the man. I wondered how long he had been there, sitting on that park bench, in childlike faith that some day a stranger would come past, who would know about the veld and who would listen to his story. There was something very strange about this patience. Something frightening, almost. Like a poet waiting for the fairies to return.

Subsequently, when I had tea with him in Aldwych, I related this incident to another South African, Mr. Lionel Alfred, Junior, of Amalgamated Advertising Contractors. I discussed the matter in terms of abstract philosophy. 'It's queer how London always seems to lead the world in art and literature,' I said. 'Here I have had to come all the way to London, to Hyde Park, to hear the world's best Afrikaans story.'

'Yes,' Lionel Alfred answered, looking at me significantly, 'and that man is not the only South African who has slept in Hyde Park before today.'

I coughed then, and changed the subject.

But later on, when I remembered the sombre tone in which he had spoken, I began to think things about Lionel Alfred. I mean, I wonder what he did in London before he started working for Schlesinger?

But that man on the bench, there ... always he will remain for me a strange and disturbing symbol of Africa. And I haven't even bothered to write down his story.

Two kinds of people live in England. One kind is very tall, and breathes only the best available air, which is located in the upper regions of the atmosphere. This kind is known as the upper class. The other kind is very short. It is termed the lower class. These social distinctions follow a man wherever he goes. Even when a lower class man is seated right on top of a bus, you can still tell what class he belongs to: you can tell by the expensive cigar-ash that has been dropped on to his hat by a member of the upper class. Sometimes you see a man making furtive attempts at brushing off the cigar-ash in question. This process is known as social climbing.

They tell me that since the war class-distinctions have grown less marked. That makes me wonder what things were like before the war. It would be interesting to know what an upper class man dropped on to a lower class man's hat besides cigar-ash. Used tram-tickets, maybe.

There is also another class in London. Its members are found mostly in the parks on the Embankment. I don't know what is the position of this class in relation to society; but I do know that in relation to geometry its position is horizontal. I have only once seen a member of this class move out of the recumbent posture. That was near the Serpentine. This man raised his head and shoulders from the ground, very slightly, in order to expostulate with a passing duck.

'Second time I told you not to walk on my face,' he said, in tones of calm reason, 'with wet feet.'

I understand that this class's main grievance is concerned with the question of ducks walking on its face with muddy feet.

I once wrote a couple of articles for a newspaper, foretelling the downfall of civilisation. That was almost two years ago. A few weeks back the editor asked me for another article along those lines. 'Write me some more of that coming doom of civilisation dope,' he requested, elegantly.

But I told him it was too late, then. 'The doom,' I said, 'has already happened.'

They are nice boys, the journalists of Fleet Street, and in outlook they are very much in advance of the newspapers they work for. Perhaps that is why the Fleet Street journalists of today write so much better than the novelists and dramatists; better, even, than the professional writers of anonymous letters.

And at striking an effective literary pose they have got the poets here stone cold. Look at Hannen Swaffer, for instance.

The quality that has most impressed me about life in England is its simplicity. Europe seems to be very childlike and ingenuous next to Africa, with her old disquiet.

They accept life simply here. They feel no things deeply. You may call it civilisation, if you like; more probably you will call it decadence. And yet I think it is better so. I think it is better when the hearts of men are free from the turmoil of aspirations; from wayward dreams, and old and far-off longings, and wistful things, and they seek no more. It is as though hope has cast away her burden, in the way that a prisoner, summoned for release from a weary sentence, flings down his hammer by the stone-pile.

Or on a warder's foot.

• LIFE AWAKE •

Charles Lamb (1775–1834)

Charles Lamb lived all his life in London. He was educated at Christ's Hospital, where he formed a lifelong friendship with the Romantic poet Coleridge. His writings include essays, poetry and prose, but he is probably most remembered for the book **Tales from Shakespeare,** *which he and his sister Mary wrote in order to make Shakespeare accessible to young people.*

This passage is an extract from a letter he wrote to William Wordsworth in January 1901 which was published in R C Bald's collection titled Literary friendships in the age of Wordsworth. *Wordsworth's Lake District, which inspired so many of his poems, obviously did not appeal to Lamb, who was a committed Londoner.*

I ought before this to have replied to your very kind invitation into Cumberland. With you and your Sister I could gang any where. But I am afraid whether I shall ever be able to afford so desperate a Journey. Separate from the pleasure of your company, I don't much care if I never see a mountain in my life. I have passed all my days in London, until I have formed as many and intense local attachments, as any of you mountaineers can have done with dead nature. The Lighted shops of the Strand and Fleet Street, the innumerable trades, tradesmen and customers, coaches, wagons, playhouses, all the bustle and wickedness round about Covent Garden, the very women of the Town, the Watchmen, drunken scenes, rattles – life awake, if you awake, at all hours of the night, the impossibility of being dull in Fleet Street, the crowds, the very dirt mud, the Sun shining upon houses and pavements, the print shops, the old book stalls, parsons cheap'ning books, coffee houses, steams of soups from kitchens, the pantomimes, London itself a pantomime and a masquerade, – all these things work themselves into my mind and feed me, without a power of satiating me. The wonder of these sights impells me into night-walks about her crowded streets, and I often shed tears in the motley Strand from fulness of joy at so much Life. – All these emotions must be strange to you. So are your rural emotions to me. But consider, what must I have been doing all my life, not to have lent great portions of my heart with usury to such scenes?

My attachments are all local, purely local. I have no passion (or have had none since I was in love, and then it was the spurious engendering of poetry books) to groves and valleys. The rooms where I was born, the furniture which has been before my eyes all my life, a book case which has followed me about (like a faithful dog, only exceeding him in knowledge) wherever I have moved – old chairs, old tables, streets, squares, where I have sunned myself, my old school, – these are my mistresses. Have I not enough, without your mountains? I do not envy you. I should pity you, did I not know, that the Mind will make friends of anything. Your sun and moon and skies and hills and lakes affect me no more, or scarcely come to me in more venerable characters, than as a gilded room with tapestry and tapers, where I might live with handsome visible objects. I consider the clouds above me but as a roof, beautifully painted but unable to satisfy the mind, and at last, like the pictures of the apartment of a connoisseur, unable to afford him any longer a pleasure. So fading upon me, from disuse, have been the Beauties of Nature, as they have been confinedly called; so ever fresh and green and warm are all the inventions of men and assemblies of men in this great city. I should certainly have laughed with dear Joanna.

Give my kindest love, and my sister's, to D. and yourself and a kiss from me to little Barbara Lewthwaite.

C Lamb

• THE REELING EARTH •

Sarah Gertrude Millin (1889–1968)

Born in Lithuania, Sarah Gertrude Millin grew up near the diamond diggings on the lower reaches of the Vaal River. Her writings include a number of novels, short stories and biographies. J M Coetzee, one of South Africa's foremost contemporary writers, has referred to her as 'certainly the most considerable novelist writing in English in South Africa between Olive Schreiner and Nadine Gordimer.' She became a well-known and widely-travelled literary personality in her time.

The following extracts are from a diary kept during the second year of World War Two, which was published in **The Reeling Earth** *and* **World Blackout***. The selection is based on entries she made about the effects of the war on England in the 1940s. They show how the German blitz on London was perceived and interpreted by a British supporter living thousands of kilometres away. For those who lived through that year in England, her account reads like an exact account of a long, complicated nightmare, and it has been said by those who lived through the destruction that she saw better than they did, what was actually happening.*

5 September 1940 – 'The world', says Hitler (like everyone else, summing up the first year of war) 'must be set free. For good and all, we must do away with the absurd state of affairs where one nation is in a position, at its own sweet will, to blockade an entire continent ... and one pirate state expose over 450,000,000 people to poverty and misery ... The rule' (says Hitler) 'of pitiable, dishonourable warmongers must be abolished ....

When England realizes the seriousness of the game she is playing,' said Napoleon in 1805, 'she will be forced to give up the blockade.' And Hitler, too, means by his words England.

I sometimes wonder if Hitler hasn't a colossal sense of humour which makes him love to turn things upside down and then watch people take him seriously.

Here he enjoys himself taunting the English. For instance the way they find everything to their advantage: the Polish collapse: 'Now we can concentrate on the West.' The Norwegian collapse: 'The British war reports rejoiced over the enormous mistakes we Germans made.' The French collapse: 'At last England can concentrate all her forces.' England's allies: 'General Revolution. General Hunger. General Winter. General Bluff' ... to whom Germany will simply oppose General Fact, and 'see who is the better man ....'

'The British once said the war would last three years. We will prepare ourselves for five years. I said to Reichsmarschal Goering: "Prepare everything for five years." The British ask: "Why don't you come?" I reply: "Calm yourselves. We shall surely come!"'

9 September 1940 – Last night there was an air raid on London even more intense than that of Saturday night, the seventh. One hundred and fifty planes attacked London alone. They penetrated north of the Thames. All night the people were kept awake by warning sirens and screaming bombs. Churches, museums, hospitals, were hit. Houses were demolished, and people – perhaps as many as the night before – were killed and injured. Those caught at a distance from their homes, spent the night in bomb shelters. Now the trapped and injured are being sought among the debris; mobile canteens feed the homeless; thousands are moving away from their wrecked districts to districts less dangerous. Theatres are closing down. Children are too weary to attend school.

10 September 1940 – For the third night in succession London has been bombed. St. Paul's, says a cable, is safe after an all-night struggle by hundreds of firemen. I have a superstitious feeling that St. Paul's, if it symbolizes the Nation's faith, will survive.

The bodies of children are being taken from a wrecked school in the East End. The babies, in a maternity hospital that was bombed, were placed in cots under the beds of their mothers; and mothers and babies were finally taken in ambulances, guarded, during a raid, by police, to the country. Thousands of families are being moved from devastated East End districts; and, from wealthier districts, furniture and valuables are being deposited in safe places. The Archbishop of Canterbury tells of sleepless nights, 'with hideous bombings, not at intervals, but every minute'; 'of not knowing where the next bomb will fall or the next fire will break out.'

The people of Berlin should experience such nights. They like total things. Let them have nights of total horror.

In London they are carrying on business – not quite – as usual. The

A.R.P. workers, fighting fire and destruction night after night, without self-regard, are the new heroes. But one can't go on being heroic without sleep. Let the people of Berlin, not the people of London, go mad in this madness they have loosed on the world. Berlin 'is become a habitation of devils and a hold of every unclean spirit ... her sins have reached even unto heaven ... Render unto her even as she rendered, and double unto her the double according to her works .... In one day shall her plagues come, death and mourning and famine. And she shall be utterly burned with fire .... And shall be found no more at all'.

12 September 1940 – Mr Churchill has broadcast to the people of England and the Empire his thought that there may be an invasion of England – perhaps next week. He compares the days with those 'when the Spanish Armada was approaching the Channel, and Drake was finishing his game of bowls; or when Nelson stood between us and Napoleon's Grand Army at Boulogne.' He tells his listeners what they have to fear, and what to hope:

'The effort of the Germans to secure daylight mastery of the air over England is, of course, the crux of the whole war. So far it has failed conspicuously ....'

Mr Churchill tells how England will oppose the Germans with her fleets and flotillas, her Air Force 'conscious of its proved superiority, not indeed in numbers, but in men and machines. Our shores are well fortified and strongly manned, and, behind them, ready to attack the invaders, we have a far larger and better-equipped mobile army than we have ever had before.'

'This wicked man,' Mr Churchill describes Hitler in his out-of-date, Drury Lane, startling way, 'has now resolved to break our famous island race by indiscriminate slaughter and destruction. What he has done is to kindle a fire in British hearts ... which will burn with a steady and consuming flame until the last vestiges of Nazi tyranny have been burnt out of Europe, and until the Old World – and the New – can join hands to rebuild the temples of man's freedom and man's honour, upon foundations which will not soon or easily be overthrown.'

I am often reminded by Mr Churchill, not only of Drury Lane, but also of Shakespeare – of Henry V speaking Shakespeare's words.

But these days, when England stands alone defending civilization, are nobler than the days when kings fought for fun – holier, too, than the times of the crusades when, first exaltation past, men went, for fun again, for adventure and profit, to 'tread the wine-press of the Lord'.

13 September 1940 – The world is waiting to see if England will be blotted from the Book of Life. Yesterday the Germans came three times over London and lost 91 aircraft to the British 24 – seven pilots safe. A delayed action bomb exploded in the grounds of Buckingham Palace and damaged the Palace.

Today six more bombs were dropped on Buckingham Palace, and the Royal Chapel was wrecked. The King and Queen, in an air raid shelter, escaped injury.

The House of Lords has been damaged. Bombs have fallen in Downing Street, Bond Street, Regent Street, the Burlington Arcade. Several churches, the offices of the *Standard* and *Herald,* Madame Tussaud's, have been damaged. The Bank of England 'has not escaped'.

17 September 1940 – Within the last few days bombs have fallen in Park Lane, Bond Street, Regent Street, Bruton Street, Berkeley Square, Oxford Street, Piccadilly, Piccadilly Circus; in the courtyards of the British Museum and Wallace Collection; in the library of the Inner Temple; on Somerset House. They have damaged or destroyed some of London's greatest shops, hotels, cafes, houses. Lord Londonderry's house has been hit, which he offered as a shelter to families rendered homeless by bombs.

Desolate East Enders are now camping in many of the great West End homes. The air-raid warnings went on last night for ten hours.

25 September 1940 – They are behaving in Europe as if England is finished; yet, alone, England does still stand. It is the greatest drama, the greatest time, in history.

Only, the actors in this immortal drama, these supermen, have to express their glory by scurrying underground like animals – among their maimed and destroyed and the litter of their inheritance.

9 October 1940 – Mr Churchill has told the House that England's casualties to date are 8 500 killed and 13 000 wounded; and since the heavy September raids the figures have declined by a thousand a week from 6 000 to 3 000.

But the destruction of property, he says, is considerable. He speaks in particular of the small houses, whose people are the worst sufferers, but who say 'We can take it', and also 'Give it 'em back' ... 'We will rebuild them (these houses), says Mr Churchill, 'more to our credit than some of them were before. London, Liverpool, Manchester, Birmingham, may have much to suffer, but they will rise from their ruins, more healthy, and, I hope, more beautiful.'

He approaches his end:

'Long dark months of trials and tribulations lie before us. Not only great dangers, but many misfortunes, many shortcomings, many mistakes, many disappointments will surely be our lot. Death and sorrow will be the companions of our journey; hardship our garments; constancy and valour our only shield ....'

5 November 1940 – England had last month her heaviest shipping losses of the war – over 172 000 tons. There were nearly 7 000 civilians killed in air raids and over 10 000 injured. Nevertheless, she would have been glad in July, says Mr Churchill, to foresee her position in November. 'Surveying the whole scene, alike in its splendour and its devastation, I see no reason to regret that Herr Hitler tried to break the British spirit by the blind bombing of our cities and our countryside.'

'Herr Hitler,' says Mr Churchill, 'declared on 4th September that, as we would not bend to his will, he would wipe out our cities .... The cities of Britain are still standing, they are quite distinctive objects on our landscape.'

The people of England (34 000 killed and injured) are standing too, he proudly claims. They face 'a mighty army crouching across the Channel and the North Sea'. We face one gigantic army across the waters of the Channel. We face another very powerful army on the frontier of the Libyan Desert ... In the circumstances there is only one thing we can do. We shall do, 'says Mr Churchill, 'our best.'

10 November 1940 – Hitler, celebrating the abortive 1923 Putsch, has spoken of Germany's battle (her crusade) against the Jews and Jew-controlled England: the 'small clique of international democrats, Jews and plutocracies ... Churchill and Company'.

He claims that the Germans carried out no night raids on Poland, Norway, Holland, Belgium, France until suddenly Mr Churchill had bombs dropped on the German civil population. 'I waited in patience, thinking, 'the man is mad: such action can only lead to Britain's destruction!' I made my plans for peace .... In vain. They wanted to fight, and they are going to get it ....

'The German people', says Hitler, 'ask for a peace ... which will make it impossible for an international crook to incite other nations against us .... Mr

Churchill, that arch-liar, was recently forced to give up lying about submarine losses. He now has to admit that German submarines have increased in number. I can assure you that they will go on increasing, and that one of these days there will be no Mr Churchill, but there will still be German U-Boats.'

16 November 1940 – Waves of heavy bombers flew over Coventry city on the night of the 14th and made a hell of it. The news says nothing of any opposition. 'A hail of fire bombs', it says, 'began a series of fires which lit up districts for miles around, and cascades of bomber formations plastered the floodlit areas hour after hour. Within a few minutes the centre of the town was ablaze. Factories, offices, shops, banks, hospitals, hotels and cinemas were all an inferno, and the fourteenth-century cathedral is reduced to ruins.'

There are a thousand and fifty casualties.

Hundreds of German raiders yesterday attacked London and the Midlands. In London seven hospitals and five convents were hit. Buckingham Palace has been hit again. St. Martin-in-the-Fields has been hit. The bomb tore a hole in the pavement, pitted the wall with splinters, decapitated the figure of Christ in the stained glass window over the altar, and made holes in the Apostles. Down in the crypt, 600 people sang – not hymns, but 'Annie Laurie.'

25 December 1940 – In Greece the bells are ringing this Christmas Day to celebrate the capture of Chimara and all the other successes of the Greeks.

Marshal Pétain, following some new Fascist measure, has spoken to his people, comparing the birth of Christ with the rebirth of France: 'It is the feast of the Nativity. A new France has been born.'

In Bethlehem itself there was a blackout for Christmas. The tawdry lamps of the Church of the Nativity remained unlit.

'A proper Christmas', says King Haakon, 'cannot be celebrated by Norwegians in a Norway in chains.'

Queen Wilhelmina says that 'all the evil in the world has not been able, through the ages, to change or weaken God's eternal, impenetrable, inexhaustible, merciful love' .... She innocently adds: 'I think of threatening hunger, cold, lack of clothing and shelter ... of the many tears shed for the loved ones who have departed, of all the deep heartfelt suffering under injustice that is being committed, of down-trodden freedom, shattered happiness, joy extinguished.'

Hitler is spending Christmas with his troops in the West. General von Brauschitsch says: 'We are convinced that the war is already won, and that Hitler will end it in the way needed by our nation for the security of its future. I know that you are burning with desire at last to engage the English. I know how eagerly you are awaiting Hitler's order.'

Rudolf Hess says a German victory will be 'a blessing for Europe' and 'perhaps bring true peace to the world .... Divine justice', he says, 'has turned against England .... The Almighty has created the German people. To serve this people is thus also to serve the Almighty who created it.'

Dr Frank, Governor of German Poland, says: 'Adolf Hitler is called upon to be the leader of the world, unhampered by anyone .... It is the greatest gift of Heaven to be able to call oneself a German. We are proud to master the world as Germans.'

And here I go round asking myself how Germans are not horrified at being Germans, not frightened that they are made in the image of their god, Hitler.

28 December 1940 – London has again been heavily bombed. A Church of England review of the past year says that over a thousand of its churches, schools, halls and vicarages have suffered through enemy action.

The miners of Durham (whose Cathedral, the loveliest in England, has not yet, I think, been bombed) have sent a message to miners in German occupied territories:

'Whatever the toll to be paid, whatever the sacrifice involved, we will face it cheerfully in the realization that there can be no hope for mankind so long as the Nazis exist .... We urge you to trust the words of men who have never dishonoured their pledge and who have never shirked danger and death in fulfilment of rescue.'

The message sounds as if those Durham miners saw the comrades they were addressing entombed: and, through gas, fire and crashing rock, were tunnelling their way to them. It moves me, as I have not been moved by Mr Churchill's messages to France and Italy. Perhaps Mr Churchill's voice is not adapted to the dulcet tone.

Still, there is this: Mr Churchill *will* stand, and, in the last war, the miners always – struck.

• THE ARTIST AND • THE WAR

Virginia Woolf (1882–1941)

Virginia Woolf was born in London, and became an important figure in a circle of writers known as the 'Bloomsbury Group'. In 1912 she married Leonard Woolf, another member of the group, and together they founded the Hogarth Press in 1917, which published many famous works, including the poems of T S Eliot. Her first books were novels, and at the time of her death she had won foremost place among English fiction writers. In 1941, experiencing a depth of depression exacerbated by the war, she committed suicide by drowning.

Virginia Woolf was a prolific letter-writer and more than 4 000 of her letters have been published – although she once described her letter writing as 'a mere tossing of omelettes'. The letters selected here span the years 1938 to 1941, during which Virginia and Leonard were forced to move, for safety's sake, from their home in London to their country home. Virginia's writings of this time are filled with a mixture of horror and fascination with both the beauty of the countryside and the destruction in the cities. Broken by the devastation of London, she found it difficult to write, and fell into an increasingly disturbed state of depression.

To Vanessa Bell *1st October 1938*

Monks House, Rodmell,
Lewes, Sussex

In London it was hectic and gloomy and at the same time despairing and yet cynical and calm. The streets were crowded. People were everywhere talking loudly about war. There were heaps of sandbags in the streets, also men digging trenches, lorries delivering planks, loud speakers slowly driving and solemnly exhorting the citizens of Westminster 'Go and fit your gas masks.' There was a long queue of people waiting outside the Mary Ward settlement to be fitted. Leonard went off at once to see Kingsley Martin. Then he came back and said Kingsley was in despair, they had talked for two hours; everybody came into the *New Statesman* office and talked; telephones rang incessantly. They all said war was certain; also that there would be no war. Kingsley came to dinner. He had smudges of black charcoal round his eyes and was more melodramatic and histrionic than ever. Hitler was going to make his speech at 8. We had no wireless, but he said he would ring up the BBC after it was over and find out the truth. Then we sat and discussed the inevitable end of civilisation. He strode up and down the room, hinting that he meant to kill himself. He said the war would last our life time; also we should very likely be beaten. Anyhow Hitler meant to bombard London, probably with no warning; the plan was to drop bombs on London with twenty minutes intervals for forty-eight hours. Also he meant to destroy all roads and railways; therefore Rodmell would be about as dangerous as Bloomsbury. Then he broke off; rang up Clark, the news man at the BBC, 'Ah – so its hopeless ....' Then to us, 'Hitler is bawling; the crowds howling like wild beasts.' More conversation of a lugubrious kind. 'Now I think I'll ring up Clark again .... Ah so it couldn't be worse .... To us: Now Hitler is more mad than ever .... Have some whiskey Kingsley, said Leonard. Well, it don't much matter either way, said Kingsley. At last he went. What are you going to do? I asked. Walk the streets. It's no good – I can't sleep. So we clasped hands, as I understood, for the last time.

Next morning Tuesday every one was certain it was war. Everyone, except one poor little boy in a shop who had lost his head and was half crying when I asked for a packet of envelopes (and he may have been in some sort of row) was perfectly calm; and also without hope. It was quite different from 1914. Everyone said probably we shall win but it'll be just as bad if we do. I went to the London Library to look up some papers about Roger. I sat in the basement with the *Times* open of the year 1910. An old man was dusting. He went away; then came back and said very kindly, 'They're telling us to put on our gas masks, Madam'. I thought the raid had begun. However, he explained that it was the loudspeaker once more addressing the citizens of Westminster. Then he asked if he could dust under my chair, and said they had laid in a supply of sand bags, but if a bomb dropped there wouldn't be many books left.

To Vanessa Bell *Monday, October 3rd 1938*

Monks House, Rodmell,
Lewes, Sussex

Gwen St Aubyn arrived from Lewes; she had been taking her daughters school [Frances Holland] from London to Stanner Park. Miracles of organisation had been performed by everyone. The roads, she said were crowded with lorries full of escaping schools. Vita said it was known for certain that London was to be attacked at twenty minutes intervals for twenty-four hours with gas and bombs. Also that Mussolini had been stiffened at the last moment by the king of Italy who had said he would abdicate. Hence his pressure upon Hitler; which had turned the tide at the last moment. We came back, half expecting to find our refugees waiting us at Monks House. Mercifully there was no one.

Then next day we all turned rather cynical, and were sure of peace with dishonour. Then the BBC kept on saying that nothing was safe, we were all to go on expecting war; until finally Chamberlain arrived; and we heard him read the terms from Heston; frantic cheers; hysterical cries from old ladies; then the Archbishop praying; then bells pealing; while here at Rodmell a service was hastily got up; our bells made a perfectly infernal din; Mrs Ebbs [wife of the rector] in vain tried to whip up the villagers to some excitement; but one and all they remained perfectly sure that it was a dirty business; and meant only another war when we should be unable to resist. Of course the country was much calmer than London. Leonard was amazed by the sagacity of the old gaffers. The Postman stayed and talked good sense for about half an hour. The BBC however still announced that all reptiles would be shot at the Zoo; and any tiger that escaped killed at sight. I think they were so proud of their organisation that they wanted to air it, though it began to leak out that the air defence had been found full of holes; and that the carnage would have been immense in London.

We all analysed our complexities of shame, and fear; Lydia said Maynard had really been a great deal alarmed; and excited. Of course the truth was that one felt all along that Chamberlain had something up his sleeve; only one couldn't say how much. Also the feeling of despair and coming death was very genuine in London, however irrational. I am proud to say that my last words on leaving the Press were 'There won't be war' but I was hooted down. I suppose everyone, except Kingsley Martin, chopped and changed. For instance some of the Gordon Square pundits – friends of Maynard's – refused to agree to trenches being dug in the square and held out that war was impossible. On the other hand, the whole Royal Society has fled to the country; and Cambridge was so disorganised – all the colleges fitted up as hospitals – that it has had to put off term for some days. It it was all a piece of stage management on Chamberlain's part, he took in a great many authorities.

To Vanessa Bell *Saturday October 8th 1938*

Monks House, Rodmell,
Lewes, Sussex

You say you want details. England has now settled down to the usual cat and dog; I mean, I told you so, it's your fault no it's not; kettle yourself; pot yourself; or whatever the phrase is. Trenches were dug because if you lie at the bottom of a sloping hole, a shell will burst at either side and miss you. Two workmen were buried alive making them. As for gas masks, many have died through testing them on the exhaust pipes of cars. Government has now issued an edict that they're not to be tried on gas pipes as they don't work. Black boxes are being issued to keep them in against the next war.

To Vanessa Bell *24th October 1938*

52 Tavistock Square, W.C. 1.

London is appalling, but also I admit fascinating – in its meretricious way. Also Exmouth Street Market, with a black corpse of a horse among flowers and cheap glass has its appeal; also Hampton Court where we went yesterday in the balm of a perfect summers day, was worth all your black-visaged spectacular south. We roamed the park, smelt the flowers, and mooned along the galleries where, thanks [to] Roger, I'm now seeing in chairs, pictures, tapestries, a remote world of inexplicable significance. I think the art of painting is the art for one's old age. I respect it more and more. I adore its severity; its bareness from impurity. All books are now rank with the slimy seaweed of politics; mouldy and mildewed. I wish I could settle to pure fiction; indeed had to rush headlong into a novel as a relief; but am now back at Roger and the compromise of biography again.

To V Sackville-West *Tuesday 29th August 1939*

Monk's House, Rodmell,
near Lewes, Sussex

Well, there's another day of peace – I mean we've just listened in to the Prime Minister. I suppose Harold came back [from the House of Commons], so you didn't come [to Rodmell].

I can't help letting hope break in, – the other prospect is too mad.

But I don't think I'm philosophic – rather, numbed. It's so hot and sunny on our little island – Leonard gardening, playing bowls, cooking our dinner: and outside such a waste of gloom. Of course I'm not in the least patriotic, which may be a help, and not afraid, I mean for my own body. But that's an old body. And all the same I should like another ten years: and I like my friends: and I like the young. That'll all go forever if – Meanwhile, not a van will come to unpack furniture or remove books at 37; all's held up: publishing and moving blocked. We go up on Thursday to see what's to be done.

Otherwise come at any time, and indeed, my dearest creature, whatever rung I'm on the ladder is a great comfort in this kind of intolerable suspension of all reality – something real.

But isn't it odd? – one can't fold it in any words.

To Angelica Bell *Monday 16 October 1939*

37 Mecklenburgh Square, W.C.1.

Dearest Pixie,

You can't think how difficult it is to write a letter in this doomed and devastated but at the same time morbidly fascinating town. Also there's a dearth of pens and a prevalence, indeed a pullulation of chamber pots. Oh and the books: all over the floor: oh and the pictures: all on their heads. Oh oh oh ....

We lunched with Mrs Drake to meet Mrs Webb: and she was like a dead leaf spotted with fire – so crinkled; so curled; but invincible in spite of bladder trouble and cancer by the sheer might of disinterested intelligence. Her nephew at the War Office says there'll be a raid tonight: (so this is no doubt my dying word) and the War will be over by Xmas, because its a fact that the German army is already in disruption. Hitler's last fling will be at our heads tonight and tomorrow.

You don't know what a queer place London is – here we are running in and out of each others' houses with torches and gas masks. Black night descends. Rain pours. Vast caterpillars are now excavating trenches in the Square. Shops shut at 5 or so. Many windows remain black all day. The streets are a hurry scurry of people walking. Ambulances abound. Very stout women wear blue trousers. No one ever sits down. The buses are quick but rare. And in short – I've just pulled down the black blinds – rats in caves live as we do.

To Benedict Nicolson *13 August 1940*

Monk's House, Rodmell,
Lewes, Sussex

Dear Ben,

Just as I began to read your letter, an air raid warning sounded. I'll put down the reflections that occurred to me, as honestly, if I can, as you put down your reflections on reading my life of Roger Fry while giving air raid alarms at Chatham.

There goes that damned siren, I said to myself, and dipped into your letter. You were making extracts from Roger's letters as you listened. 'Returning slowly through France he stopped in many of the towns and villages ....'

Here the raiders came overhead. I went and looked at them. Then I returned to your letter. 'I am so struck by the fools' paradise in which he and his friends lived. He shut himself out from all disagreeable actualities and allowed the spirit of Nazism to grow without taking any steps to check it ....'

Here the raiders began emitting long trails of smoke. I wondered if a bomb was going to fall on top of me; I wondered if I was facing disagreeable actualities; I wondered what I could have done to stop bombs and disagreeable actualities .... Then I dipped into your letter again. 'This all sounds as though I wish to say that the artist, the intellectual, has no place in modern society. On the contrary, his mission is now more vital than it has ever been. He will still be shocked by stupidity and untruth but instead of ignoring it he will set out to fight it; instead of retreating into his tower to uphold certain ethical standards his job will be to persuade as many other people as possible to think and behave in the same way – and on his success and failure depend the future of the world.'

Who on earth, I thought, did that job more incessantly and successfully than Roger Fry? Didn't he spend half his life, not in a tower, but travelling about England addressing masses of people, who'd never looked at a picture and making them see what he saw? And wasn't that the best way of checking Nazism? Then I opened another letter, as it happened from Sebastian Sprott, a lecturer at Nottingham; and I read how he'd once been mooning around the S. Kensington Museum: '... then I saw Roger. All was changed. In ten minutes he caused me to enjoy what I was looking at. The objects became vivid and intelligible .... There must be many people like me, people with scales on their eyes and wax in their ears ... if only someone would come along and remove the scales and dig out the wax. Roger Fry did it ....'

But what I'd like to know is, suppose we both survive this war, what ought we to do to prevent another? I shall be too old to do anything but write. But will you throw up your job as an art critic and take to politics? And if you stick to art criticism, how will you make it more public and less private than Roger did?

Well, the hostile aeroplanes have passed over my head now; I suppose they're dropping bombs over Newhaven and Seaford.

I hope this letter doesn't sound unkind. Its only because I liked your being honest so much that I've tried to be. And of course I know you're having a much worse time of it at the moment than I am ... Another siren has just sounded.

To Ethel Smyth *11th September 1940*

Monk's House, Rodmell,
near Lewes, Sussex

Yesterday we were up in London, and there was a crowd at Meck Square: a policeman stopped us: we got out – saw that the house just opposite ours across the road had been entirely crushed that night. A direct hit on top. It was nothing but a heap of bricks, smoking still. And we weren't allowed to go to 37, as a bomb was still in the square unexploded. Our house wasn't touched, but the windows are broken. So there was nothing for it but to come away. Everyone apparently in that house – one of those lovely houses at the side – had sheltered in the basement. All killed I suppose. We go up on Friday to arrange about moving the Press [to Letchworth, Hertfordshire], and to bring back some of our valuables, that is if we're allowed. But everyone has been evacuated; the Press can't work – and then we went and saw Holborn – my word – it's like a nightmare. All heaps of glass, water running, a great gap at the top of Chancery Lane; my typist's office demolished.

I've just seen a plane shot down on the hill beside Lewes. We heard firing, ran out, and saw the plane swerve and fall, and then a burst of black smoke. Then the English plane circled and made off. There's the all-clear.

That's why it's so difficult to write a coherent letter. I try to write of a morning. Its odd to feel one's writing in a vacuum – no-one will read it. I feel the audience has gone. Still, so oddly is one made, I find I must spin my brain even in a vacuum.

But I want to know about you. Vita was coming but at the last moment she rang up. Bombs were dropping round Sissinghurst, and she had to stay, as she drives an ambulance. Rose Macaulay is doing the same in London. I admire that very much. Here we lead a disjointed jumping life. I had a niece staying here; another in a cottage. They collected friends in the airforce and so on. We had a féte: also a village play. The sirens sounded in the middle. All the mothers sat stolid. I also admired that very much.

Post Script *Thursday 12 September*

I've been up on the hill picking blackberries for dinner, and lost a glove that was to have lasted a winter, and suddenly conceived the idea of a new book, and really I think I can weather – I mean weather cock – I mean brain spin – another ten years if Hitler doesn't drop a splinter into my machine. Churchill cheered me up. Also this great gale that's blowing as it must have blown the other Armada. What touched and indeed raked what I call my heart in London was the grimy old woman at the lodging house at the back, all dirty after the raid, and preparing to sit out another. We, after all, have at least been to Italy and read Shakespeare. They haven't: dear me, I'm turning democrat. And then, the passion of my life, that is the City of London – to see London all blasted, that too raked my heart. Have you that feeling for certain alleys and little courts, between Chancery Lane and the City? I walked to the Tower the other day by way of caressing my love of all that. We might be in the Strand, here at night the raiders make such a noise of traffic – like buses and drays – in the sky. Now and then a bomb drops – but far away – Eastbourne I think.

To Ethel Smyth *14th November 1940*

Monk's House, Rodmell,
near Lewes, Sussex

Another bomb in Meck Square: did I tell you? All the books down again. Did I tell you we half think of moving the furniture here? We brought down a car load last week. Then, to my infinite delight, they bombed our river. Cascades of water roared over the marsh – All the gulls came and rode the waves at the end of the field. It was, and still is, an inland sea, of such indescribable beauty, almost always changing, day and night, sun and rain, that I can't take my eyes off it.

To Ethel Smyth *12th January 1941*

Monk's House, Rodmell
Sussex

How odd it is being a countrywoman after all these years of being Cockney! For almost the first time in my life I've not a bed in London. D'you know what I'm doing tomorrow? Going up to London Bridge. Then I shall walk, all along the Thames, in and out where I used to haunt, so through the Temple, up the Strand and out into Oxford Street, where I shall buy macaroni and lunch. No. You never shared my passion for that great city. Yet it's what, in some odd corner of my dreaming mind, represents Chaucer, Shakespeare, Dickens.

To Ethel Smyth *February 1st 1941*

Monk's House, Rodmell,
Sussex

Did I tell you I'm reading the whole of English literature through? By the time I've reached Shakespeare the bombs will be falling. So I've arranged a very nice last scene: reading Shakespeare, having forgotten my gas mask, I shall fade far away, and quite forget.... They brought down a raider the other side of Lewes yesterday. I was cycling in to get our butter, but only heard a drone in the clouds. Thank God, as you would say, one's fathers left one a taste for reading! Instead of thinking, by May we shall be – whatever it may be: I think, only three months to read Ben Jonson, Milton, Donne, and all the rest!

To Elizabeth Robins *March 13th 1941*

Monk's House, Rodmell,
Lewes, Sussex

It's amazingly peaceful here, you can almost hear the grass grow; and the rooks are building; you wouldn't think that at 7.30 the planes will be over. Two nights ago they dropped incendiaries, in a row, like street lamps, all along the downs. Two hay stacks caught and made a lovely illumination – but no flesh was hurt. Indeed, every bomb they drop only casts up a crater so far. It's difficult, I find, to write. No audience. No private stimulus, only this outer roar.

To Vanessa Bell *Sunday 23 March 1941*

Monk's House, Rodmell,
near Lewes, Sussex

Dearest,

You can't think how I loved your letter. But I feel that I have gone too far this time to come back again. I am certain now that I am going mad again. It is just as it was the first time, I am always hearing voices, and I know I shan't get over it now.

All I want to say is that Leonard has been so astonishingly good, every day, always; I can't imagine that anyone could have done more for me than he has. We have been perfectly happy until the last few weeks, when this horror began. Will you assure him of this? I feel he has so much to do that he will go on, better without me, and you will help him.

I can hardly think clearly any more. If I could I would tell you what you and the children have meant to me. I think you know.

I have fought against it, but I can't any longer.

To Leonard Woolf *28 March 1941*

Monk's House, Rodmell,
Sussex

Dearest,

I want to tell you that you have given me complete happiness. No one could have done more than you have done. Please believe that.

But I know that I shall never get over this: and I am wasting your life. It is this madness. Nothing anyone says can persuade me. You can work, and you will be much better without me. You see I can't write this even, which shows I am right. All I want to say is that until this disease came on we were perfectly happy. It was all due to you. No one could have been so good as you have been, from the very first day till now. Everyone knows that.

V.

• BOWLED OVER •

Kingsley Fairbridge (1885–1924)

Born in Grahamstown, Kingsley Fairbridge moved with his parents to what was then Rhodesia, where he worked as a bank clerk, journalist and market gardener. He visited England in 1903 and then returned in 1906 as a Rhodes Scholar. He later moved to Australia, where he died in 1924.

His only volume of poems, entitled **Veld Verse and Other Lines,** *was published in 1909, while his* **Autobiography,** *from which the following extract is taken, was published posthumously in 1927.*

All of a sudden his heart and will
Cried out to God for a wild bird's wings
To fly from the snares and the cruelties
Out to the veld, where men are few,
Where Peace is rous'd by each sunrise new,
And God leans down from His lonely skies!

Arthur Shearly Cripps: *A Way Out*

I set foot in England for the first time in March, 1903. The first thing that I remarked was the apparent nearness of the grey sky. In quick succession I was surprised by the youthful look of the people, by the fresh damp smell, by the dirtiness of the walls of the houses, by the vivid green of the fields, and last – but by no means least – by curious stripes that lay across many of the meadows. It was not till years later that I discovered that these stripes were caused by rolling the grass in spring.

As we drove along the narrow, winding streets of London, a sense of keen disappointment came over me. I had expected a city of gold and white, mighty thoroughfares, imposing edifices, solemnity. Instead straggled long lines of grimy three-storied living-houses, ill-lit and uninviting. Instead of stately processions of dignified citizens, conscious of the responsibilities of Empire, I found throngs of smallish, active, young-looking people, shouting, running hither and thither, vending papers and posies and penny toys. Cartoons and advertisements flared at me from every hoarding.

This was Saturday evening; I had only about seventeen shillings in my pocket, and my grandmother had told me she was moving, so I set about waiting as cheaply as I could until I got her address from her bank on Monday. I got my bed and breakfast for, I think, 5*s*; for lunch I ate nothing, and I converted dinner into a fairly light afternoon meal which consisted of a cup of cocoa, 2*d*, and a bun, 1*d*.

My amusements had to be cheap also. Two or three of us went down the Strand to Piccadilly that Saturday night, and I was accosted by a benevolent old gentleman who presumed that I belonged to the Wild West show at Olympia. I had never heard either of this entertainment or of Olympia; and I was highly indignant that an Englishman could not recognize a fellow Englishman when he saw him. But this incident called my attention to my sun-bleached peaked hat, upon the rim of which was scored my big game kill on the Mazoe. I determined to get a bowler.

I awoke the next morning to a tremendous silence reigning over the City of London, a silence broken only by the twittering of numbers of sparrows down in Charterhouse Square. As soon as I had had breakfast I hurried outside to see London. The sparrows appealed to me tremendously; every breath of the damp air seemed fraught with new things .... I peered through the iron railings at old Charterhouse School; I found an old friend, a very grimy fig-tree, growing against a wall in the Square. Then I went forth into Aldersgate Street and discovered St. Paul's. I knew it was really St. Paul's because a policeman told me. I did not go inside, not because I did not want to see the inside, but solely because I did not want to go 'to church' that morning.

The following morning, Monday, was a revelation to me. Instead of my empty Aldersgate Street and my deserted Cheapside, I found the City throbbing with life. Great tides of people swept the pavements, the roads were invisible for the throngs of drays and cabs and buses.

I love England. She cured me of a bitter sickness, of bitter hatreds, of bitter ignorance. The English summer filled my ears with song, and my heart with gladness. The grey keen winter rested eyes that were over-tired with gazing against the sun, and healed nerves that were frayed and ragged. In the quiet cold of autumn, in the dark rains of winter, in the boisterous keenness of spring, I discovered a plodding energy of which I had never dreamed. I love England for her surpassing history, and I love her for her youth.

I was never weary of exploring London streets, travelling on unfamiliar buses, and watching the people. I was fond of dropping in at out-of-the-way eating-houses, for there I had opportunities of meeting many strange people. After the purchase of a bowler hat I was never taken for anything but a Londoner. Now and again while 'taking a glass' with some friendly carter or publican I divulged the fact of my South African birth, and this never failed to elicit surprise. I was, on these occasions, invariably complimented on my correct English; and I never escaped a certain inward bitterness when the fact that I was *white* was commented on.

• EISTEDDFOD •

Dylan Thomas (1914–1953)

Dylan Thomas was born in Swansea, Wales, but later moved to London. His writings reflect his Welsh background, but he himself spoke disparaging of the country of his birth, once saying of it, 'The land of my fathers. My father can have it.'

Although famous mainly for his poetry, he also published a number of prose works and a play. By the time that he died during a lecture tour of the United States, he was already something of a legend as a poetry reader and broadcaster, and for his rather bohemian lifestyle. The coroner said he died of 'an insult to the brain' after drinking eighteen straight whiskys in a night.

Twenty-seven years after his death, in 1981, he was accorded an honour he would never have dreamt of, when he was buried in Westminster Abbey – the traditional burial place of England's greatest writers. Most of the delay had to do with widespread beliefs that his lifestyle should have excluded him from a church burial.

Llangollen. A town in a vale in rolling green North Wales on a windy July morning. The sun squints out and is puffed back again into the grey clouds blowing, full to the ragged rims with rain, across the Berwyn Hills. The white-horsed River Dee hisses and paws over the hills of its stones and under the greybeard bridge. Wind smacks the river and you, it's a cold, cracking morning; birds hang and rasp over the whipped river, against their wall, as though frozen still, or are wind-chaffed and scattered towards the gusty trees. As you drift down Castle Street with your hair flying, or your hat or umbrella dancing to be off and take the sky, you see and hear all about you the decorous, soberly dressed and headgeared, silent and unsmiling inhabitants of the tame town. You could be in any Welsh town on any windy snip of a morning, with only the birds and the river fuming and the only brightness the numberless greens and high purples of the hills. Everything is very ordinary in Llangollen; everything is nicely dull, except the summer world of wind and feathers, leaves and water. There is, if you are deaf, blind, and dumb, with a heart like cold bread pudding, nothing to remark or surprise.

But rub your eyes with your black gloves. Here, over the bridge, come three Javanese, winged, breastplated, helmeted, carrying gongs and steel bubbles. Kilted, **sporraned**, tartan'd, daggered Scotsmen reel and **strathspey** up a sidestreet, piping hot. Burgundian girls, wearing, on their heads, bird-cages made of velvet, suddenly whisk on the pavement into a coloured dance. A Viking goes into a pub. In black felt feathered hats and short leather trousers, enormous Austrians, with thighs big as Welshmen's bodies, but much browner, yodel to fiddles and split the rain with their smiles. Frilled, ribboned, sashed, fezzed, and white-turbaned, in baggy-blue sharavari and squashed red boots, Ukrainians with Manchester accents gopak up the hill. Everything is strange in Llangollen. You wish you had a scarlet hat, and bangles, and a little bagpipe to call your own, but it does not matter. The slapping bell-dancers, the shepherds and **chamois**-hunters, the fiddlers and fluters, the players on gongs and mandolines, guitars, harps, and trumpets, the beautiful flashing boys and girls of a score and more of singing countries, all the colours of the international rainbow, do not mind at all your mouse-brown moving among them: though you long, all the long Eisteddfod week, for a cloak like a blue sea or a bonfire to sweep and blaze in the wind, and a cap of bells, and a revelling waistcoat, and a great Alphorn to blow all over Wales from the ruins of Dinas Bran.

Now follow your nose, and the noise of guitars, and the flying hues and flourish of those big singing birds in their clogs and aprons and bonnets, veils, flowers, more flowers, and lace, past the wee Shoppes, through the babel of the bridge, by the very white policeman conducting from a rostrum, and up the tide of the hill, past popcorn and raspberryade, to the tented field.

Green, packed banks run, swarming, down to the huge marquee there that groans and strains and sings in the sudden squalls like an airstrip crewed full of choirs. Music spills out of the microphones all over the humming field. Out of the wind-tugged tent it rises in one voice, and the crowd outside is hushed away into Spain. In a far corner of the field, young men and women begin to dance, for every reason in the world. Out skims the sun from a cloud-shoal. The spaniel ears of the little tents flap. Children collect the autographs of Dutch farmers. You hear a hive of summer hornets: it is the Burgundian *vielle*, a mandolin with a handle. Palestrina praises from Bologna to the choral picnickers. A Breton holiday sings in the wind, to clog-tramp and ***biniou***.

Here they come, to this cup and echo of hills, people who love to make music, from France, Ireland, Norway, Italy, Switzerland, Spain, Java, and Wales: fine singers and faulty, nimble dancers and rusty, pipers to make the dead swirl or chanters with crows in their throats: all countries, shapes, ages, and colours, sword-dancers, court-dancers, cross-dancers, clog-dancers, dale-dancers, **morris**, **ceilidhe**, and highland, **bolero**, **flamenco**, heel-and-toe. They love to make music move. What a rush of dancing to Llangollen's feet! And, oh, the hubbub of tongues and toes in the dark chapels where every morning there's such a shining noise as you'd think would drive the Sunday **bogles** out of their doldrums for ever and ever.

All day the song and dancing in this transformed valley, this green cup of countries in the country of Wales, goes on until the sun goes in. Then, in the ship of the tent, under the wind-filled sails, watchers and listeners grow slow and close into one cloud of shadow; they gaze, from their deep lulled dark, on to the lighted deck where the country dancers weave in shifting-coloured harvests of light.

When you leave the last voices and measures of the sweet-throated, waltzing streets, the lilt and ripple of the Dee leaping, and the light of the night, to lie down, and the strewn town lies down to sleep in its hills and ring of echoes, you will remember that nobody was surprised at the turn the town took and the life it danced for one week of the long, little year. The town sang and danced, as though it were right and proper as the rainbow or the rare sun to celebrate the old bright turning earth and its bullied people. Are you surprised that people still can dance and sing in a world on its head? The only surprising thing about miracles, however small, is that they sometimes happen.

• AN APPROACH TO • OXFORD

John Betjeman (1906–1984)

Educated at Oxford University, John Betjeman established a reputation in his lifetime as a poet of note. He received numerous major British literary prizes, and was appointed Poet Laureate in 1972. Betjeman was also a well-known broadcaster and a leading authority on architecture, with a special interest in Victorian architecture.

The following essay on Oxford was published in 1938.

The approaches to Oxford are the worst thing about it. None of them prepare you for a vision of the home of learning nestling grey among the elm surrounded meadows. I have made a mistake. There is *one* route, too circuitous and too laborious to be taken by any but the most romantic minded. You turn off the main road from High Wycombe just beyond Wheatley and make for Chipping Norton. After a few miles you branch left by shut-in lanes through grey Elsfield downhill to Marston. Here you take the footpath to Marston Ferry. At the ferry you board a punt or canoe or rob roy and paddle down the stream of the Cherwell to Magdalen Bridge.

The Cherwell is a romantic as it ever was – willows, meadows in which **fritillaries** have been found, a few boathouses and tea gardens with parents pouring out tea for self-conscious undergraduates. Under willows you will see punts moored close into the bank. The intellectual head of an undergraduette appears above the cushions, the pipe smoke of her admirer winds up among the leaves. A gramophone plays a dance tune. Gradually the subtle variations of a Bach fugue break in upon the dance. A punt rounds the corner, full of clever looking men in grey flannel trousers and shirt sleeves – sleeves of what shirts setting off what Czechoslavakian peasant-art ties! – this probably contains one of the younger dons with some promising pupils. Soon they will all be off on a reading party to the Pyrenees and when they return very few of them will be on speaking terms.

But let us not look into the future while we can see so much of the past.

As the shouts of the boys and the encouragement of the swimming instructors die away from the bathing place of the Dragon School behind us, the river takes a turn at a discreet female bathing place, and part of Oxford University is before us. We are in the University Parks where, of an afternoon, games are played on those dreary levels of sparse grass. In the distance Keble College pricks the skyline with its turrets and iron decorations. The river is spanned by an elegant concrete foot bridge, which humps itself like a Magpie Moth Caterpillar. The effect is quite Japanese. This is the prettiest bridge for miles, a delicate piece of engineering unspoiled by 'architectural' additions.

Hoarse shouts, splashes, and screams sound above the thunder of a weir. We are at Parson's Pleasure, the open-air bathing place. There may be many parsons there, for all we can tell – clergymen are a great feature of North Oxford – but everyone is naked. Bodies lie stretched on the grass, looking up between the poplars, pipes jammed into mouths, sunlight dappling bald or long-haired heads.

We pull the boat over the rollers and the Cherwell winds on through the meadows of Mesopotamia to Magdalen Bridge. A gravel walk follows the river. Earnest students walk briskly along it, airing their brains before an evening's study. Snatches of conversation float down to us – 'Herodotus ... first class mind ... an alpha man ... Aristotelian ... Hegelian ... economic ...' The conversation dies away. The river bends. The banks are steep and scooped away by the narrow stream. The trees of Addison's Walk hang over us. We are shut in by mud and grass. Somewhere about here it is, that you can hear the bells of Oxford better than from anywhere else. The sound sifted from the motor traffic carries across the meadows. I cannot particularise the bend in the stream without going in a boat to show you. It is some yards from Magdalen Bridge for the roar of the main road traffic is scarcely audible. Then you have to be spared the blaring of portable gramophones. But there is such a bend and no time is better to hear the bells than shortly before six on a still summer evening.

One – two, *One* – two, *One* – two. New College Tower is calling to choral evensong. Elsewhere college chapels and little high church places of worship where a lonely vicar will run through evensong to an old lady from North Oxford, keep up an insistent tinkle. Then Magdalen Tower breaks into a chime quite near, one two three four, four three two one, one two three four, four three two one. This sets the bells going all over the town. Finally the heavy boom from Tom Tower, Christ Church strikes the hours and puts an end to the dispute. Now the bells start for evening chapel at Magdalen, and somewhere a church tower, probably Carfax, strikes a belated six to defy the thunderings of Tom.

People have noticed these bells across the Oxford rivers for years. At the end of the eighteenth century, Cowper's friend, the Reverend James Hurdis, Professor of Poetry, thus remarked them:

So have I stood at eve on Isis' banks,
To hear the merry Christ-church bells ring round.
So have I sat too in thy honoured shades
Distinguish'd Magdalen, on Cherwell's brink,
To hear thy silver Wolsey tones so sweet.
And so too have I paus'd and held my oar
And suffer'd the slow stream to bear me home,
No speed required while Wykeham's peal was up.

With a bump we knock into the cluster of boats round Magdalen Bridge, thread our way through cushioned empty punts shaded by Magdalen Tower. So by willows, lovers, intellectuals, boys, bathers, bells, we have come right into the High Street of the University City; what more appropriate approach?

• OF ECCENTRICS AND • ECCENTRICITIES

Richard Rive (1931–1989)

Richard Rive was born in District Six in Cape Town. Having obtained his BA at the University of Cape Town, he studied at Columbia University in the United States, and later at Oxford, where he completed a doctoral thesis on Olive Schreiner. At the time of his death, he was a lecturer in English at the University of the Western Cape.

Rive's writings covered a wide range of genre, and include short stories, plays, essays and two novels – some of which have been translated into as many as fifteen languages.

Writing Black, *his autobiography, was published in 1981, and gives an account of his life, travel and friends. This extract describes his experience as a student at Oxford University in 1971.*

My leaving for Oxford in August 1971 was uneventful except that I innocently became a drug-pusher. I did this unwittingly and for no gain. As a farewell present a friend of mine who was a medical doctor gave me a small collection of medicines and pills to tide me over the years. To facilitate matters she had carefully labelled the separate items with instructions which even I could understand, such as 'For headaches take two', 'Take one a day for severe backache', 'If you can't sleep take a tablet every three hours'. She had included some pills as soporifics as I was overwrought and was bound to sleep badly. Their potency had not yet been realised and I received the drug under her prescription. I myself never had cause to use it.

At Oxford station we stood in a long queue waiting for a taxi to take us to our various Colleges. In front of me was a tall, slender Asian student. His luggage was beautiful and he seemed wealthy and sure of himself. He had dyed a gold streak into his jet-black hair, and his finger-nails were polished purple. Although I appreciate odd people and odd situations I was unsure whether I would like Oxford if any other undergraduates looked like that. But once I had seen the gardens of Magdalen and sat reading in Duke Humphrey's room in the Bodleian, I knew I was going to enjoy my stay in the ancient university city. A friendly porter helped carry my luggage, and my scout introduced herself as Mrs Davis. How could I cope with a servant to clean my rooms and wash my dishes? Mrs Davis was Welsh to the core and had her rooms, which she shared with her husband, at the foot of our staircase. Mr Davis was phlegmatic and seemed to have a personal grudge against all students. He once stopped a party in my rooms when an American Rhodes Scholar tried to throw a bicycle out of the window. I felt it was unreasonable of Mr Davis. My scout had a cigarette permanently dangling from her lips. She was a staunch Conservative Party supporter and I spent some of my time at Oxford persuading her to vote Labour. Sometimes I would drive her to her Bingo hall in North Oxford. Often, especially at Christmas and Easter, I would return to my rooms to find my desk laden with food and delicacies she had left for me.

One day she was cleaning my sitting-room when she noticed copies of *Emergency* piled on my desk.

'Isn't that your name on the cover, luv?' I said it was. 'You mean you wrote that book?' I said I had and offered her a copy. I inscribed it to 'the best scout at Magdalen' and she left starry-eyed clutching it to her ample bosom. My rooms were on the second floor of the staircase. I noticed that undergraduates living above me would race down the stairs, pull up and tiptoe past my rooms, then race on as before. I could never understand this odd behaviour until I taxed one of them. I was then told that Mrs Davis always gave an initial lecture to all members of our staircase, during the course of which my book was produced (bound in a cloth cover she had specially made for it), and the subdued and overawed students were admonished not to make a noise when passing my rooms as I was busy thinking. I did not disillusion them.

I took quite easily to most Oxford customs. I enjoy eccentricities and eccentrics, and Oxford had enough of both. I liked the don who mumbled Latin to himself on his cycle as he creaked down the High. I enjoyed the sight of the don who hurried past me near Queen's, his gown flapping while he exclaimed to all who cared to hear him, 'They nearly all failed palaeography again.' And the scholar of Christ Church who, when taking his entrance examination for All Souls, was asked to translate a piece of Ionian

Greek and did so into Serbo-Croat. And the elderly don who, because of advanced age, had insisted on having only one student for tutorials. Times were hard, so the college insisted that he take an extra one. He objected vehemently but, when he realised that the college would not budge, he contemptuously gave the additional students to his scout for tutorials. The scout was no ordinary servant, had intellectual aspirations, and belonged to the public library in the Westgate. He took out books and conducted tutorials. So successful were these that his student scored a second in the preliminary examinations while the don's student could only manage a third.

And there was old Kobus from Stellenbosch University, who had been notorious back in South Africa for his way-out liberal oratory at mass meetings. He sported an enormous beard and resembled an emaciated Karl Marx. He was a Rhodes Scholar at Keble College. I visited him there and found it difficult to imagine more depressing surroundings. His rooms were gloomy and Victorian with oilcloth shades over the fanlight, imparting an air of decadence. Kobus was heavily depressed from the moment he arrived and the atmosphere at his college was certainly not conducive to expelling his gloom. One evening he was in my rooms feeling very sorry for himself. This was infectious and I was also becoming depressed. He mentioned that he could hardly sleep at night and I then displayed immediate interest. I had pills which could help him. I gave him a few. He returned to his college, climbed into bed and immediately went on a trip. Pleasant night followed exciting night. When he ran out of supplies he came back for more. Finally, when even these did not help he went to see his psychiatrist, to whom he mentioned that his depression had initially been lifted by pills from a friend at Magdalen. I was admonished to throw all the remainder into the Cherwell, which I hastily did.

My biggest ***faux pas*** happened at my first formal dinner in hall. I sat there complete in dark suit and gown. I knew no students yet at the college so sat quietly, making little conversation other than asking for the salt to be passed or my wine glass to be filled. Having finished the meal I was in a hurry to leave as I was expecting someone in my rooms. I rose, pushed back my chair and mumbled an apology to the student sitting nearest me. Those around stopped what they were doing and stared. A **phalanx** of scouts barred my path.

'Where do you think you're going, sir?'

'To my rooms, I have finished.'

'You can't just leave like that without permission from High Table. I would suggest you return to your seat, sir.'

I learnt afterwards that there was a complicated ritual that had to be adhered to before leaving a formal dinner. The senior student sitting at the head of this table called the chief scout and sent him with a request to the President at High Table to allow the gentlemen to leave. The President nodded his approval, which was conveyed by the chief scout to the senior student. The latter then rose, bowed to the President, who acknowledged it, and only then were the gentlemen allowed to leave without doing irreparable harm to custom. I learnt fast and to my chagrin discovered that I actually enjoyed all the rituals. During my final year I was as horrified at anyone who inadvertently broke any of the rules.

• STRANGE THINGS •

Wole Soyinka (1934–)

Akinwande Oluwole Soyinka was born in Abeokuta in western Nigeria, where he spent his childhood. After two years at the University College of Ibadan, he took an Honours Degree in English at Leeds University in England. In 1960, he returned to Nigeria to do research, write and direct. His international reputation has grown since the early 1960s, boosted by the publication of novels, poetry, an opera and an autobiography, as well as the productions of his plays and by his presence in America and Europe as a teacher, lecturer and director. In 1986 he became the first African writer to win the Nobel Prize for Literature.

In his autobiography, **Aké** *(1981), he gives an account of his first eleven years and provides vivid portraits of his Yoruba parents and of Aké, the quarter of Abeokuta in which he lived with them. His father was headmaster of St Peter's Primary School in Aké. His mother, dubbed 'Wild Christian' in* **Aké**, *came from a family which had played a pioneering role in spreading Christianity in western Nigeria. An extroverted and energetic woman of many accomplishments, she was a teacher, performer, political activist and trader, who was a major influence on the young Soyinka.*

The sprawling, undulating terrain is all of Aké. More than mere loyalty to the parsonage gave birth to a puzzle, and a resentment, that God should choose to look down on his own pious station, the parsonage compound, from the profane heights of Itoko. There was of course the mystery of the Chief's stable with live horses near the crest of the hill, but beyond that, this dizzying road only sheered upwards from one noisy market to the other, looking down across Ibàràpa and Ita Aké into the most secret recesses of the parsonage itself.

On a misty day, the steep rise towards Itoko would join the sky. If God did not actually live there, there was little doubt that he descended first on its crest, then took his one gigantic stride over those babbling markets – which dared to sell on Sundays – into St Peter's Church, afterwards visiting the parsonage for tea with the Canon. There was the small consolation that, in spite of the temptation to arrive on horseback, he never stopped first at the Chief's, who was known to be a pagan; certainly the Chief was never seen at a church service except at the anniversaries of the Alake's coronation. Instead God strode straight into St Peter's for morning service, paused briefly at the afternoon service, but reserved his most formal, exotic presence for the evening service which, in his honour, was always held in the English tongue. The organ took on a dark, smoky sonority at evening service, and there was no doubt that the organ was adapting its normal sounds to accompany God's own sepulchral responses, with its timbre of the ***egúngún***, to those prayers that were offered to him.

Only the Canon's residence could have housed the weekly Guest. For one thing, it was the only storey-building in the parsonage, square and stolid as the Canon himself, riddled with black wooden-framed windows. BishopsCourt was also a storey-building but only pupils lived in it, so it was not a house. From the upper floor of the Canon's home one *almost* looked the top of Itókò straight in its pagan eye. It stood at the highest lived-in point of the parsonage, just missing overlooking the gate. Its back was turned to the world of spirits and ghommids who inhabited the thick woods and chased home children who had wandered too deeply in them for firewood, mushrooms and snails. The Canon's square, white building was a bulwark against the menace and the siege of the wood spirits. Its rear wall demarcated their territory, stopped them from taking liberties with the world of humans.

Only the school-rooms of the primary school shared this closeness to the woods, and they were empty at night. Fenced by rough plastered walls, by the windowless rear walls of its houses, by tumuli of rocks which the giant trees tried vainly to obscure, Aké parsonage with its corrugated roofs gave off an air of fortifications. Secure within it, we descended or climbed at will into overlapping, interleaved planes, sheet rock-face drops, undergrowths and sudden hideouts of cultivated fruit groves. The hibiscus was rampant. The air hung heavy with the perfumes of lemon leaves, guavas, mangoes, sticky with the sap of *boum-boum* and the secretions of the rain-tree. The school-compounds were lined with these rain-trees with widespread shade filled branches. Needle-pins rose above the acacia and forests of bamboos kept us permanently nervous; if monster snakes had a choice, the bamboo clumps would be their ideal habitation.

Between the left flank of the Canon's house and the School playing-fields was – the Orchard. It was too varied, much too profuse to be called a garden, even a fruit-garden. And there were plants and fruits in it which made the orchard an extension of scripture classes, church lessons or sermons. A leaf-plant, mottled white-and-red was called the Cana lily. As Christ was nailed to the Cross and his wounds spurted blood, a few drops stuck to the leaves of the lily stigmatizing it for ever. No one bothered to explain the cause of the abundant white spots which also appeared on every leaf. Perhaps it had to do with the washing of sins in the blood of Christ, leaving even the most mottled spots in a person's soul, snow-white. There was the Passion fruit also, born of another part of that same history, not however a favourite of any of us children. Its lush green skin was pleasant to fondle in one's palm, but it ripened into a dessicated yellow, collapsing like the faces of the old men and women we knew. And it barely managed to be sweet, thus failing the infallible test of a real fruit. But the queen of the orchard was the pomegranate which grew, not so much from a seed of the stone church, as of the lyrical Sunday School. For it was at the Sunday School that the real stories were told, stories that lived in the events themselves, crossed the time-border of Sundays or leaves of the Bible and entered the world of fabled lands, men and women. The pomegranate was most niggardly in producing. It yielded its outwardly hardy fruit only once in a while, tended with patience by the thick-veined hands and face which belonged to someone we only knew as Gardener. Only Gardener could be trusted to share the occasional fruit among the small, dedicated band of pomegranate watchers, yet even the tiniest wedge transported us to the illustrated world of the Biblical Tales Retold. The pomegranate was the Queen of Sheba, rebellions and wars, the passion of Salome, the siege of Troy, the Praise of beauty in the Song of Solomon. This fruit, with its stone-hearted look and feel unlocked the cellars of Ali Baba, extracted the genie from Aladin's lamp, plucked the strings of the harp that restored David to sanity, parted the waters of the Nile and filled our parsonage with incense from the dim temple of Jerusalem.

It grew only in the Orchard, Gardener said. The pomegranate was foreign to the black man's soil, but some previous bishop, a white man, had brought the seeds and planted them in the Orchard. We asked if it was *the* apple but Gardener only laughed and said No. Nor, he added, would that apple be found on the black man's soil. Gardener was adjudged ignorant. It was clear that only the pomegranate could be the apple that lost Adam and Eve the joys of paradise. There existed yet another fruit that was locally called apple, soft yet crisp, a soft pink skin and reasonably juicy. Before the advent of the pomegranate it had assumed the identity of the apple that undid the naked pair. The first taste of the pomegranate unmasked that imposter and took its place.

Swarms of bats inhabited the fig tree, their seed-pocked droppings would cake the stones, lawns, paths and bushes before dawn. An evergreen tree, soft and rampant bordered the playing-field on the side of the bookseller's compound, defying the Harmattan; it filled the parsonage with a tireless concert of weaver-birds.

An evil thing has happened to Aké parsonage. The land is eroded, the lawns are bared and mystery driven from its once secretive combs. Once, each new day opened up an unseen closure, a pocket of rocks, a clump of bush and a colony of snails. The motor-hulk has not moved from its staging-point where children clambered into it for journeys to fabled places; now it is only a derelict, its eyes rusted sockets, its dragon face collapsed with a progressive loss of teeth. The abandoned incinerator with its lush weeds and glistening snakes is marked by a mound of mud. The surviving houses, houses which formed the battlements of Aké parsonage are now packing cases on a depleted landscape, full of creaks, exposed and nerveless.

And the moods are gone. Even the open lawns and broad paths, bordered with whitewashed stones, lilies and lemon grass clumps, changed nature from season to season, from weekday to Sunday and between noon and nightfall. And the echoes off the walls in lower Parsonage acquired new tonalities with the seasons, changed with the emptying of the lawns as the schools dispersed for holidays.

BishopsCourt, of Upper Parsonage, is no more. Bishop Ajayi Crowther would sometimes emerge from the cluster of hydrangea and bougainvillea, a gnomic face with popping eyes whose formal photograph had first stared at us from the frontispiece of his life history. He had lived, the teacher said, in BishopsCourt and from that moment, he peered out from among the creeping plants whenever I passed by the house on an errand to our Great Aunt, Mrs Lijadu. BishopsCourt had become a boarding house for the girls' school and an extra playground for us during the holidays. The Bishop sat, silently, on the bench beneath the wooden porch over the entrance, his robes twined through and through with the lengthening tendrils of the bougainvillea. I moved closer when his eyes turned to sockets. My mind wandered then to another photograph in which he wore a clerical suit with waistcoat and I wondered what he really kept at the end of the silver chain that vanished into the pocket. He grinned and said, Come nearer, I'll show you. As I moved towards the porch he drew on the chain until he had lifted out a wholly round pocket-watch that gleamed of solid silver. He pressed a button and the lid opened, revealing, not the glass and the face-dial but a deep cloud-filled space. Then he winked one eye, and it fell from his face into the bowl of the watch. He winked the other and this joined its partner in the watch. He snapped back the lid, nodded again and his head went bald, his teeth disappeared and the skin pulled backward till the whitened cheekbones were exposed. Then he stood up and, tucking the watch back into the waistcoat pocket, moved a step towards me. I fled homewards.

That Bishop Ajayi Crowther frightened me out of that compound by his strange transformations only confirmed that the Bishops, once they were dead, joined the world of spirits and ghosts. I could not see the Canon decaying like that in front of my eyes, nor the Rev. J. J. who had once occupied that house, many years before, when my mother was still like us. J.J. Ransome-Kuti had actually ordered back several ghommids in his life-time; my mother confirmed it. She was his grand niece and, before she came to live at our house, she had lived in the Rev J.J.'s household. Her brother Sanya also lived there and he was acknowledge by all to be an *òrò,* which made him a home in the woods, even at night.

•

Workmen came into the house. They knocked lines of thin nails with narrow clasps into walls. The lines turned with corners and doorways and joined up with outside wires which strung across poles. The presence of these workmen reminded me of another invasion. At the end of those earlier activities we no longer needed the oil-lamps, kerosene lanterns and candles, at least not within the house. We pressed down a switch and the room was flooded with light. Essay's instructions were strict – only he, or Wild Christian could give the order for the pressing of those switches. I recalled that it took a while to connect the phenomenon of the glowing bulb with the switch, so thoroughly did Essay keep up the deception. He pretended it was magic, he easily directed our gaze at the glass bulb while he muttered his magic spell. Then he solemnly intoned:

'Let there be light.'

Afterwards he blew in the direction of the bulb and the light went out.

But finally, we caught him out. It was not too difficult to notice that he always stood at the same spot, that that spot was conveniently near a small white-and-black object which had sprouted on the wall after the workmen had gone. Still, the stricture continued. The magic light was expensive and must be wisely used.

Now the workmen were threading the walls again, we wondered what the new magic would produce. This time there was no bulb, no extra switches on the wall. Instead, a large wooden box was brought into the house and installed at the very top of the tallboy, displacing the old gramophone which now had to be content with one of the lower shelves on the same furniture. The face of the box appeared to be made of thick plaited silk.

But the functions continued to be the same. True, there was no need to put on a black disc, no need to crank a handle or change a needle, it only required that the knob be turned for sounds to come on. Unlike the gramophone however, the box could not be made to speak or sing at any time of the day. It began its monologue early in the morning, first playing 'God save The King'. The box went silent some time in the afternoon, resumed late afternoon, then, around ten or eleven in the evening, sang 'God Save The King' once more and went to sleep. Because the box spoke incessantly and appeared to have no interest in a response, it soon earned the name *As'oromagb'esi.*[1]

At certain set hours, the box delivered THE NEWS. The News soon became an object of worship to Essay and a number of his friends. When the hour approached, something happened to this club. It did not matter what they were doing, they rushed to our house to hear the Oracle. It was enough to watch Essay's face to know that the skin would be peeled off the back of any child who spoke when he was listening to The News. When his friends were present, the parlour with its normal gloom resembled a shrine, rapt faces listened intently, hardly breathing. When The Voice fell silent all faces turned instinctively to the priest himself. Essay reflected for a moment, made a brief or long comment and a babble of excited voices followed.

The gramophone fell into disuse. Christmas carols, the songs of Marian Anderson; oddities, such as a record in which a man did nothing but laugh throughout, and the one concession to a massed choir of European voices – the Hallelujah Chorus – all were permantly interned in the same cupboard. Now voices sang, unasked, from the new box. Once that old friend the Hallelujah Chorus burst through the webbed face of the box and we had to concede that it sounded richer and fuller than the old gramophone had ever succeeded in rendering it. Most curious of all the fare provided by the radio however were the wrangling of a family group which were relayed every morning, to the amusement of a crowd, whose laughter shook the box. We tried to imagine where this took place. Did this family go into the streets to carry on their interminable bickering or did the idle crowd simply hang around their home, peeping through the windows and cheering them on?

---

1 *As'oromagb'esi – One who speaks without expecting a reply.*

We tried to imagine any of the Aké families we knew exposing themselves this way – the idea was unthinkable. It was some time, and only by listening intently before I began to wonder if this daily affair was that dissimilar from the short plays which we sometimes acted in school on prize-giving day. And I began also to respond to the outlandish idiom of their humour.

Hitler monopolised the box. He had his own special programme and somehow, far off as this war of his whim appeared to be, we were drawn more and more into the expanding arena of menace. Hitler came nearer home every day. Before long the greeting, Win-The-War replaced some of the boisterous exchanges which took place between Essay and his friends. The local barbers invented a new style which joined the repertory of Bentigo, Girls-Follow-Me, Oju-Aba, Missionary Cut and others. The women also added Win-de-woh to their hair-plaits, and those of them who presided over the local foodstalls used it as a standard response to complaints of a shortage in the quantity they served. Essay and his correspondents vied with one another to see how many times the same envelope could be used between them. Windows were blacked over, leaving just tiny spots to peep through, perhaps in order to obtain an early warning when Hitler came marching up the path. Household heads were dragged to court and fined for showing a naked light to the night. To reinforce the charged atmosphere of expectations, the first aeroplane flew over Abeokuta; it had a heavy drone which spoke of Armageddon and sent Christians fleeing into churches to pray and stay the wrath of God. Others simply locked their doors and windows and waited for the end of the world. Only those who had heard about these things, and flocks of children watched in fascination, ran about the fields and the streets, following the flying miracle as far as they could, shouting greetings, waving to it long after it had gone and returning home to await its next advent.

One morning The News reported that a ship had blown up in Lagos harbour taking some of its crew with it. The explosion had rocked the island, blown out windows and shaken off roofs. The lagoon was in flames and Lagosians lined the edges of the lagoon, marvelling at the strange omen – tall fires leaping frenziedly on the surface of water. Hitler was really coming close. No one however appeared to be very certain what to do when he finally appeared.

There was one exception: Paa Adatan. Every morning, Paa Adatan appeared in front of Wild Christian's shop opposite the Aafin, before whose walls he passed the entire day. Strapped to his waists was a long cutlass in its scabbard, and belts of amulets. A small Hausa knife, also in its sheath, was secured to his left arm above the elbow and on his fingers were blackened twisted wire and copper rings.

Paa Adatan patrolled the Aafin area, furious that no one would take him into the Army and send him to confront Hitler, personally, and end the war once and for all.

'Ah, Mama Wole, this English people just wan' the glory for den self. Den no wan' blackman to win dis war and finish off dat nonsense-yeye Hitler one time! Now look them. Hitler dey bombing us for Lagos already and they no fit defend we.' He spat his red kola-nut juice on the ground.

'Let him come! Make him step anywhere near this palace of Aké and that is how I go take in head for my mouth and bite am off.'

Head erect, chest defiant, he resumed his patrol.

• WEST AFRICA •

Guy Butler (1918–)

Born in Cradock, Guy Butler, noted poet and playwright, studied English at Rhodes University and Oxford. He became a lecturer at the University of the Witwatersrand, and in his early 30s was appointed as Professor of English at Rhodes University, a post which he held with great distinction until his retirement in 1983.

The following account of pre-independence Nigeria in the 1950s comes from the third volume of his autobiography, **A Local Habitation**, *which was published in 1991.*

In 1954 Jean and I with our baby Patrick went to Britain on a Nuffield Foundation Fellowship. I was deep into my poetic phase. After a wintry spell in London we moved north to Oxford, where we enjoyed a beautiful spring, and made the acquaintance of the poetry of John Betjeman in such poems as 'Belbroughton road is bonny, as pinkly blooms the May'.

We also renewed several friendships, before moving to a house south of Bristol in the village of Winscombe. It was also the time when I met Roy Campbell, William Plomer and David Wright.

On 3 December Jean returned to South Africa ahead of me. After a spell back in London, I followed. I asked the British Council to arrange for me to fly back via Nigeria and the Gold Coast. I wished to look at the new African universities which were springing up in those British colonies which were moving to independence most quickly.

January 1955 was an exciting time to visit Nigeria. It seemed to be a country where a period under a colonial power might achieve some sort of vindication. Under the guiding hand of Lord Lugard some 60 million people of 250 ethnic groups had been gradually brought together under some sort of government by district officers and indigenous councils for the main regions. By 1954 this artificially created country had become a federal state. The regional councils had increased greatly in importance. Much would depend on the collaboration between these regions.

I shall have to rely heavily on recollection for this month-long visit to Nigeria and Ghana. My memory is full of vivid images and incidents, but I know enough about its vagaries to wish that I had kept a diary.

I have a clear recollection of coming in to land at Kano under a vast orange sky. The runway was not far from a huge treeless city of sunbaked mud houses. Not round huts, but houses whose characteristic form was cubic, not spherical. Space galore. And strange as it all was, the light and the smell meant home to me. It was unmistakably African – dust and powdered dung, I think.

At Lagos I was met by a driver from the University of Ibadan. He was suffering from a bad asthmatic attack and drove as though death's winged chariot were behind the old Ford V8 sedan. He was, however, determined to die at home in Ibadan. He did not steer that vehicle, he aimed it. His rivals for road space were mostly five-ton Dodge or Ford trucks adapted for passenger use: they were crowded with happy humanity, bulging in all directions, decorated in bright bandanas and prints, gourds of fruit, and unhappy chickens. These trucks were known as Mammy Wagons.

Evidence of a passion for the written word was everywhere. The city traffic had been so slow that I had time to read the legends outside the diminutive booths from which people traded or did their business. London was the reference point for Lagos:

THE MAYFAIR PARADISE LADIES HAIRDRESSING SALOON
and
MAN-ABOUT-TOWN TAILORS
(Branch Office in Bond Street, London)

Any bare space, whether fixed or mobile, was regarded as waste and lost until redeemed by the written word. So, on the tailboards of Mammy Wagons I read a succession of adverts for various goods, religious exhortations and personal messages from the driver/owner to his passengers, such as 'Hurry up, don't waste my time!'

My driver wasted no time in overtaking him and, by a miracle, dodged into a gap, almost colliding with the tailboard of the truck ahead which told me, in huge African gothic letters, 'Prepare to meet thy Maker.'

I assured my Maker that I was not ready to meet him yet and prayed for time to prepare.

The road was a bad strip of tar under enormous cottonwood trees which met overhead, creating a hazy tunnel through which we hurtled, overtaking

Mammy Wagons whenever the oncoming traffic allowed the gasping driver to risk another head-on crash. I thought of Othello, 'Of hair-breadth 'scapes in th' imminent deadly breach ...'

Then the stream slowed down and one caught glimpses of a village thatched with palm leaves in the dappled shade. Fairly close to the road was a spacious rectangular meeting-place under a large pitched roof supported on poles about six feet apart, between which, except for the entrances, were mud walls about two feet high. These were used as seats and even as reclining couches for the customers, all of whom seemed to be asleep or comatose. One patron lay prone with his spine along the wall and his hands clasped across his chest. His left foot was flat on the top of the wall, with the knee raised, on which knee the right foot rested. He seemed to be dreamily admiring the silhouette of his five toes against a far, vague sky. Over the entrance to this place of peace was a large sign, in Roman capitals – THE PUB.

The stream of traffic drew to a halt. There was no oncoming traffic. My driver explained – 'Level Crossing'. I got out to stretch my legs. In the distance I could see the horizontal prohibition of the boom.

Suddenly the bush on either side of the road blossomed with white eyes and white smiles. These soon acquired heads with baskets of fruit and gourds of palm wine for sale. For half an hour the road became a market in which the villagers did a roaring trade with passengers. I bought a banana the size of a policeman's truncheon. It was coarse and tasted of nothing. Then the boom was lifted, no train having passed in the meantime. I deduced that the boom operator must be in the pay of the villagers, or that he lived under such threats that he elevated their demands above those of the Nigerian Railways.

I stayed with the principal of the emergent university, a no-nonsense ex-navy or army man who had seen enough of the worldwide empire not to be surprised by the conventions and customs of its different peoples. What should one expect? He lived simply and gave some startling answers to my questions.

'What is the most reliable way of getting a letter from Lagos to Kano? Train or bus?'

'Neither. Cleft stick.'

I was both impressed and disturbed by the campus. It seemed to bear absolutely no relation to what I had seen – and what I was soon to see – of Ibadan.

Ibadan in 1954 was a city of about a million, spread out on seven (or was it seventeen?) hills – a set of villages which had grown until they had merged. It was intersected by a spider's web of tarred main roads, along which rose occasional European-style structures, seldom more than one or two stories. Commerce seemed to be run by the Lebanese. I had been told that the heart of the place was the market, so to the market I went.

Again the small crowded booths. I needed razor blades. These I found in a booth which also stocked razors and soaps and powders, and combs and Brylcreem – everything in a Western barbershop in fact. It smelt of scented soap.

Next to it was a medicine shop with not a single patent medicine in it – not even an aspirin. Instead exotic pods and roots and seeds, and grains such as would delight my vegetarian relatives, but also a variety of medicines that would not: dead beetles and other brittle arthropods; defunct lizards; fragments of birds, and on skewers a number of dried-out rodents about the size of rats, still squinting, rather surprised at the stakes emerging from their mouths.

Next to the medicine man was a camera shop which sold not only cameras and films but nude photographs. A black adolescent was staring mesmerised at a photograph of an amply endowed white woman in the never-never, smiling in a way white women in West Africa were not expected to smile at black people. Next, brightly coloured enamelware – yellow basins and blue colanders, and scarlet tea and coffee pots and green mixing bowls – really a delight to the eye. Nearly all the owners and shopkeepers were vital and voluble women. Some said women were the financial bosses of Nigeria.

But the magic rose as the sun went down. I don't know the name of the religious sect responsible, but its followers gather at key points all round the outskirts of the city with torches and drums. Singing, they moved towards the city centre, gathering worshippers en route. I moved closer to the road along which one of the bands would pass. At my elbow a young man next to a stall was examining a mouth-organ, turning it this way and that. Then the sound of the drums must have got through to him like a current catching hold of an idling leaf in a stream. He put the mouth-organ down and floated off into the procession, his feet already obeying the beat. And this hypnotic incrementation was happening on all the main roads into the centre of the city, along irregular lines of light and song converging in the dark. It was both beautiful and magical.

What shocked my subconscious was the lack of straight lines: with few exceptions the roads of Ibadan twist and turn and writhe like unhappy worms. How people find their way is a mystery. I was also shaken by the lack of water supply and a sewerage system. Ibadan's drains were open, the original streams and gullies of those hills, but the fluid in them looked like a thick pus.

However, the people give the overwhelming impression of abundant energy and happy-go-lucky zest. Life is for now.

The campus, some distance outside Ibadan, was beautifully planned. Its buildings employed the best insights of Western architecture. They were elegant, clean, bright shapes against the surrounding forests. But as the dusk settled down, those trees looked like praying mantises to me, hovering above delicate structures as pale as moths.

Molly Mahood arranged a cocktail party so that I could meet members of the faculty. I remember three conversations. The first was about a crisis that had developed in the play-school run for the children of faculty members. English, Scots, Yoruba, Ibo, you name it. A slender black mother was objecting, gently but firmly, to her child's literary diet of *Hickory Dickory Dock*, *Goosey Goosey Gander* and *Jack and Jill.* This raised the whole question of mother-tongue education in a piquant manner – a problem with which the Molteno Project of Rhodes University has had to come to terms.

The second was a crisis in the Registrar's department. Exam questions had been stolen and fed to a poor candidate, who had been sent to university by contributions from his extended family. In most of Africa one's duty to one's family take precedence over obligations to any other body. The 'guilty' clerk was in an impossible moral dilemma: between his duty to the university, who paid his salary, and his duty to his family, who needed this particular member to qualify and become a breadwinner. The argument was interminable. Some said that, while Africa remained Africa, such things were inevitable. One African proposed, with just a ghost of a smile, that the staff of the examinations section of the Registrar's department should all be well-paid expatriates. They were unlikely to be tempted by the importunities of poor relatives in the exam hall.

The third crisis was raised by my presence, apartheid. Towards the end of the party an earnest New Zealander, who felt that someone should question my **bona fides**, cleared his throat:

'Professor – you are returning to South Africa?'

'Yes.'

'In spite of Dr Malan and apartheid?'

'It is my home.'

'But are you not afraid of going back?'

'Of what?'

'Of violence, of revolution.'

'That has always been a possibility. If the Nats stay in power they will make it probable.'

'How can you contemplate living on the edge of a volcano?'

'It is better than trying to adjust to life in someone else's wasteland. It is, after all, my own volcano.'

The phrase appealed to several of the Africans who repeated it with chuckles. They were living on a volcano of their own which would erupt in the Biafran war.

At another later party – a jolly one – I got on to a very convivial wavelength with a large ebullient Yoruba in flowing robes, who looked and behaved like a Roman **epicure**. He admitted that he did not like the Ibo from eastern Nigeria, small, neat, usually in European suits and probably related to the Vice-Chancellor. I had been speaking of the great variety of people, 250 ethnic groups each with its own language, that he must have to consider in his job. He spoke tolerantly enough of the Hausa, but 'as for the Ibo, we westerners regard them as little monkeys recently fallen from the trees'. He sounded like a Transvaler from the Waterberg talking of the Venda or the Pedi.

In the event, Nigeria has proved to be quite as volcanic as South Africa: the oil-rich Ibo had to pay dearly for their hankering after independence from the Yoruba westerners and the Muslim north. But most of the whites were optimistic – the Muslims needed the carbohydrates of the south, and the south needed the protein of the cattle-keeping north. Intelligent self-interest would ensure success.

• TINKA-TINKA •

Evelyn Waugh (1903–1966)

Evelyn Waugh was born in London and educated at Lancing and Oxford. His novels, which were mainly sophisticated and witty satire, include **The Loved One** *and* **Men at Arms**. *In 1958, when Waugh decided that he couldn't bear another winter in England, he set sail for the warmer shores of Africa. When he published an account of his travels,* **A Tourist in Africa**, *he wrote, 'My hope ... in publishing this diary is that the things which amused and interested me on my little tour may amuse and interest others.' His diary is a portrait of Kenya, Rhodesia (Zimbabwe) and Tanganyika (Tanzania), as they were when on the edge of independence.*

The extract below is taken from a chapter describing an excursion to the Masai in what was then Tanganyika, to witness a great assembly of this nation for the ceremonial initiation of elders.

The Masai are, I suppose, the most easily recognizable people in Africa. Their physical beauty and the extreme trouble they take to adorn it have popularised their photographs in geographical magazines and tourist advertisements all over the world. Every writer on East Africa has paid his tribute to their pride and courage. A generation back they still carried the long spear, hunted lion with it and defended their grazing rights over a huge region much of which is now the 'white highlands' of Kenya. They gleefully pointed out at the time of the Mau Mau rising that it was the English who introduced the supposedly docile Kikuyu into those lands and they enjoyed their small part in the pacification. For a generation they had been punished for raiding the Kikuyu; now they were paid to do so. The story is told that a patrol was sent out with orders to bring in any Kikuyu 'arms' they could find; next morning the commanding officer's tent was surrounded with a heap of severed limbs. Fighting, hunting and herding cattle, sheep and goats – but primarily cattle – are the only occupations suitable for a man.

The Matabele, an equally brave people, when conquered, immediately became the servants of their conquerors. No one has ever made a servant of a Masai; nor were they ever conquered; they have been cheated a little, but they have always negotiated with the white man as equals. They employ a servile tribe as blacksmiths and themselves practise no crafts except those of the beauty parlour. Four Holy Ghost Fathers work among them, but by far the greater part remain pagan and polygamous. Nor have they been influenced by the Mohammedan missionaries who are making more converts than the Christians in some areas round the Lakes. At the time of writing, it is announced that they have elected a Catholic paramount chief. There was no paramount chief before; authority resided in an intricate system of local chiefs and elders; the new office is, I think, that of an ambassador rather than of a ruler. They have found it convenient to appoint an educated spokesman to deal for them, not so much with the British Commissioners who understand them, as with the educated Africans of other tribes who will shortly be assuming power; who would like to despise them because they do not wear shorts but have inherited an ineradicable awe. The Masai are not primitive in the way that pygmies and bushmen are. They are an intelligent people who have deliberately chosen to retain their own way of life. Tobacco, snuff and South African sherry are the only products of white civilization which they value. Like the French they recognize nationality by social habits rather than by race. Men and women from other tribes who marry among them and conform to local custom are accepted. In one boma near Arusha I saw a head-man who was by origin a Sikh. I had always thought Sikhs a remarkably handsome people until I saw him beside the Masai. Those who have been encouraged to seek higher education outside their pastures usually return and at once eagerly readopt the costume and customs of their people. The few who go to the cities are said to turn criminal. Thirty years ago it was predicted that the Masai would become extinct. In fact they have slightly increased in numbers.

•

The excursion to the Masai was not quite as exhilarating as I had hoped. Early on the cold grey morning the Acting Provincial Commissioner called with the news that the officer who had volunteered to accompany me had gone sick. 'But you'll be all right,' he said, 'your driver knows where to go. You will find the District Commissioner Peebles in camp there and he will show you everything. The place is called Tinka-Tinka. Better take sandwiches with you.'

He presented a police driver to me and addressed him in Swahili; the words 'Tinka-Tinka' occurred in the introduction. The man, who came from Tanga, repeated 'Tinka-Tinka' in a knowledgeable way. It was arranged that he should return in a Landrover after I had breakfasted.

I secured a packet of food and by nine I and my monoglot driver were on the road, the main road north to Nairobi. We drove for two hours, passing the police post which marked the Kenya frontier. It struck met as odd that an officer of the Tanganyika service should be presiding in Kenya, but I had no means of communicating my doubts and was dulled by the blank monotony of the countryside. The sun was now out. At length we turned off the road and came to a stop at a clearing where there stood six little tin market stalls. The name of the place was plainly displayed on a painted board 'NGUTATEK'.

'Tinka-Tinka?' I asked

'Tinka-Tinka.'

I pointed to the sign board but my guide was not only monoglot but illiterate. 'Tinka-Tinka,' he said firmly.

'Bwana Peebles?' I asked.

'Bwana Peebles,' he replied. Then he got out of the car and lay down in the shade of a tree.

Great clouds of flies and bees surrounded the little shops. They were kept by Africans and were stocked with identical, miscellaneous goods. I entered one and asked 'Ngutatek?'

'Ngutatek,' the shop keeper confirmed.

'No, Tinka-Tinka?'

'Tinka-Tinka.'

'Bwana Peebles?'

An emphatic shake of the head. 'No Bwana Peebles.'

'D.C.?'

'No D.C.'

I went to my supine driver. 'No Bwana Peebles. No D.C.'

He nodded vigorously. 'Bwana Peebles, D.C. Tinka-Tinka.'

I despaired and returned to the Landrover. Presently there appeared a small group of unmistakable Masai, young warriors covered in ochre; their hair plaited and coated with red; bracelets and necklaces and ear-rings of copper and beads; spears and knobkerries in hand; their ruddy togas falling loose and open to reveal their dyed flanks. They stared at me and the car. I attempted my little catechism about Tinka and Bwana Peebles. They spat (a politeness, I was told later) and sauntered away. They swaggered into the shops and bought nothing. They swaggered on to my driver and stared at him. He got up and moved further away to the shade of another tree, plainly scared of them. An hour passed. Then there appeared a Kikuyu boy.

I welcomed, as I little expected to do when I set out, the evidence in shorts and shirt of European influence. He had a few words of English.

I begn my little catechism. No D.C. here. D.C. not coming here. A big meeting of Masai? Not here. Where? That way; pointing vaguely into the bush. But is this Tinka-Tinka. Tinka that way, just here. He pointed to some huts half a mile distant. Show me. I roused my driver. We bumped along the track and found a well with a mechanical pump. This was Tinka. There was no one about. 'Tell this boy in Swahili where the Masai are meeting.' Some conversation ensued, after which my driver got into the car and drove off very crossly in my opposite direction to the one indicated. We drove another twenty miles into Kenya and came to an Indian shop. Here the driver made some enquiries as the result of which he turned the car round and drove furiously back over the road we had travelled.

'Arusha?' I asked.

'Arusha.'

At a river-crossing near the Tanganyika border we had passed an agreeable looking little road-house. Here I made him stop. I did not want to accept defeat without one more effort. The hotelier was English and kindly disposed. Yes, he knew about the Masai gathering, but he thought it was to be a week or two later. He knew where the D.C. was in camp. He explained the mystery of Tinka. It is an onomatopoeic word used in those parts for any mechanical device. The pump at the well was a Tinka. There were Tinkas all over the place, one at the site of the D.C.'s camp, which was below the western slopes of Kilimanjaro. The hotelier came out to my driver and explained to him in great detail how to get there. The man repeated the route sullenly but apparently with accuracy. All now seemed set fair. I parted from my rescuer with warm thanks at one o'clock. I ate my luncheon which the driver refused to share, whether from religious scruples or sheer bad temper I do not know. We stopped and refilled with petrol at the frontier post. Presently we left the main road and took to dirt tracks. Then it came on to rain.

We were now, it was plain from the quality of the cattle, in an area of European occupation. It seemed an improbable venue for Masai initiation ceremonies. We passed various signs illegible to my driver which indicated farms and government establishments, but he drove on through the mud and rain as fast as he could go with a grim lack of curiosity which suggested confidence. He was following instructions, I assumed. It was three hours before I realized he was completely lost. Then I said 'Arusha', and we were looking for a place to turn in the deep lane when there appeared on foot two uniformed Askaris. These were men from the camp we were seeking. They climbed into the car, directed us and at last, with an hour of daylight left, I met Bwana Peebles, who had expected me at ten o'clock that morning and now greeted me with good humour.

There was no assembly of the Masai, such as I had been led to expect. That, as the hotelier had said, was in the future. The holy hill where the initiation had to take place was separated from the main tribal grazing grounds by the European farms and it was to arrange a corridor through which the assembly and its herds could pass that the D.C. and his vet were now in camp. The holiness of the hill was traditional; the Masai resolutely maintained their rights to its use, despite any inconvenience to the 'immigrant races', but I gathered the initiation ceremony would be convivial rather than devotional. A warrior may not marry, but he enjoys wide privileges among the unmarried girls of the tribe. When he becomes an elder, he marries, his wife's head is shaven to make her unattractive and an operation is performed which is thought to make her impervious to the temptations of love. His diet is reduced, but his influence in conference grows. It was this transition, in early middle age, that was being prepared at this new Tinka. Half a dozen of the prospective candidates for maturity were there, living in a neighbouring boma. I was invited to enter this little enclosure, where each family has its own hut and its own entrance to the thorn stockade, and the cattle are penned at night among the surrounding dwellings. Cow dung was the main constituent of the architecture.

'If only people would realize that the Masai are just men with two legs,' said the D.C. 'Europeans go quite dotty about them one way or another.'

'Doesn't everyone love them?'

'No, indeed.'

As we were talking a neighbouring farmer, of Boer extraction, came into camp. It was plain that he for one did not at all relish the passage of the Masai through his property. Mr Peebles disabused me of many popular fallacies, such as that the Masai bleed their cattle and subsist on their blood as a staple diet. It is only done, he told me, either ceremoniously or to stop them straying in time of drought. Also of the belief that they are totally untouched by the modern world. When he first came to the district, he told me, before he had learned the language, he was confronted in his office by a Masai warrior in full rig, standing on one leg. He turned to his clerk and said in Swahili: 'Can you find someone to interpret?'

'That will not be necessary,' said the Masai in English. 'I have come to ask for a passport to attend a Boy Scouts' Jamboree in London.'

The rain had passed. Under a watery sunset my dull driver, who had refused food from the Askaris also (I suppose he simply lacked appetite), was given instructions for his return journey which he successfully followed.

• BRIGHT LIGHTS •

Shiva Naipaul (1945–1985)

Shiva Naipaul was born in 1945 in Port of Spain, Trinidad. He was educated in Trinidad and at Oxford. He and his brother V S Naipaul are both renowned travel writers.

V S Naipaul wrote of travel writing in 1987, that 'there is a way currently in vogue of writing about degraded and corrupt countries. This is the way of fantasy and extravagance. It dodges all issues; it is safe. I find the way empty, morally and intellectually; it makes writing, literature, the opposite of what it should be; it makes writing an aspect of the corruption of the countries out of which it issues. I find my brother's tragic sense, his insistence on rationality and the intellect, and his high artistic conscience, exhilarating.'

The following extract is taken from Shiva Naipaul's **North of South** *which was published in 1978.*

How recent it is. How startlingly recent! A century ago, city life in East Africa was confined to the Islamicised, Swahili-speaking coast- to towns like Mombasa, Malindi (flourishing kingdoms when Vasco da Gama visited them at the end of the fifteenth century) and Lamu. But these towns belonged to the relatively sophisticated trading arena of the Indian Ocean and were only marginally of Africa. Up-country tribes, like the Kikuyu, living in scattered homesteads, knew nothing of urban life. Even as late as the Mau Mau emergency, the pattern persisted. For purely military purposes, a compulsory 'villagisation' program was adopted. Elspeth Huxley, writing in 1955, could foresee some unintended good arising out of this measure; she believed it would speed up the rate of Kikuyu cultural advance.

At the turn of the century, Nairobi could hardly be said to exist. In 1913 it consisted of little more than the railroad, a network of dusty lanes, a hotel or two and the ramshackle Indian bazaar.

•

The primitive world is a realistic world. Within it, vision and ambition and desire are controlled. Magic and superstition operate within a known sphere and on a familiar scale. The tribal man knows what is possible. He is at home. His means fit his ends. He is sane. It is this wholeness that we really ought to admire. His dignity arises from it. The primitive, existing within his own terms, cannot be mocked. His is a complete and undefiled self-realization. This may help to explain some of the traditional difference between the European attitudes toward the Masai on the one hand and the Kikuyu on the other.

The Masai – a condensation of the dark heart of Africa – have consistently aroused the admiration of Europeans. They have seemed (borrowing the language of Joseph Conrad) 'savage and superb, wild-eyed and magnificent.' Karen Blixen provides the classic summary in her well-known book *Out of Africa*: 'A Masai warrior is a fine sight ... daring, and wildly fantastical as they seem, they are still unswervingly true to their own nature, and to an immanent ideal ...'

The sedentary Kikuyu, living in closer proximity to Europeans, were more adaptable – and vulnerable – to outside influence. They were condemned for their avarice and their cunning; and they paid the inevitable price the primitive must pay when he dilutes his authentic existence.

The tribal world was real; the new world, lacking definition and solidity, fades away into the dimmer reaches of fantasy. This sense of people's having lost touch with reality, of a constraining dam's having burst, arises whenever one contemplates the lusts that disfigure African societies – and not only African societies, but the societies of the poor and backward in general.

It has all happened before. The insatiable appetite for slaves in the seventeenth and eighteenth centuries stimulated the equally insatiable appetite of African chiefs for brandy, beads, tobacco and guns – all the gaudy bric-a-brac of European civilisation. The desire to get hold of these things unleashed an orgiastic frenzy that devastated the land and wrecked the societies of West Africa. In its essence, the nature of the ties linking the African with the European has not really changed since the first Portuguese ships went sailing down the west coast of the continent: the sophisticated magic of the white man remains irresistibly alluring to the black. Transistor radios and cassette recorders have taken the place of glass beads and mirrors.

At the height of the slave trade, African rulers seemed literally to have gone mad. To get hold of the guns and tobacco and brandy they craved, some chiefs betrayed and enslaved their own people. The desire to possess had spiraled out of control. Their successors behave no differently. Slavery, of course, is now illegal. But are there any moral distinctions to be drawn between a chief who, in order to satisfy his lust for brandy, sells his own people into slavery and the contemporary politician who, coveting a Mercedes-Benz, embezzles the funds of a charity set up to help orphan children? It is no accident that **Uhuru** is thought of as a 'fruit' – something to be eaten, something to grow fat on. Africans are content with the political kingdom.

•

Andrew, I would guess, was in his early twenties. We had met in the street when I stopped him to ask the way. He wore a striped suit, platformed shoes and carried a leather briefcase. Rather than explain, he offered to escort me personally, brushing aside my objections. 'I'll take you,' he said firmly.

Having delivered me safely, he announced his intention to wait for me.

'That isn't necessary,' I said, wary now of his generosity.

'I'll wait.'

'But I don't know how long I'll be.'

'That's all right. I have nothing else to do.' He was quietly adamant.

He was as good as his word. An hour later I found him where I had left him. He fell in step a pace or two behind me, as self-effacing as a shadow, and followed me back to the hotel. He touched my arm as I entered the lounge. No doubt he was expecting to be paid for his services. Hesitantly, not knowing whether it was too much or too little or – come to that – whether he would be offended by my presumption, I offered him ten shillings. He took the note, folded it neatly and put it in his breast pocket. But he still showed not the slightest inclination to depart.

'You want *more* money?'

'I don't want more money,' he said. 'I want to give you this.' He held out a stylishly printed calling card. 'Andrew Njenga. Office Furniture Salesman.' An address and telephone number were supplied.

I returned the card. 'I don't need any office furniture. Sorry.'

'You keep it,' he said. 'It's for you. If you give me your card, we could write to each other.'

'I don't have a card.'

This appeared to astonish him. However, ready for any emergency, he produced an address book and a pencil. 'You can write your address in here,' he said.

'But why do you want us to write to each other?'

'I would like you as a pen pal,' he said. 'I like writing to pen pals.'

I was touched, rebuking myself for my churlishness. I wrote my address in his book. Anxious now to make up for my gracelessness, I offered to buy him a drink. He accepted the invitation with alacrity. [...]

'My real ambition,' he said suddenly, 'is to be a lawyer or an engineer. But for that I need a scholarship.'

'Won't the government give you one?'

'I have tried. I don't have the correct qualifications.' He stirred the frothy crest of his beer with a finger. 'My only hope is that one day I might be lucky enough to meet some rich person who will help me. I know somebody who got a scholarship like that.'

'Who gave it to him?'

'A German lady. I hear the Germans are nice people. I keep hoping I would meet someone like that. Someone who will take me away with them and give me good studies.'

'Maybe you will.'

'Maybe.' He gazed despondently around the room. [...]

He finished his beer. 'Come,' he said, abruptly cheerful. 'I'll take you for a walk. I'll show you some of the sights of Nairobi.'

Kenyatta Avenue was crowded with office workers on their way home. The late-afternoon light, luminously yellow, was hazed with the fertile red dust of Kikuyuland. Spaced like sentries at regular intervals along the pavement, the shoeshine boys, surrounded by an array of tins and bottles and brushes, kept their eyes fixed on the shoes of the pedestrians. On the numerous newsstands, row upon row of the latest pornographic magazines from the West were on display. What did someone like Andrew make of these provocative displays? Did he regard it as one more token of the new-forged 'equality' between black and white? More than time seems to have flown since the days when 'respect' was regarded by the European settlers as a near-mystical tribute to be paid by black to white, a surer safeguard of their survival than superior firepower. Respect, Elspeth Huxley has candidly observed, was, for the European, 'an invisible coat of mail ... the least rent or puncture might ... split the whole garment asunder and expose its wearer in all his human vulnerability.'

Exposure has come in a more literal way than she could ever have imagined. That very week, at the Sombrero Night Club, Beauty Lee, 'the International Striptease Artiste' (European, but of no precise provenance) was supposed to be performing on stage three times nightly. The Monro Massage Salon was enticing customers with its African, Asian and European masseuses. Naturally, not everyone approves. The long-settled British, those to whom the Norfolk Hotel is a last embattled outpost of settler civilisation, remain aloof and tight-lipped. The blame is generally – and quite rightly – placed on those Europeans without adequate colonial experience – the Swedes, the Danes, the Germans, even the Swiss. One Swiss lady had caused a minor ripple of scandal when she disappeared into the bush with her African lover.

Andrew stopped and stared into the window of a shoe shop. He said he needed new shoes. 'Those are nice,' he said, pointing at a multicoloured, platformed pair.

I pretended not to hear. We walked on, turning left up a side street lined, I noted anxiously, with clothes shops. I tried to divert his attention. 'What would you do if you became a lawyer – or an engineer – and made a lot of money?'

'I'd buy a big farm and grow tea on it.' He looked at me wisely. 'You get a very good price for tea these days.' He paused by a shop window. 'Those are nice jeans.'

'And what else would you do if you were rich?' We walked on.

'I would buy a Mercedes-Benz.' He laughed. 'Then I'd get all the beautiful women. The Wabenzi always have beautiful women.' ('Wabenzi' is the pleasantly jocular term used to describe the **nouveau-riche** black middle class – they who have eaten well of the fruit of Uhuru. They signal their status by the acquisition, at the first opportunity, of a Mercedes-Benz. Hence, the Wabenzi – the Benz tribe. [...]

Andrew paused by one of the pornographic displays. He picked up a magazine.

'You will buy this for me?'

I was too tired to argue. I bought it for him. He slipped it into his briefcase.

Andrew accompanied me back to the hotel. 'Tomorrow,' he said, 'I go home to my ***shamba*** near Kisumu. Every weekend I go there.' He laughed. 'I am a different man when I work on my *shamba*. When I take off all these clothes, you would find it hard to recognize me. You will write to me?'

'I will write to you if you write to me.'

We shook hands. He wandered off, swinging his briefcase, dreaming, perhaps, of the rich German lady who might stop him on the street any day to ask the way; of the 'scholarship' she might offer him; of the Mercedes-Benz that might one day be his and the beautiful women it would bring. What a ragbag of fantasies must whirl in that head! Within twenty-four hours, the office-furniture salesman with his elegantly printed calling cards would, as he himself had said, become unrecognizable. He was an unstable compound of urban and peasant man.

•

'The settler's town,' Frantz Fanon wrote, 'is a strongly built town, all made of stone and steel. It is a brightly lit town ... a town of white people, of foreigners. ... The look that the native turns on the settler's town is a look of lust, a look of envy; it expresses his dreams of possession: to sit at the settler's table, to sleep in the settler's bed, with his wife if possible ... there is no native who does not dream at least once a day of setting himself up in the settler's place.'

Nairobi, with its broad avenues, its multistoreyed hotels, its travel agencies, its boutiques, its nightclubs, its striptease 'artistes' and massage parlors, its two casinos, is not even a settler's town – not any more. It is a tourist town; and the tourist town is, by its very nature, a fantastical place, a kind of ***papier-mâché*** confection. Its quintessential expression is the international hotel. In the eyes of native and tourist alike, international hotels are dream palaces. But the tourist has this advantage: he *knows* it is a dream; he knows that at the end of two or three weeks he will fly away and return to an everyday world. The native cannot make the distinction. The abnormal becomes the stamping ground of his visions of 'progress' and 'development' because it is only the abnormal he sees. He is vulnerable. He is defenseless. Culturally, he is in much the same position as those aboriginal peoples who were wiped out by imported Old World diseases. Black and white meet and mingle at the point of fantasy, aggravating an already deformed vision. Fantasy is piled on fantasy. For as long as he can afford it, Andrew will sit in darkened, air-conditioned bars and dream of miraculous rescue.

• AMONG GREAT • GHOSTS

Guy Butler (1918–)

Guy Butler served in the Second World War in the North African and Italian Campaigns. During 1943-44 he was an information officer in Egypt, whose function was to provide a kind of adult education programme for the soldiers to combat boredom. This account of some of his experiences in Egypt is taken from the second volume of this autobiography, entitled **Bursting World**, *published in 1983.*[1]

It was some weeks before I got into Cairo on two days' leave, with Bill Fielding. It was my first big old city, and I found it fascinating. I had picked up the soldier's prejudices against **'Gyppos'**, and found the unceasing pressure of salesmen and hawkers a trial. It was commercialism gone mad. Everything was being sold on the streets: food, shoeshine, leatherwork, and 'my sister, who is not black like me but white, like Lady Lambson' (the British Resident's wife). This proposition was put to Bill by a sweet little boy about 10 years old.

In a dilapidated taxi, we crossed the Nile to the Pyramids. I quote from my letter to Jean.

> We mounted our camels, which sneered at us. Our guide Suliman besat a donkey so small that his feet nearly touched the ground. And so up the road to the great monuments to man's dread of death. After the congestion and complexity, the clashing colours and sounds in the bazaars, the sandstone simplicity of the huge triangular silhouettes against the clean

1 *Guy Butler's life and writings are introduced on page 98.*

desert sand was disconcerting. There were only two colours, yellows and the pale blue sky. The running to and fro of human beings became suddenly a silly thing, the bargains in bazaars a vulgar impertinence before these stony statements in the sun. Then down the hillside to the Sphinx. Her eyes are tired of curious humanity, blind with sunlight, the pupils half eroded by cataracts of wind. Like everything else in Egypt, the Sphinx and the pyramids were up for sale: this time in the form of exotic background to a photograph of oneself on a camel. We declined.'

That evening Bill and I were introduced to Cairo night-life by my cousin Amy Collett, who had been in Cairo for over a year: a bright redhead I had known all my life. She was engaged to a paratrooper. She took us to the Roof Garden of the Hotel des Roses, where a South American orchestra was playing rumbas, and soldiers from all the Allied forces in the Near and Middle East were trying to get on to a dance floor the size of a sixpenny bit.

•

Every so often I would run into a **Rhodian**. It was a great pleasure to encounter Aitchie in Cairo. Aitchie said we simply must have an evening together. He would rustle up some girls from somewhere, God knows where, but there must be some around. He had some sort of an admin. job at Ishmailia, and a billet with a living-room that opened on to a pleasant garden.

The party was not a success. Still the incorrigible romantic, he had borrowed a portable gramophone and some suitably atmospheric music; there was also a large flask of wine. The book of verse was, in fact *The Rubaiyat of Omar Khayyam.* But the girls (two pretty typists in uniform, one a Palestinian) were untouched by Tchaikowsky's heartbroken yearnings, and it was quite apparent after Aitchie had read no more than two stanzas that neither was aspiring to be a moon of delight for either Aitchie or me. They sat tight in their garden chairs. No amount of rearranging of the cusions on the deep lawn could persuade them to budge.

I lay back among my own cushions and watched the searchlights holding practice. Suddenly all the beams went out together, returning us to the unfamiliar stars. A violin turned the silence of each into an electric cell, filled with the voltage of longing or **ennui**. No one was capable of discovering a circuit in which that current could be released even to glow-worm pitch. It seemed as if the very ground 'shamed us into pettiness'. Egypt, the burnt-out country, was no help; she had seen too much of humanity, too many wars, more than enough of casual parties between transient soldiers and females found almost by serendipity.

'So burnt-out', I wrote; possibly because that morning I had visited Memphis and the tombs at Sakara. There I had found an image of early Egyptian vitality, in the tombs of the sacred bulls. There is one tomb, about seventeen metres underground, consisting of a tunnel three hundred metres long, with compartments on either side for the gigantic polished-granite coffins of the splendid bulls. There was something very African about a cult centering on a sacred bull.

•

In addition to absorbing history and ancient culture, we made efforts to maintain our own. Cedric Messina of Signals, later of SABC and BBC, produced a highly successful concert. One of the battalions staged *Journey's End*, surely one of the least suitable plays for men preparing for battle. The Divisional magazine encouraged scribblers to send in contributions. The first issue of the *Sable* published one of my efforts.

El Kahira

In a doorway, half-ajar,
She pauses, sways and throws -
Not cassia or jasmin,
Nor oleander, rose,
Not even a flamboyant
That burns beside the Nile -
But the withered flower of the streets,
A stale commercial smile.

A soulless comedy in the streets, straight sex in the cabaret:
Time has burnt man's soul to ash, but left his flesh to play
A pantomime of appetites that have no rein or leash.

Mohammed Ali's minarets are grey through the ***khamseen's*** *red;*
The geometric pyramids are plundered of their dead -
And the Past is sold by ***dragomen****, piecemeal, for more* ***Bakshessh'****.*

I was re-reading Shakespeare, and found myself returning over and over again to *Antony and Cleopatra. There* were lines which one could quote, lines so much more effective than anything written since, let alone anything I could write.

Shall I abide
In this dull world which in thy absence is
No better than a sty? ...

... The odds is gone,
And there is nothing left remarkable
Beneath the visiting moon.

I gave a talk, which the Brig attended, entitled 'They saw the Pyramids' – I started with Jacob and Moses, mentioned Alexander the Great, Caesar and Pompey, Antony and Cleopatra, Joseph and Mary, Saladin, St Louis of France, Napoleon and Lawrence of Arabia.

Cleopatra worried the Brig. She put a tin whisker on him. He shook his head over that affair. That chap Antony, as a general, should have known better.

•

'Imagine a dry dry heat and a flat grey-yellow sea of sand and little stones. Your moving truck is the centre of a slowly turning horizon under a colossal cloudless sky. You crest one of the rises and suddenly below you in a shallow pan a few ragged trees are dancing high off the ground, changing shape in the liquid glass of the heat. Suddenly your heart and head are filled with a tumult of sweetness – the scent of mimosa, the definite Karoo smell of mimosa in bloom. Though the leaves are smaller the tree has the same white thorns. What luxury! You are suddenly alive, yourself, Guy Butler, the boy from Cradock; a scent you have grown up with, smelt every spring of your childhood, is here, in this place in nowhere, this vacuum of the world. The shock to your memory stimulates your whole being, and you hunger for Jean to be there to see the yellow pom-poms of the flowers, and the hundreds of butterflies fluttering over them.'

You may have lost your bearings, but you have found the delicate core of the desert.

There were other surprises in the desert besides mimosa scent and butterflies. One day while travelling we pulled off the road to look at the Bitter Lakes.

'Imaginc a yellow sand valley about four miles wide, and at the bottom the irregular bright pattern of the bitter lakes – one blue as delphiniums, another red as wine. We just couldn't believe our eyes – and on the other side, blending with the sand, the **Coptic** monasteries jotted haphazard here and there. I dipped my hands in the water. When it dried it left a little fringe of salt crystals on my fingers.'

Life was getting so terribly monotonous that it was hard to keep one's sense of proportion. The smallest thing – a fly buzzing round one's face in the early morning – could make one go nearly mad with fury. I felt dry inside like sand.

• THE AMBIVALENT • CAPE

Laurens van der Post (1906–)

Born at Phillipolis, Laurens van der Post has spent most of his adult life with one foot in Africa and one in England. He served during the Second World War in Africa, Indonesia and Burma. Since 1949 he has undertaken several official missions exploring little-known parts of Africa. His independent expedition to the Kalahari Desert in search of the San was the subject of an acclaimed documentary film and of **The Lost World of the Kalahari** *(1958). This book is an account of the author's attempts to rediscover the spiritual and historical origins of humanity. Van der Post has published numerous books. The following extract is taken from a reflective and philosophical work, titled* **Yet Being Someone Other,** *which features what could be described as episodes of autobiography.*

Until it was all over, I had no idea how deeply I would be affected by my last voyage in the last liner from the Cape. Although it is several years now since I made that round voyage in the *Windsor Castle* from Southampton, I have not yet made my peace with the event and doubt if I ever shall. Whenever I return to the Cape, as I do regularly, and look down on Table Bay from the slopes of the mountain which gives it its name, it looks like a ghost harbour. It is still full of shipping but not the kind which made it, for me, one of the most exciting harbours in both the world and history. Unless there happens to be one of the rare cruise liners which treat the sea and its ports as sites for floating Butlin camps, I see only tanker after tanker, one more gigantic and unprepossessing than the other, interspersed with the proliferating classes of container ships, even uglier in line and general appearance than the greasy giant oilers.

The absence of these ships is what makes Table Bay such an empty and reproachful scene for me now. The loss of the beauty itself is hard enough to bear because the ships of the line, of which the *Windsor Castle* was the last, were perhaps the most beautiful ever built. From the moment they first appeared in the blue South Atlantic water, they caught the imagination of all and held it attentive until the end.

Hard to bear as the loss of such beauty is, yet harder still is the knowledge that they were the end not merely of a line but of a long and significant era of history, leaving us deprived and unprepared on the hazardous frontier of an undiscovered world of mind and spirit and universe. That last voyage compelled me to look, as I had not previously looked, into the paradox implicit in the fact that someone born so far in the interior of Africa as I was should be so deeply concerned over the event, and prompted me to uncover in myself a sense of history and the sea which was in many ways not only a dominant factor in the evolution of my own life and spirit but of some importance for understanding what happened, is happening and is about to happen in our time.

I begin therefore in Africa and with this unusual sense of sea and ships.

•

The great Cape itself, like the grit in the oyster on which the mystery of the pearl turns, was fixed firmly in my imagination at first sight and then transformed into a permanent point of growth for my love of the sea. My first view of it was towards evening from among the milk-bushes and dunes beyond Blueberg Strand. To look at Table Bay and Mountain from that point and at that hour was part of a solemn ritual of my father's life. He would always say it was the nearest he could get to reliving his first view of the Cape from the deck of a sailing ship some fifty-five years previously after a voyage of seventy-nine days from Europe. It had been visible like a smudge of cloud on the horizon of the blue sea on that morning so long ago. But then on a day made unbearably long, he emphasised, by an extreme hunger for land after so many confined days at sea, he and the whole crew had had to watch it acquiring substance with ponderous slowness until it stood in front of them tall and majestic, and much as we were seeing it at that moment. The view was more beautiful than anything the sailors had foreseen, and for him lifted the experience to an almost religious dimension.

The discovery that all this was an immediate part of my own family story, as well as the history of my native country, subsequently had a great deal to do with the impact of the experience. My impressions too were inflamed by the nature of that particular hour.

There is always for us who are truly born of the earth of Africa a kind of drama in the sunset hours, which no contrived theatre can equal. They are not merely remote impersonal moments confined to the external world. They are events joining the wheeling systems of a universe beyond even the light-year limits of our discerning, in a single totality because they correspond to a pattern within the human spirit, charged with a natural mythological import as of participation at that precise moment in some kind of cosmological sacrament. I remember that even my father's voice as he talked to me about it was not quite normal.

When he did speak again it was to stress how uncanny it was that he could show me the view exactly as it had been that evening, fifty-five years before, when the ship was preparing to beat up and down the Roadstead stained with sunset so as to be ready for disembarkation at dawn the next day. Devil's Peak, which he pointed out to me on the left of the central mountain, the Lion's Head on its right, falling away into its rump at Signal Hill, they all stood just as boldly then as they did now, except that Table Mountain itself, contained as it was in its own halo of light, seemed perhaps higher, wider, more authoritative and imperious than it had been in the past. And so much did he appear to relive the hour that it was as if the years in between had become a weight of some kind which caused his shoulders to sag whenever he pointed out the scene. And that alarmed me. But the difference, he feared, was subjective, because there was still no doubt in his mind that the objective message was the same. The empire of the sea ended there and an imperative of land as great, of which the mountain was the plenipotentiary, began right there where it stood. His voice, still in the grip of the original emotion, deepened as he spoke, and indeed every inch of the mountain's height confirmed what its name implied – The Cape of Good Hope – of great and new good hope for all of them perhaps. He understood why his own father had referred to David the psalmist, who had once called on his own fatigued self in another land of promise to lift up his eyes to the hills from whence would come his help.

It was just as well to remember, my father reminded me, history being such an unpredictable and contradictory process, that not everyone who had seen the Cape in the past had thought of it in terms of hope. The first name bestowed on it by Europeans was the Cape of Storms. There was no doubt that where the Cape drove a wedge into the sea for some ninety miles between the Indian and Atlantic Oceans, the greatest storms of wind and water of which nature was capable were constantly born and reborn. Looking at the cold Atlantic, utterly resolved and at peace in the bay as if already curled up for sleep in the curve of the arm of land which kept it from the warm Indian Ocean only some thirty miles to the east, such duplicity seemed unbelievable.

But our farewell visit provided a disturbing confirmation of what my father meant. At first glance Table Bay was tranquil and full of light. But as the sun began to go down, the green-blue sky turned sulphur and suddenly, between it and the mountain, we noticed a strange kind of murk, half mist and half cloud, smoking over the sea towards the south before it fanned out and came racing towards us. A moment before, the long level light had so enveloped the mountain that it seemed not lit up from without but rather glowing from within like a lamp from its own flame.

After the untroubled calm and sense of magisterial benevolence which had been my experience until then, the transformation was frightening. For me the Cape, in an instant, had become a living and vengeful gigantic presence. The impression went so deep that when, many years later, I was to encounter its personification as the resentful Titan, Adamastor, in the *Lusiad* of Luis de Camões, I instantly understood what had inspired him.

By the time we arrived back at our hotel a south-east gale was racing down the face of the mountain, pouring through the spaces between Devil's Peak and the Lion's Head, and testing every anchor of that line of ships that we had seen riding so confidently in the darkening Roadstead as they waited for room and shelter in the crowded dock at the far end of the Bay. Before long it turned into one of the most fearful of south-easters ever unleashed over the Town and Bay. We heard its music riding high and wild all through the night. The thick walls of the building shook, shuddered and at times felt as if they were reeling like a ship under the blows of the wind. Such sleep as I had was troubled perhaps by the first inkling that life was not made with the clear-cut simplicity for which one longed, but that the reality might be profoundly ambivalent and the manifest appearance only skin deep.

There is not another cape that has so dominated not only my own but also, I believe, the imagination of the world. Alone among the great capes of the world, the Cape of Good Hope seems to have been dressed to perfection by both earth and fate for the two-sided reality that it was destined to play in our history: at one moment an image of hope, at another the ultimate symbol of storm.

• A GLIMPSE OF CAPE TOWN IN THE 1870s •

Olive Schreiner (1855–1920)

Born at a mission station near Lesotho, Olive Schreiner spent her early years in various places, including Kimberley and Matjiesfontein, a small town in the western Karoo. She later settled at Matjiesfontein, the drier air of which she hoped would relieve her severe asthmatic condition. She also spent a number of years overseas.

Schreiner's main literary achievement was the novel **The Story of an African Farm** *(1893), which won world-wide acclaim, and is generally regarded as the first South African novel of merit. She has also published other novels, numerous essays, political pamphlets and allegories.*

This extract appeared in **From Man to Man,** *a book she wrote during her years as a governess in the 1870s. It was never completed, but was published posthumously in 1926.*

Tucked away among the great oak avenues in the suburbs of Cape Town was Rebekah's home. You might ride mile after mile on a hot summers' day and never feel the sunshine on you, for the great oak trees met over your head; and here and there to the right and left were houses buried behind hedges, with trees touching the roofs, and verandahs, and flower gardens.

Everywhere was the scent of fir trees; and pine plantations stretched away up the mountain sides; and now and then there were vineyards stretching acre on acre, with the sunlight shimmering through their leaves, and with white and purple grapes kissing the ground. Behind all rose the mountain's side, sloping away towards the Devil's Peak. On sunny days, as you looked up at it, it seemed as though that side of the mountain were a giant, tranquilly leaning backwards and watching with great godlike, placid eyes the pine woods and the dwellings of men curled about his feet.

It was very peaceful in the great avenues. Sometimes carts drove along and foot-passengers walked there; in summer the acorns fell, and in winter the leaves strewed the side-walks, and the beautiful tracery of the bare oak branches showed against the clear blue sky, and the lovely green of the pines and of the flower gardens seemed the brighter because the oak trees were bare.

In the houses at night you always heard the trees everywhere rustling with a sound like the distant moaning of a sea. Yet, if you entered a train at one of the little stations, in half an hour or a little more you might be on the other side of the mountain and in the old seaport town itself, with its long streets, principally of single storied houses, but also here and there of double, with small-paned windows, much as the old Dutch loved to build a hundred years ago. In the streets were Malays; and fish carts blowing their horns; and Dutchmen, and Englishmen, and men of all nations and colours and mixtures; and in the side streets were little Malays and coloured children playing happily in the gutters before their doors, or sitting on the stoep steps with a bunch of grapes in the one hand and a lump of bread in the other; and everywhere the peaceful, sleepy life of the old South African town crept on slowly; with its open drains, and its old families, and its old quiet methods of business, still prevailing. And above it all towered the stupendous front of Table Mountain, its beetling crags seeming to look down always with a stern calm contempt on the little seething world of men below.

Round the Peninsula swept the Southern Sea, pale blue and deep green in fair weather, and black in storms; but always, whether in storm or in fair weather, restless and passionate as no other sea on earth is – the Cape of Storms.

• LIFE IN DISTRICT • SIX

Richard Rive (1931–1989)

The following extract is from Richard Rive's second novel, **'Buckingham Palace', District Six** *(1986), which features the experiences of the people of 'Buckingham Palace', a dingy row of cottages situated in the heart of District Six. District Six was a sub-economic area at the foot of Table Mountain which in 1966 was declared for white occupation only. Local inhabitants were cleared out and buildings demolished. District Six was left derelict for many years and became a controversial symbol of the effects of apartheid. As such it has featured in much South African art and literature.*[1]

I remember those who used to live in District Six, those who lived in Caledon Street and Clifton Hill and busy Hanover Street. There are those of us who still remember the ripe, warm days. Some of us still romanticize and regret when our eyes travel beyond the dead bricks and split treestumps and wind-tossed sand.

When I was a boy and chirruping ten, a decade after the end of the Second World War, when I was Tarzan and Batman and could sing 'Rainbow on the River' like Bobby Breen – in those red-white-and-blue days I remember especially the weekends, which began with the bustle of Friday evenings when the women came home early from the factories and the men came home late although they had been paid off early – and the feeling of well-being and plenty in our house on the upper left-hand side of Caledon Street near St Mark's Church. We lived in the fourth in a row of five mouldy cottages called 'Buckingham Palace' by the locals. The first, 201, the one far-

---

1 *Richard Rive's life and work is introduced on page 86.*

thest from the church as if by design, was a bluepainted House of Pleasure called the 'Casbah'. In it lived Mary and The Girls. Next to them at 203, painted bright pink, was 'Winsor Park' (spelt like that), which was occupied by Zoot and The Boys. Then came 205, the cottage of The Jungles, then ours, then at 209 that of Last-Knight the barber, his wife and three daughters. A sprawling open field overgrown with weeds and rusty tin cans separated Buckingham Palace from the church.

Friday evenings were warm and relaxed. We felt mellow because it was the week-end and payday. While my sister got dressed to go to the Star or National Bioscope with her boyfriend, since there was no time for her to cook I was sent to Millard's Fish and Chips shop beyond Tennant Street to get the evening's supper. I raced with the south-easter and then forced my way into the shop crowded with customers, the air thick with the smell of stale sawdust, boiling fish oil and sweaty bodies as steam rose from the frying-pans. When I had wriggled my way through the forest of grown-up legs and torsos, I found myself jammed against the counter, always just too late to order from the last batch of fish and chips, and then had to wait, fighting to prevent the breath from being squeezed out of my body, until the next batch of gleaming stockfish and thick fingers of potato chips were hoisted, dripping oil, and spewed out onto the warmers. On the way home I raced to keep the parcels hot, but not so fast that I could not pierce a small hole in the packet and remove a few chips. But this was finally detected by my hawkeyed mother, who knew what was happening in spite of my denials.

Saturdays and Sundays were different.

Saturday mornings were brisk, for some men must work and all women must shop. And Hanover Street was crowded and the bazaars and fish-market did a roaring trade. There were groceries to buy on the book and clothes on hire-purchase.

Katzen, who was the landlord of Buckingham Palace, had his emporium on the corner of Hanover and Tennant Streets. His shop windows were cluttered with bric-a-brac such as celluloid dolls, huge glass tankards still celebrating the Coronation, rolls of crepe-de chine, gramophones and framed and mounted prints of a violently pink-faced King George VI and Queen Elizabeth. After his premises had been broken into six times in so many weeks, Katzen displayed a notice outside his shop, 'Although Katzen has been burgled again, Katzen will never burgle you!'. We all knew that there was no chance of the small, Jewish shopkeeper with his walrus moustache and large feet ever climbing through our back windows to steal our radios, but we also felt that he could rob us in other ways. The thieves always seemed to steal his gramophones and crepe-de-chine and patriotically left the prints of King George VI and his queen.

Saturday mornings Tennant Street, Hanover Street and Castle Bridge heaved and bustled with housewives, peddlers, skollies, urchins, pimps and everybody else. Everybody bought everything on lay-bye and it was all written down in exercise books; Moodley, the Indian general dealer in Caledon Street, scribbled it on the back of brown paper-bags which he lost when he absent-mindedly used them as containers for sugarbeans or rice. Everyone also knew they would have to pay in the end, even those who owed Moodley, although when that end was, was extremely flexible and it could be next week or next year or next never.

Near Seven Steps Mr Angelo Baptiste owned a dark Italian shop from the ceiling of which hung strings of garlic. His shop also smelt of macaroni and olive oil. We would tease him in order to hear him swearing volubly in his native language.

On Saturday afternoons I went to Star Bioscope with Estelle, Manne and Broertjie to see that week's exciting episode of 'Zorro Rides Again' in black in white. We could not stand in any queue to get in because the idea of queues had not yet reached District Six. So we pushed and tugged and sweated to slip through the narrow opening in the iron gates which would allow us into the foyer where we could purchase tickets. Estelle, who never feared anyone, simply climbed onto the nearest pair of shoulders at the back of the heaving mass and then crawled over heads. Once through the gates, we bought our tickets to sit on the hard seats downstairs, where ushers in soiled, prison-warder khaki, shouted loudly and forced us to share seats with whomever they shoved down beside us. If you raised any objections you were meanly clouted. (One sadistic usher took to riding up and down the aisle on a bicycle, lashing out with his belt at any unfortunate urchin who provoked his displeasure.) When Estelle, resplendent in his cowboy shirt, three-quarter pants and high-heeled boots arrived late and stood in the lighted entrance, he would cup his hands to his mouth and blow a loud strident whistle which only he could blow. It rose above the packed and heaving auditorium to Manne, who sat in the farthermost corner tight between his girl and the one he was keeping for Estelle. Manne, heeding the whistle of his leader, would throw lighted matches into the air, regardless of anyone on whom it landed, like a ship sending up distress flares. And then Estelle would wade over seats and frightened urchins in a straight line to his minion and the girl reserved for him.

We sat goggle-eyed in the thick, cigarette-smoke dark, watching Zorro carve out Z's with his whip on the foreheads of those crooks stupid enough to challenge his dexterity with inferior weapons like six-guns. We munched our way through half-loaves of split-open brown bread that had whole pieces of fried fish placed in between. Estelle, who was a successful pickpocket, always paid for the refreshments. When they played the movie of *Hamlet*, Estelle whistled and shouted derisively that it was a lot of balls, and Alfie, who was in Junior Certificate at Trafalgar High and a budding critic, said the outjie spoke far too much and who ever saw a ghost that looked like that.

And in the evenings we would stand in hushed doorways and tell stories about the legendary figures of District Six, Zoot, Pretty-Boy and Mary, or show off about our prowess with the local girls, or just talk about the ways of white folks and how Cissie Gool was fighting for us and showing the white people a thing or two. And how wonderful it was to live in America and talk like Charles Starrett and sing like Gene Autry. The young men went to parties or bioscope, and the older men played dominoes and klawerjas on the stoeps, holding the huge boards between them on their laps, and when they banged down the dominoes or the cards, hordes of flies would spin up and then settle down again. The young girls waited for the men to fetch them, all coy, demure and made up in the latest fashions. The older housewives came out with their wooden benches and sat apart from the men on the stoep and gossiped the mild evening away.

And the apricot warmth of a summer Sunday morning when almost everyone slept late and mouldy cocks kept in postage-stamp, asphalt yards crowed their confined calls to wake no-one in particular. Then the sun rose over-ripe although it was barely six o'clock and the whole District was snoring and blowing away the fumes of Saturday evening. The gaiety and sheer abandonment of the previous night had given way to the exhausted sleep of Sunday morning.

I would be sent to buy koeksisters for breakfast at a house next to Bernstein's Bottle Store, where three unmarried Muslim sisters lived. Their house always smelt of aniseed and rose water. I would stand in the dark passage awaiting my turn, watching them fry the light dough until it was golden brown, then dip it hot and sugary into coconut. They had taken a liking to me and always gave me an extra one wrapped separately which I ate on the way back.

When the first people had woken from their smoke-filled sleep, the more righteous washed themselves in zinc tubs in their yards or kitchens (with the curtain drawn), then put on their Sunday best and searched for hymn-books and bibles neglected during the rest of the week. They put on tight patent-leather shoes, had a hurried breakfast of hot coffee and koeksisters, and walked wincingly up Caledon Street to attend the morning service at St Mark's. Those less virtuous tossed dreamlessly, fading out the monotony of the week before at the same job in the same factory for the same wages which were never enough for groceries and rent and a bit of booze and maybe an evening with the girls at Mary's.

At midday we were served with the heaviest meal of the week. We sat around the dining-room table stiff and uncomfortable in our navy-blue best. After a long drawn-out grace we started with curry and yellow rice rich with raisins and cinnamon. The curry was pale and anaemic because my aunt, who always lunched with us on Sundays, claimed to suffer from acid winds. But after that we had thick slices of roast and potatoes smothered in gravy, and red beetroot salad. And finally jelly and custard and sometimes bread or rice pudding.

In the afternoon, when the adults were snoring heavily, we children would roam the streets, always careful not to soil our Sunday suits. On rare occasions we ventured downtown to the Museum to see the models of Bushmen with big bums or furtively glance at the nude statues in the Art Galleries. What a wicked and enjoyable place the world was. What goings-on. And then we walked back through the Botanical Gardens whooping and shouting and raising havoc deliberately to frighten fragile little white ladies sitting on quiet benches, who would then complain to the attendants about those rude slum children.

Back home the darkness descended from Table Mountain and the street-lamps flickered to life at the tops of their stalks, leaving pools of light at their bases in which we played our games till called inside because it was school tomorrow. It was always school tomorrow on Sunday evenings when we were enjoying ourselves, even when we knew it was vacation time. The hush crept over the District as one by one the lights were switched off or paraffin lamps blown out until there was only the basin of darkness at the foot of the mountain illumined by rows of lamp-post stalks. The streets would empty until in the small hours there were only stray dogs, prowling cats, solitary drunks and hawkers' carts leaning awkwardly with their long shafts against the walls.

And I still clearly remember the characters and the incidents.

• THE HAPPY ISLE •

Lawrence G Green (1988–1973)

Lawrence Green was born during the siege of Kimberley and died in 1973. He was a retiring type of person who collected all his material personally and published numerous narrative works describing his experiences in different places.

The piece which follows is taken from his collection titled **A decent fellow doesn't work: experiences of an easy-going traveller in search of pleasure, interesting people and places inside and outside Southern Africa – with a little wisdom gathered along the way.** *In the extract, Green's account of Robben Island provides a colourful picture of the state of the island as it was before it became a prison for many political prisoners, such as Nelson Mandela.*

Truly the island could a tale unfold
Of many a dark deed done in days of old,
And many a treasure lies beneath its sands
Hid in those early times by shipwrecked hands.

Cannon G.F. Gresley, a
Robben Island chaplain.

Often and often in my wanderings I have discovered that the happiest groups of people are to be found in places more or less isolated from the teeming, restless human race. And so it was on Robben Island.

Robben Island is small and low, a sandy island crouching in the Table Bay entrance rather like a brown whale with a lighthouse on its back. I first went there as a schoolboy before World War I, and I have landed many times since then. The whole world is my stage, but I never overlooked the queer and interesting places on my own doorstep.

I saw Robben Island at its best. Heaven knows, there have been dark pages in this island story. Any place where prisoners, lepers and lunatics were put away must have its tortured ghosts. The island was the scene of cruelty and scandals at various times. Then came a merciful transformation, a period when hundreds of islanders formed happy memories.

At first sight Robben Island is a forbidding scene. Mariners shudder as they watch the long ocean swells breaking on dangerous reefs. It is a mere two miles long by one mile at the widest point, and in midsummer this tiny area seems desolate and waterless indeed. Only when you land in spring does the rough oval of the island reveal its green fields or arum lilies, daisies and buttercups and golden wattle.

'Only the ignorant speak of the island with horror', one of the former residents told me. 'Talk to any children born on the island and hear what they have to say. Even when we spent only a few days in Cape Town there was the thrill of coming home. We roamed at will over the island, wandered in the woods among the turtle-doves, walked on sandy beaches and bathed in lonely bays. When we moved about the veld in September the quail flew up before us, and on the rocks there were the gulls. We islanders had something very precious. Then came the sad day when we had to leave and settle on the mainland.'

'Sometimes we found ways of returning to the abandoned island for a picnic in the ruins of our happy isle. We walked silently on tip-toe in certain places for fear of disturbing the ghosts of the island of our past.'

Even as a schoolboy I sensed the tranquillity of the island. The population was large when I first landed there a few years before World War I: five hundred officials with their families in the village called Irish Town; one hundred convicts kept for sanitary duties and as labourers; five hundred mental patients and one thousand lepers.

•

After the war I owned a little yawl, *Amitia*. When the wind was offshore I would anchor near the island at week-ends and call on friends in the village. I went on shore often after the settlement had been evacuated, and then it was an island of memories indeed.

Come round with me in the heyday of the isle. Land at the jetty, named the Faure Pier after Sir Pieter Faure who carried out the opening ceremony towards the end of last century. Someone stole the champagne intended for the naming, and Faure had to smash a bottle of ginger-pop against the crane.

Irish Town stands near the south-east corner of the island. Some have declared the name arose because of the number of Irishmen on the staff in the early days; but it is also said that most of the houses had green roofs years ago.

Finest house was the Residency, a cool stone mansion with seventeen rooms and lawns running down to the sea. A commissioner who valued privacy added a sort of observation tower on the roof. It was reached precariously by a cat-walk over the ceiling. There the bygone commissioners sat in state with their after-dinner cigars gazing at the lights at Cape Town six miles away. The medical superintendent ruled the island until the eighteen-nineties. Then the posts were separated, and civil servants were appointed.

Government offices were in Irish Town. Officials lived there; the Anglican church and rectory and the Dutch Reformed Church parsonage were in the village. So were the male and female mental hospitals, and many people employed well-behaved patients as cooks and servants. Police barracks, the public works department, the convict station and the lighthouse were set apart.

Lamp-posts of London design were provided in the main street of Irish Town. Mr. Gerber the lamplighter (who was also a leper attendant) went round with a ladder in the evening putting a match to the paraffin lamps.

Irish Town had a government store. At one period Pereira, a boatman, kept a shop there; and there was a restaurant with a liquor-licence. Food and drink were cheap, but the staff and their families relied on visiting the Cape Town shops once a month for all but the simplest items. 'Chits' were used at the island shops, the butcher, baker and dairy. Some of the young children had never handled money or visited the mainland. They had never seen a train, and never had they known the dangers of city streets. I believe it was in 1920 that the first motor-car reached Robben Island.

Across the island runs a diagonal path which separated the lepers from the rest of the community. Leper compounds were fenced off, and there was a gate which the lepers called the 'Gate of Tears'. Rarely were they allowed to pass that barrier. When some well-known island personality died, however, the lepers were conducted to the wall of the graveyard in Irish Town, and thus segregated they joined in the singing.

Men have lived on Robben Island for three and a half centuries; or more than four centuries if the legend of a Portuguese settlement can be proved.

Canon G.F. Gresley, one of the island's chaplains last century, dug for weeks near Blue Stone Quarry in an effort to discover clues to the early history of the island. All he found was an old copper measure, six inches long, apparently used in the slate quarry during the Dutch occupation.

Canon Gresley thought the Portuguese had started a penal colony there early in the sixteenth century. It has been stated that the Portuguese built themselves a stone house on the island, but I have never been able to trace the source of this statement. Possibly the truth will still be found in the Lisbon archives.

•

In the eyes of government officials, islands have always seemed ideal places for prisons and the safe incarceration of prisoners. Strange to say, prisoners always manage to escape from time to time, whether the island is Alcatraz or Robben Island. Islands are never as safe as they look.

Convicts were dumped on the island all through the eighteenth century. When two guns were fired on the island it meant that convicts had escaped. This alarm was given in September 1731, and the guardians reported that seven men had put off in a little boat made of skins. They reached the mainland in spite of heavy weather, but three were drowned while landing. The other four were recaptured. Among the convicts was a former naval man, who took command of the ship *Elizabeth*, shook off all pursuers, and sailed away for an unknown destination.

Convicts built the handsome Anglican Church in the main street under Wolfe's supervision in 1841, and the church is now an historical monument, Hough, the chaplain who held the first service, selected as his text: 'It is good to be here.' I do not know whether the soldiers and convicts were in sympathy with that sentiment, but there have been many Robben Island dwellers since then who would have said it was an inspired sermon.

Robben Island first became a leper settlement shortly before the middle of last century. Convicts were moved away to the mainland. Moravian missionaries accompanied the lepers from the former hospital at Hemel en Aarde in the Caledon district.

Lunatics were sent to the island soon afterwards and able bodied men among them were called upon to carry out many tasks which the convicts had done. Years passed before convicts were again sent to the island to work as boatmen and sanitary labourers.

• HOME TOWN •

Herman Charles Bosman (1905–1951)

Here, Bosman describes his return to his home town of Kuilsriver, outside Cape Town, after an absence of many years. The extract was originally published in the collection titled **Just Jerepigo** *in 1957.*[1]

Last week I revisited Kuils River, a village that is a few miles outside of the Cape Town municipal area and that enjoys the questionable distinction of being the place in which I was born. How shall I describe my feelings on alighting at the shabby little railway station and gazing about me at my unfamiliar birthplace, which I saw again, now, for the first time since the age of four? I felt very lonely. There was nothing about the place I recognized. And if it wasn't for the fact that Table Mountain looked quite near – through its proximity at least giving me some sort of a clue as to whereabouts I was – I feel sure that I would have caught the next train back again. I felt so lost both emotionally and geographically.

I had only one conscious memory of Kuils River. That was when I was about two. I was seated on the grass, wrapped around in a blanket and there was a soft wind blowing, because it was getting on towards sunset, and two young girl-cousins, a few years older than I, were dancing about me on the grass. And I suddenly burst into tears, just like that, without reason. And the sadness of that memory has, at intervals, haunted me throughout the rest of my life.

But as I strolled down a quiet little road in the direction of the village, with the station behind me, it suddenly struck me that while I remembered nothing at all of the external features of my birth-place, there was something

1 *A background to the writings of Herman Charles Bosman appears on page 9.*

else, something timeless and more vivid than memory, that made me intimately acquainted with my surroundings even though I didn't know where the path on which I was walking, that lay deep in white dust, would lead to. In the stir of the noonday breeze was something anciently familiar. And the patches of bluish-coloured grass, sifted around with dunesand: were these not the things I had always known?

And a sudden fragrance, coming off from the warm earth and blending with the subtle odour of black-wattle, overwhelmed me for a moment, almost, as though I had left Kuils River only yesterday.

Far from requiring Table Mountain any longer as a comforting landmark, I now began to feel that I could show other people the way around here in this village. Even though I had to enquire of passing strangers the way to the main street, where the village stores were, and the post-office, and the local pub.

And because life in Kuils River is very leisurely, with the pace of things smooth and unhurried, I found many people who were glad to hold converse with a visitor from Johannesburg, and they told me many things, and at great length, about my home town from which I had emigrated at the age of four. And from numerous enquiries I made, putting my questions judiciously and in all sorts of roundabout ways, I elicited the fact that nobody in Kuils River had ever heard of me.

At least, the first lot of enquiries I made were of a tentative nature. I would ask, clearing my throat somewhat selfconsciously, whether Kuils River did not perhaps have a few literary traditions, kind of; whether there was any local knowledge of anybody, distinguished, sort of, having been in Kuils River during the present century, sort of – in the literary like? All sorts of different, indirect questions like that. That was how I started off. But afterwards I just began asking them straight out. And the replies were always, monotonously, the same. There was Dr F C L Bosman, they said, of Cape Town University. Well, he was a writer, of course. And he was born in Kuils River. And C H Kuhn ('Mikro'), the author of the Afrikaans bestseller *Toiings*, had come to settle in Kuils River some years ago, to write, and everybody in the village was very proud to have him there, of course. And it was well-known that the local dominee had been contributing morally uplifting stories to the Afrikaans religious press for a good number of years. That was the sum total of Kuils River's literary associations, but for a small place like that it wasn't at all bad, they said.

'No, it isn't at all bad,' I agreed, each time.

Taken all round, it seemed to me that there could be such a thing, in Kuils River, as overdoing the old truth about a prophet not being without honour.

I enquired, later in the afternoon, as to whether there were any historical monuments in Kuils River – any ancient, time-worn edifices, any noble and inspiring ruins. And they said yes, there was. They said there was Colonel Creswell. They said he lived at the top end of Kuils River, on an estate barricaded with palisades and with savage dogs roaming the grounds. They said that several English families had settled in Kuils River and that they all went in for tall stake-fences and fierce mastiffs.

I dashed off in the direction of where they indicated to me Colonel Creswell's house was, after they had again cautioned me about the Hounds of the Baskervilles loping about the wooded grounds with slavering jaws. Colonel Creswell. I couldn't believe it. What volumes of water had not flowed under Vaal River bridge, in dry seasons and all, since I had last seen Colonel Creswell's name in a newspaper.

I found the place, huge, rambling, closed in with pointed poles like what Harold's army erected before Hastings. I located the gate with some difficulty. It was a good distance up the driveway to the house, and I had to kick a big dog out of the way that was lying asleep in the sun. He disappeared into the undergrowth with a yelp. I was still considerably out of breath when, having been admitted by a servant into the drawing-room, I sat down to wait for Colonel Creswell to appear.

But I was glad I had come. I stayed there all afternoon. Towards evening we went and sat on the stoep. In appearance Colonel Creswell was more like the cartoons of him that had appeared in anti-Pact newspapers in those far-off days than he resembled a studio photograph of himself in the drawing-room. But that was all the years had done to him. His mind was as bright as ever. He was a fund of enthralling reminiscences. Intimate little stories about Merriman and Botha and Hertzog. And when he said that Smuts had never forgiven him he wiped his left eye, which was watering. He spoke about his birth-place, Malta or Gibraltar – I forget which he said – and about the first mine he worked on on the Rand, the Durban-Roodepoort, and about his having had to sever his connection with the Chamber of Mines in rather a big way, on account of some Chinamen he had kicked out.

'Don't you go back to the Rand sometimes?' I asked, 'to go and have a look at the Durban-Roodepoort again, for instance – all the old scenes?'

But Colonel Creswell said that he was already 85, and that while he would like to visit the Rand some day, there was hardly anybody there that still knew him. So he preferred Kuils River. It seemed very sad, somehow. And so I told Colonel Creswell – and he was the only person in the village in whom I had confided this fact – that I was born in Kuils River – and that there was not a soul in my birth-place that knew me. We sat for a good while after that in silence.

The wind of early evening, sweeping across from the dunes, stirred through the tangled undergrowth. And it seemed chillier than the wind that blew from over the dunes when I was a child.

• LANDING AT ALGOA BAY •

Thomas Pringle (1789–1834)

Thomas Pringle was the leader of a small party of Scottish settlers who set sail for South Africa in 1820. He subsequently moved to Cape Town, where he followed an academic and journalistic career, which brought him into conflict with the rather autocratic governor Lord Charles Somerset.

He is regarded by many as 'the father of South African poetry'. The editors of the Companion to South African English Literature *comment that his 'enduring creative achievement is that, working without models, he procured some of the first convincing South African, as opposed to British-humanist, poetry.'*

The following extract is from **Narrative of a Residence in South Africa.**

On the 15th, and late in the afternoon [we] came to an anchor in Algoa Bay, in the midst of a little fleet of vessels, which had just landed, or were engaged in landing, their respective bands of settlers ...

It was an animated and interesting scene. Around us in the west corner of the spacious bay, were anchored ten or twelve large vessels, which had recently arrived with emigrants, of whom a great proportion were still on board. Directly in front, on a rising ground a few hundred yards from the beach, stood the little fortified barrack, or block-house, called Fort Frederick, occupied by a division of 72nd Regiment, with the tents and marquees of the officers pitched on the heights around it. At the foot of those heights, nearer the beach, stood three thatched cottages and one or two wooden houses brought out from England, which now formed the offices of the commissaries and other civil functionaries appointed to transact the business of the emigration, and to provide the settlers with provisions and other stores, and with carriages for their conveyance up the country. Interspersed among these offices and among the pavilions of the functionaries and naval officers employed on shore, were scattered large depots of agricultural implements, carpenters' and blacksmiths' tools, and iron ware of all descriptions, sent out by the home government to be furnished to the settlers at prime cost. About two furlongs to the eastward, on a level spot between the sand-hills on the beach and the stony heights beyond, lay the camp of the emigrants. Nearly a thousand souls, on an average, were at present lodged there in military tents, but parties were daily moving off in long trains of bullock wagons, to proceed to their appointed places of location in the interior, while their place was immediately occupied by fresh bands, hourly disembarking from the vessels in the bay. A suitable background to this animated picture, as viewed by us from the anchorage, was supplied by the heights over the river Zwartkops, covered with a dense jungle, and by the picturesque peaks of the Winterhoek and the dark masses of the Zuurberg ridge far to the northward, distinctly outlined in the clear blue sky.

The whole scene was such as could not fail to impress deeply the most unconcerned spectator. To us, who had embarked all our worldly property and earthly prospects – our future fortunes and the fate of our posterity, in this enterprise, it was interesting and exciting to an intense degree.

It being too late to go ashore that evening, we continued gazing on this scene till long after sunset – till twilight had darkened into night, and the constellations of the southern hemisphere, revolving in cloudless brilliancy above, reminded us that nearly half the globe's expanse intervened between us and our native land – the homes of our youth and the friends we had parted from for ever; and that here, in this farthest nook of Southern Africa, we were now about to receive the portion of our inheritance, and to draw an irrevocable lot for ourselves and for our children's children. Solemn reflections will press themselves at such a time on the most thoughtless; and this night, as we swung at anchor in Algoa Bay, so long the bourne of all our wishes, many a wakeful brain among us was doubtless expatiating, each according to the prevailing current of thought, in serious meditation on the future or the past. A long sea voyage, and, far more, one with such an object as we had before us, totally disconnecting us for a time from the bustling world behind and before, and from the great political and social interests of humanity, appears as it were, like a pause or interlude between the acts of the busy drama of human life, and deepens the interest both of the past and the future by affording a convenient space for reflection. The quiet interval was about to close with us; and we now waited with anxiety for the curtain to draw up, and unfold in all the distinctness of reality the scenes of novelty and adventure to which we had so long looked forward.

Early next morning, in order to make arrangements for the disembarkation of our party, I went ashore with Lieutenant Pritchard, the government agent who had accompanied us from London. There is no landing-place at this bay, except on the open beach; and when the wind blows strong from the south-east there is a tremendous surf, which totally precludes all communication between the shore and the vessels at anchor, and even renders the roadstead extremely hazardous. At this time, however, the weather was favourable, and we dashed boldly through the breakers in the captain's gig.

The disembarkation of the emigrants from the other transports was proceeding with alacrity. Party after party were conveyed safely and rapidly through the breakers by the surf-boats (managed by seamen from the sloop of war), and then borne ashore 'high and dry' on the shoulders of fatigue parties of the military. The beach was all alive with bustle and confusion, and the boisterous hilarity of people who felt their feet on firm ground for the first time after a wearisome voyage. Bands of men and women were walking up and down, conversing and laughing; their children gambolling around them, and raising ever and anon their shrill voices in exclamations of pleasure and surprise, as some novel object excited their attention. Other groups were watching their luggage, as it was carried from the boats and piled in heaps upon the sand; or were helping to load the wagons appointed to convey it to the settler's camp. Bargemen and soldiers were shouting to each other across the surf. Tall Dutch Boers, with broad-brimmed white hats, and huge tobacco-pipes in their mouths, were brawling in colonial Dutch. Whips were smacking, bullocks bellowing, wagons creaking; and the half-naked Hottentots who led the long teams of draught oxen, were running and hallooing, and waving their long, lank swarthy arms in front of their horned followers, like so many mad dervishes.

•

I then strolled along the beach to survey more closely the camp of the settlers, which had looked so picturesque from the sea. On my way I passed two or three marquees, pitched apart, among the evergreen bushes which were scattered between the sand-hills and the heights behind. These were the encampment of some of the higher class of settlers, and evinced the taste of the occupants by the pleasant situations in which they were placed, and by the neatness and order of everything about them. Ladies and gentlemen, elegantly dressed, were seated in some of them with books in their hands; others were rambling among the shrubbery and over the little eminences, looking down upon the bustling beach and bay. One or two handsome carriages were standing in the open air, exhibiting some tokens of aristocratic rank or pretension in the proprietors. It was obvious that several of these families had been accustomed to enjoy the luxurious accommodations of refined society in England. How far they had acted wisely in embarking their property and the happiness of their families in an enterprise like the present, and in leading their respective bands of adventurers to colonise the wilds of Southern Africa, were questions yet to be determined. Foreseeing, as I did in some degree (although certainly by no means to the full extent) the difficulties and privations inevitable in such circumstances, I could not view this class of emigrants, with their elegant arrangements and appliances, without some melancholy misgivings as to their future fate; for they appeared utterly unfitted by former habits, especially the females, for roughing it (to use the expressive phraseology of the camp) through the first trying period of the settlement.

A little way beyond, I entered the Settlers' Camp. It consisted of several hundred tents, pitched in parallel rows or streets, and occupied by the middling and lower class of emigrants. These consisted of various descriptions of people; and the air, aspect, and array of their persons and temporary residences, were equally various. On the whole they formed a motley and rather unprepossessing collection of people. Guessing vaguely from my observations on this occasion, and on subsequent rambles through their locations, I should say that probably about a third part were persons of real respectability of character, and possessed of some worldly substance; but that the remaining two-thirds were for the most part composed of individuals of a very unpromising description – persons who had hung loose upon society – low in morals or desperate in circumstances. Enterprise many of these doubtlessly possessed in an eminent degree; but too many appeared to be idle, insolent, and drunken, and mutinously disposed towards their masters and superiors. And with such qualities, it was not possible to augur very favourably of their future conduct and destiny, or of the welfare of those who had collected them in England, and whose success in occupying the country depended entirely on their steady industry.

A GLIMPSE OF • CRADOCK IN • THE 1870s

Olive Schreiner (1855–1920)

The following extract from **From Man to Man** *by Olive Schreiner was written during her years as a governess in the 1870s. It was never completed, and published posthumously in 1926.*[1]

Up-country, in the red karroo, was the town where Aunt Mary-Anna lived, red karroo to right of it, red karroo to left. A river-bed ran below the town, in winter full of dried mud banks and reaches of gravel and bare stone, but, in the summer rains, coming down red and full, the dark sand-laden water lying level with the banks and bearing on its waves trees and stumps, the carcasses of drowned animals, and even sometimes at long intervals a human corpse.

All round the plain were flat topped mountains, some broken into jagged points, but still bearing the marks, in their flat structure, of what had been the shores of seas and lakes, the remains of whose mammoth amphibious beasts lay still within the stratified shale, turned in the course of the ages to stone themselves.

There were three churches in the town and a great square full of sand with shops and houses round it, where, in the early morning, buck-wagons drawn by long teams of oxen rolled slowly in, laden with produce from the country, skins and pumpkins and firewood, bags of meal or mielies and sometimes butter and garden growths; and the little market master held the morning market. There the townsmen gathered to hear the latest news and send round the latest gossip, till by eight o'clock they had all gone home to

1 *Olive Schreiner's life and writing is introduced on page 124.*

their breakfasts, the wagons had rolled out and the square was left empty and silent enough all day, crossed occasionally by customers making their way to the different shops or business men going home to their meals, and, at eleven o'clock, by streams of men coming to the hotel at the corner where they went to have their morning drink of soda and brandy and to smoke and chat for a while on the hotel stoep.

Three times a week the post-cart with its dusty wheels and horses came in, blowing its bugle and bringing its news from the outer world, and everyone hurried to the post office to get their letters. And twice a week came Cobb and Co.'s great coaches, swinging on their great leather straps; and their teams of six horses, bearing passengers to and from the Diamond Fields, drew up before the hotel door, when for two hours the town was alive and excited with the new arrivals; then the horses would be put in again and pass away in a cloud of dust and the town would be left to its silent monotony.

There were two croquet clubs in the place frequented by the members of two churches which formed the two great cliques; there was a courthouse where occasionally the members of one church gave a dance which the other church thought wicked and never went to, and once or twice a year some travelling showman would arrive and give an entertainment there. Every year the members of each church had a large Sunday-school picnic to which all the members of that congregation went; and sometimes a lady would give a high tea and invited a few friends, for no one dined late there.

In the upper part of the town there were rows of little flat houses, generally kept shut up and empty, where the Dutch farmers stayed when they came in once in three months to the Lord's Supper ('Nagmaal') and now and then to the Sunday services in the weeks between. But on Monday they all went out again, and the houses were left empty, and the town to its English inhabitants.

During nine months of the year, while the winds blew, clouds of dust whirled along the streets before thunder-storms; when the gusts came, great clouds of sand rose from the market square and met the still mightier clouds raised from the wide sandy plain; and the town was shrouded in sand.

It was a dull narrow little life enough, lived there among the flat-roofed houses, far removed from the currents of life and thought of the great world beyond.

Yet, if some summer morning you rose at half past four and went out to the koppie at the end of the town and climbed its round black ironstones, and stood looking down at the little town with its long rows of houses and the little brown huts of the Kaffir Location sleeping at your feet in the still blue morning air, while the damp of the night yet rested on everything and nothing moved or stirred, except where here and there a Kaffir servant might be seen hurrying from the Location to the town, her shawl drawn tight about her to shut out the chill morning air; till by and by, from some of the chimneys in the town, long blue curls of smoke began to rise, standing upright and almost motionless in the still air; then suddenly the bleak moist stone on which you stood turned golden at your feet; a shaft of light shot across the plain and struck it; another came, and the little ice plant in the crevice of the rock at your feet glittered in every crystal drop; then another, and the whole plain was golden and the roofs of the little flat houses glinted – then the town was beautiful.

• WAITING FOR THE • RAINS

Guy Butler (1918–)

This account of Cradock and its environs in the 1920s and 1930s comes from the first volume of Guy Butler's autobiography, **Karoo Morning,** *published in 1977.*[1]

The winters on the Karoo plateaux are severe and dry. Sometimes soft, low, grey clouds would settle and sag over our world, making us huddle closer to our fires; sometimes we would wake to a cold crystal morning with the mountaintops miraculously white with snow. In my recollection, that mysterious powder never fell in the town itself. But the river took little notice of snow, it waited, like everything in the valley, for the thunder to speak in late October or November. No one who has not lived in a semi-desert can imagine the annual hope and anxiety with which the inhabitants wait through days of intensifying heat for the rains to come. Our eyes are on the look-out for the appearance of the first cumulus cloud, the cloud no bigger than a man's hand, which grows, and is joined by other presences, impenetrably purple below, rising through thousands of feet to their rounded heads, each head a white cerebellum, a tumultuous brain churning its intentions over and over. Then these giants step between us and the sun, the shadows disappear, earth darkens. A gust of wind bends trees, whips up dust, rattles the windows. Birds, sheep, cattle, make for shelter. The twilight is lit alternately by great aluminium flashes of sheet lightning or splintered by vicious stabs at the earth. The first thunder comes like a sinister drumroll mustering a barbarous host in the remote hills; then much closer, a growling lion's roar. Drops of water smack into the dust, making small craters like bullets, more and more, faster and faster. A hissing, swishing sound sur-

---

1 *Butler's life and writing is introduced on page 98.*

rounds us; the yard, the street, the veld, are all awash with sliding sheets whose surface is continuously riddled and dimpled with innumerable globules of water. Gutters, runnels, sluits, dongas, rivers, receive the fluid which has cut and carved them, which is cutting and carving them now. Unpredictably, the thunder wields his club, and earth and air shake and reverberate with crashing cymbals and deep, subterranean gongs. We are in the heart of the scented storm: the water has released a fragrance from the earth.

A few hours later we hear that the river has come down – a strange paradoxical phrase, quite inadequate to describe what has happened. The little trickle that connects the silver pools has disappeared under a cataract of dark brown, rough-backed water stampeding to the sea. Mingled with the intoxicating scent which the dry earth has released is the related but different flood smell of silty waters. But, as James Butler observed at Carlisle Bridge, if that water is our lifeblood, it is given indiscriminately, with a force which carries millions upon millions of tons of topsoil to the sea. From the grandstand of the Gilfillan Bridge one may see occasional drowned sheep and other animals, and great logs of dead tree, and trees with green leaves still on them, rolling and plunging downstream.

The people of Cradock would come to watch this great performance of their old river, and also the performance of those who had not come to watch but to work; the wood fishermen, who took up their positions between the bridge and the old weir near the Abattoir, where the stream flows with less speed and turbulence, and the shelving banks are favourable to their work.

The equipment of a wood fisherman is simple: a long, strong, light rope with a three-pronged grapple attached to one end of it. His eyes scan the waters upstream. When he sees a large log or uprooted tree approaching within reasonable distance of his bank, he starts whirling the anchor round and round his head, then releases is so that it splashes down just beyond his prize; then immediately he starts hauling in, hand over hand. If he has judged and thrown well, and the grapple does not slip, he will pull his plunder into shore: firewood to be stored for the winter or to be chopped up and sold on the morning market.

Anyone – whites, Coloureds, blacks – could be a wood fisherman. Sometimes a man would harpoon such a whale of a tree that it would threaten to drag him downstream unless he abandoned his precious line and grapple. Then he would sing out for help. Fellow fishermen and bystanders would rush to his aid, determined not to let the old river defeat that man. You would find all races and generations pulling on one rope then.

• ALICE AND THE • AMATOLAS

Francis Carey Slater (1876–1958)

Francis Carey Slater, whose parents were direct descendants of the 1820 Settlers, was born in Alice in the Eastern Cape. After serving as a bank manager for a number of years, he retired early to Wynberg in Cape Town to devote himself to writing. His first volume of poetry, **Footprints thro' the Veld** *(1905), reflected his love of Eastern Cape landscape and people. Subsequently he published various other volumes of poetry, as well as a novel and some short stories.*

During his last years he frequently visited the Amatola Mountains which lie on the escarpment north of Alice. This description of the region in the 1890s is from his autobiography, **A Settler's Heritage***, which was written in the late 1890s and published in 1954.*

Alice in those far-away days might well have recalled Goldsmith's Auburn. For it was the loveliest, laziest, sleepiest, shadiest village in the Eastern Province, and anyone entering it between one and two o'clock in the afternoon would find it almost a 'deserted village' as well. Waters, led in open furrows, from the clear sweet Tyumie river, whispered through the shade-flecked streets of the village, mingling their drowsy music with the absent-minded melodies of softly rustling leaves. The azure Amatola mountains signalled to it daily from great, calm altitudes; the sky beamed brightly upon it for about three hundred and thirty of the three hundred and and sixty-five days that tell the tale of the year; and it was verily a nest of singing birds, a haunt of happy lovers, and a paradise meet for meditative poets.

Time has dealt hardly with Alice: it has grown a little in size, but not in beauty. The virginal simplicity of its old-time loveliness has gone. Its ancient quietude is now disturbed by the blatant, saxophonic snortings of the motor car, and the excruciating shrieks of the locomotive – whose belching smoke stains the crystal clarity of its skies. Old landmarks have vanished: the hardy old frontiersmen and sturdy pioneers, who found amid the leafy recesses of this demi-paradise a refuge and abiding place, have all passed away. Men and women were they – simple, earnest and steadfast, lacking in learning, but abounding in wisdom; poor in worldly goods, but infinitely rich in kindness, grace, and goodfellowship. And although, in my careless and inconsiderate youth, I liked and respected these simple and humble friends, it was not until –

'The soul's dark cottage battered and decayed
Let in more light through chinks that time (had) made' –

that I began to realise how once I had walked among angels unawares.

•

On one public holiday, I joined a riding party from Lovedale to the Hogsback.

I had long worshipped from afar the Amatola Hills, of which the peaks Gaika and Hogsback form a part. But now, as I approached these magnetic mountains my worship deepened into adoration. I have written so much in verse about these scenes that are brightest to me, that I must refrain from prose, which, may prove to be an anticlimax. Although the neighbourhood, commonly known as Hogsback, is still one of the most beautiful in South Africa, in the far away and long ago days of which I speak, it was infinitely more beautiful. Its natural loveliness was then unspoiled by the encroachments and misdirected energies of iconoclastic man. Its human habitations in those days consisted of one small wayside-inn and a modest fruit farm about a mile beyond the inn. The sacred spaces of this once secluded retreat are now bespattered with numbers of wood-and-iron and other erections – some of which have no pretensions to beauty. Its great calm silences are daily shattered by the discordant vociferations of motor-car and motor-bus, and by the raucous wranglings and ribald laughters of such mortals as are irresponsive to the beauty and sanctity of their surroundings. As an added insult to the grandeur of this neighbourhood, dismal pine and wattle plantations now over-run the broad slopes – once resplendently waving with red-brown grass – which divide from each other various deep valleys, ribbed with primeval forests of noble yellowwood trees whose solemn murmurs intermingle with the unceasing song of mountain-streams.

We forced our way through the forest undergrowth until we reached the moorland above us. Upon the outskirts of this rose the triple peaks of Hogsback, and the noble head of Gaika – all of which are nearly seven thousand feet above sealevel. From the moors above the forest, we had a splendid view of the country above, below and around us. After this delightful walk we returned to the camp, and when evening prayers and supper were over, we sang various songs and choruses. Then the Paisley man and I, after promising to be at the camp by five o'clock in the morning, sought our inn.

Next morning we reached the camp slightly before the promised hour; but owing to various delays there, we did not start until nearly six o'clock. I shall never forget a sight, which sent me sky-high, when we came to, what was then known as, the 'lilybend'. The lily-bend was (and I hope still is) a little grove, starred with arum-lilies, which lay at a bend of the old, and now almost abandoned, road between Alice and Hogsback. From this point, where the descent from the highlands begins, we beheld a white, still sea of mist, which covered the Tyumie valley and Alice, stretching beyond them to the far horizon. This motionless, enveloping mist was broken at intervals by small hillpeaks. These loomed like dark islands in a ghost-white sea which gradually became luminous beneath the far-swivelling rays of the fast-rising sun. When we reached Lovedale, I hastened to my work. All through that long and unreal day, as I worked, I was haunted by beauty – by the splendour of mountain and forest, of moor and stream. All through the day, the solemn harmonies of the wind in the echoing forest intermingled with the music of many-voiced fountains and the crisp rustling of leaves reverberated in my brain. All through the day, I dreamed of that earthly paradise I had left so lately, and, in dreaming, I often found myself sliding to the giddy verge of sleep.

•

In 1896 there was much discussion in Alice as to what should be done to celebrate the Queen's Diamond Jubilee in the following year. All cricketers, and those interested in the game were very eager that a Cricket Pavilion as a Memorial should be erected on the Market Square, where the game was then played. Alice cricket had hitherto been subject to serious handicaps. The heavy, coir-matting, with which the pitch was covered when in use, was kept in the store-room of a shopkeeper. As the said room was about 150 yards away, several of us had to lug the matting to, and from, the cricket-pitch each time we played. Apart from this, there was no suitable accommodation for spectators. In the circumstances, it is not surprising that cricketers, and also spectators (who did not find sitting on the hard ground conducive to comfort) were alike enthusiastic for the erection of this precious, projected Pavilion.

A Meeting in the Town Hall, to decide this important matter was convened by the Mayor. The hall was crowded upon that exciting evening; and among others on the platform was Dr Stewart, who was soon called upon to give us his views. To the intense surprise and discomfiture of us poor, eager but thoughtless cricketers, he advocated, as a fit and proper Memorial to grace the great occasion, the establishment of a hospital at Lovedale to be called the Victoria Hospital. The hospital would be for Natives, but a ward would be reserved for Europeans as there was neither hospital nor nursing-home at either Alice or Lovedale at the time. Towards the end of his speech, Dr Stewart compared the serious necessity of saving human life with the frivolous practice of tossing balls about, and illustrated his last phrase with a pre-eminently scornful gesture – by way of a parody of the 'tossing about' process. While Dr Stewart was speaking I realized, with the keenest dismay, that our glittering prospect of a gorgeous cricket-pavilion was fast fading away. Following hard upon this, his final gesture of contempt in referring to the glorious game of cricket, stung me into unpremeditated action.

Before I realized what I was doing, I found myself upon my feet passionately defending our 'Pass' which had suddenly become so precarious. After enlarging upon the difficulties experienced by players and spectators alike, and our long-cherished hopes for the amelioration of this unhappy state of things, I had the effrontery to add that if more people exercised themselves in healthy games there would be less need of hospitals. My ignorant and impudent speech actually met with loud applause. But although I soon regretted the shameful ingratitude shown towards Dr Stewart in my hasty speech, I am happy to add that the incident made no difference whatever in his attitude to me, for he continued to treat me with the same kind helpfulness as in the past.

As to the Memorial it was finally agreed: to proceed with *both* the hospital and the pavilion. The latter was soon erected; it was a wooden structure with a galvanized iron roof and cost less than a hundred pounds. In the following Easter we had a Cricket Tournament to celebrate its opening. Cricket teams from Fort Beaufort, Seymour and Whittlesea visited us, and the result was a draw between Alice and Fort Beaufort. This was played off on the Fort Beaufort ground, about a fortnight later, and we won the tournament. The Victoria Hospital at Lovedale, on behalf of which Dr Stewart had pleaded so earnestly, was duly built. It has since been considerably enlarged and now consists of a large cluster of stately buildings.

• THE LOST WORLD OF • THE KALAHARI

Laurens van der Post (1906–)

The Lost World of the Kalahari *was published in 1958. A landmark in South African writing, the autobiographical work documents Van der Post's search for the mythical world of the Cape San (Bushmen) who were exterminated by settlers in the Western Cape, Karoo and Kalahari. The following extracts from the book are reflections by the writer on what was to become one of the most significant journeys of the many he has undertaken.*[1]

This is the story of a journey in a great wasteland and a search for some pure remnant of the unique and almost vanished first people of my native land, the Bushmen of Africa. The journey in fact was accomplished barely a year ago, but in a deeper sense it began long before that. Indeed so far back in time does all this go that I am unable to determine precisely when it did begin. I know for certain only that no sooner did I become aware of myself as a child than my imagination slipped, like a hand into a glove, into a profound preoccupation with the little Bushman and his terrible fate.

I was born near the Great River, in the heart of what for thousands of years had been great Bushman country. The Bushman himself as a coherent entity had already gone, but I was surrounded from birth by so many moving fragments of his race and culture that he felt extraordinarily near. I was always meeting him afresh on the lips of living men. Beside the open hearth on cold winters' nights on my mother's farm of Wolwekop, 'Mountain of the Wolves' (as my countrymen call the big striped hyaenas), or round the camp fire with the jackals' mournful bark raising an apprehensive bleat from a

1 *The life and writing of Sir Laurens van der Post is introduced on page 120.*

newly-lambed ewe in the flock kraaled nearby and with the night-plover wailing over the black plain like a bosun's pipe, there the vanished Bushman would be vividly at the centre of some hardy pioneering reminiscence: a Bushman gay, gallant, mischievous, unpredictable, and to the end unrepentant and defiant. Though gone from the land, he still stalked life and reality in the mixed blood of the coloured people as subtly as he ever stalked the multitudinous game of Africa.

The older I grew the more I resented that I had come too late on the scene to know him in the flesh. For many years I could not accept that the door was closed forever on the Bushman. I went on seeking for news and information of him as if preparing for the moment when the door would open and he would reappear in our midst. Indeed I believe the first objective question I ever asked of life was: 'Who, really, was the Bushman?' I asked it of people of all races and colours who might have had contact with him. They told me much. But what they told me only made me hunger for more.

The older I grew the more concerned I became over the part my own family must have had in the extermination of the Bushman. That it was considerable I had no doubt. My mother's family had been in Africa since the European beginning. By all accounts more restless, bold and adventurous than most, they had always been in the forefront of what we called 'progress' and expansion, but what must have been retrogression and contraction to the Bushman. In fact my mother's own grandfather had been one of the very first to cross the Great River with a small band of kinsmen in covered wagons and to move north across the reeking and smoking plains of the centre. My mother's father's people too, as she once told me, had always lived naturally on frontiers, and he had been one of the earliest to settle north of the Great River. It seemed to me impossible, along such an advanced line, that they could have avoided taking part in extinguishing the Bushman. But when I asked for precise information I found that the members of the family instinctively conspired to silence. They would answer questions in general readily enough, but when it came down to particulars of family history in this regard they were dumb. Their silence confirmed my worst suspicions.

In the colourful background of the wonderful home my remarkable grandfather had made of 'The Fountain of the Bushman', two little old Bushman men moved like twilight shadows. My grandfather, I believed, had found them as children, whimpering among the boulders, and taken them home to 'The Fountain of the Bushman' to grow up in his service. But found them where? What were they? Survivors? But survivors of what? Another Bushman tragedy in the long series of tragedies? And which particular one? Now I shall never know because the people who could speak of it with authority are dead. But I can only say that the whole of the Bushman past came to a point for me in those two little men. They confirmed all that I vaguely feared and wondered at, and the world of the past which I came to recreate for myself in my imagination spun on into the future and gathered substance with those two little men always at the imponderable centre.

Somehow, in my imagination, the Bushman was always with us even when the two little old men were no longer there to represent him. And in an ever more subtle way the earth too participated profoundly in the process. Ever since I can remember I have been struck by the profound quality of melancholy which lies at the heart of the physical scene in southern Africa. I recollect clearly asking my father once: 'Why do the vlaktes and koppies always look so sad?' He replied with unexpected feeling: 'The sadness is not in the plains and hills but in ourselves.'

This may be true for others, but it was not true for me. For me, the country in its own melancholy right was sad and in a deep mourning. As a young boy I came to believe that some knowledge of the tragedy of the Bushman was always deeply implicit in the physical scene, making the blue of the uplands more blue, the empty plains more desolate, and adding to the voice of the wind, as it climbed over the hilltops and streaked down lean towards the river, the wail of the rejected aboriginal spirit crying to be reborn. It seemed to me that both the earth and I were aware that spread out before us was the scene of a great play in which the principal actor was absent and He who first created it, missing.

For some years I grieved secretly in this manner until one day I heard someone volunteer casually that on a recent journey to an oasis in the Kalahari Desert he had found the authentic Bushman living there as he had once lived in the country around us. After that, I could think of nothing else. Later in the afternoon I locked myself in the study of my father, who had died some weeks before, and took out a diary in which, secretly, I had begun to write poetry and record my thoughts. The day October 13, 1914, and in High Dutch I wrote: 'I have decided today that when I am grown-up I am going into the Kalahari Desert to seek out the Bushman.'

•

We set off on a cloudless morning for the Slippery Hills in the Kalahari. Ben and Vyan went ahead with two Land Rovers to break a way through the bush: Charles, Duncan, Samutchoso and I followed at leisure in order to be free to stop and film undisturbed.

Forty years later I remembered the warning Samutchoso had delivered solemnly in the swamp: I would have to hasten if I wanted to see a gathering of Bushmen in the Slippery Hills. They would stay there only so long as the water in the crevices at the foot of the hills lasted, for they drew on the eternal sacred water at the top of the hills not as a routine but only in dire necessity. Already twelve days had passed since I promised to meet Samutchoso at 'The Place of the Eddies' to guide us to the hills. Every day had added to the power and the glory of the sun. All around us the white waters were shrinking and even the great river falling fast, while my own spirit stamped like a horse kept over-long in the stable.

We were trying to stalk a dazzle of zebra which flashed in and out of a long strip of green and yellow fever trees, with an ostrich, its feathers flared like a ballet skirt around its dancing legs, on their flank, when suddenly two shots, fired quickly one after the other, snapped the tense silence ahead.

My blood went cold within me. Instinctively I looked at Samutchoso. His face was without expression, and yet I knew he had heard and that a change accordingly had taken place within him. With an acute sense of guilt, I realized I had forgotten to keep faith with him. My anxieties in the swamp, the long journey out and back from Johannesburg, and many other things had overlaid the moment when he and I had first discussed the journey to the hills. I had completely overlooked the essential condition of the promise extracted by him from me: that there should be no killing on our way to the hills. I had forgotten to tell our companions of Samutchoso's account of the spirits' law against killing on approach to their home.

'I'm sorry,' I said at once. It's all my fault, not theirs. I forgot to tell them. I had so much trouble I forgot my promise.'

His face relaxed and he said that he understood, but the implication was that it was not for him either to understand or absolve. With that and a brief, belated explanation and warning to my hunter companions that nothing under any conditions was to be shot, I had to be content.

The sun was setting by the time we had made camp, collected wood for our fires and installed ourselves for a stay of several days. Still no sound or movement came from bush or hills. Even a stir of evening air would have been welcome to ease the immovable and shining heat hanging in the horseshoe bowl of rocks.

It is significant that none of us was at ease during all that first night in the hills. At first light the camp came alive as though glad to be rid of such darkness, and everyone, without urging from me, began preparing vigorously for the day. Just before sunrise, however, we had an abrupt and odd interruption. Suddenly we were attacked by bees. From all directions, through the trees, they came winging sonorously at this unfamiliar hour. I have never witnessed anything like it. They came to sting, not in angry militant swarms but in great, shapeless dark-brown hordes, humming an esoteric tune of exhortation, crawling all over us and our belongings as if to sweep us, by sheer weight of numbers and volume of sound, out of their way. The smell and taste of our water could not have attracted them because they ignored it, as also the sugar set out for our breakfast coffee. They seemed interested only in beating their wings against our faces, crawling up our sleeves and trousers, and from time to time driving the mysterious point of their visitation home with a perfectly timed sting in the most tender spots.

Perturbed by the thought of the retaliation the bees might provoke, I warned the camp: 'Don't kill any of them whatever else you do.'

If I had hoped to please Samutchoso by my admonition it proved vain, because his expression clearly implied that the warning would have served us better had it been delivered two days earlier.

The next day we closed in on the base of the rocks that now seemed to stare back at us in the swelling light and heat of day with a glimmer of grim satisfaction, and started to follow the rocky contour on the ground.

We climbed up to it by a clearly defined track, the natural stepping stones worn smooth and shining with centuries of traffic. The moment one began to mount steeply one was aware that it was no ordinary track. This track had been extensively decorated. At several places where the rock presented a smooth enough surface it was highly painted. One would lift oneself up from one shelf to another to find oneself staring into the face of a rhinoceros regarding one without fear or favour; or a tortoise, head out and cocked to one side as if listening to our wilful steps, would suddenly confront one as if to imply a rebuke to the sweating procession climbing so frantically towards the summit. We seemed to be in the presence of a single system of spirit dedicated to the translation of flesh and blood into a greater idiom of the world beyond, where fruit of true knowledge purported to grow by everlasting water. I even wondered whether, with our profane guns and prying cameras, we were not clambering over the forsaken altars of a great natural temple.

Samutchoso, anyway, had no doubts. The expression on his face was exalted. He was the first to go eagerly over the rim. I followed. Before us was a deep cup in the crown of the central hill. I just had time to see a gleam of water when a heartrending sob broke from Samutchoso. He had stopped to kneel on a rock by the track, and was raising his hands like a Mussulman at his devotions, when he overbalanced backwards so violently that he nearly fell. Both knees were bleeding, but it was not the injury that was troubling him.

'Did you see, Master?' he asked, profoundly troubled. 'I was not even allowed to begin to pray!'

He pointed out two deep holes in the rock in which he had tried to kneel and a third somewhat apart on the left. It was there, he said, that the greatest spirit of all had knelt with his cruse of water to pray the day he created the world. Here also he, Samutchoso, himself had knelt to pray when he visited the hills before. Yet now he had not been allowed to do so. He had been pulled backwards. He was visibly anguished, and I could say little to comfort him, but his instinctive obedience to the working of his fate still enabled him to lead us, like a man in a trance, to the pool of perennial water.

The grass around the edges of the pool was green and lush and the surface covered with growth and slime, for it was long since it had been disturbed. In that high place, and in that arid desert, its mere existence was a miracle.

Nearby grew the 'Tree of True Knowledge', as Samutchoso called it. From its branches hung large, round fruit like green navel oranges. Samutchoso announced they were still too green for eating, and that fact, too, seemed to add to his foreboding. The fruit when ripe, he said, was more delicious than honey. I would have liked to bring some of it back for identification, but Samutchoso begged me not to pick any of it. I felt I had already so hurt his spirit that I desisted and merely tried to film the fruit.

Again at first light we were invaded by bees and had to endure them until the sun rose, when they vanished as before. After that we returned to the hills, climbed up a precipitous cleft to the first painting and began to film it. Hardly had we started when the ominous blur in the precise mechanism of the camera announced another stoppage. So it went on all day.

By this time everyone in the camp knew something unusual was happening and all stopped working to crowd round the pair of us. Silently they watched Samutchoso. He stood gazing at his palm for about ten minutes and then, in a voice we had not heard before, he began to speak to presences that only he could see, saying: 'No, not you over there. Don't push so, please ... Be so good as to make way for him that is behind you ... No not you either, but the next, please ....' And so on and on until at last a deep 'Ah!' came from him, as if he had found in a great multitude the one he sought. Then he fell silent and appeared to be listening intently. Another quarter of an hour passed thus and then, like a man awaking, he rubbed his eyes, shook his head and, seeing me again, said slowly: 'Yes! Master, it is as I thought, the spirits of the hills are very angry with you, so angry that if they had not known your intention in coming here was pure they would long since have killed you. They are angry because you have come here with blood on your hands. They are angry because you have not behaved like a leader of your men. You allowed men who are less than you to come into their presence before you did. You allowed them to trample all over the hills and drink of the water they provide for men and beasts without first saying their prayers and asking permission to do so. You should have come first with me and, as the leader, paid your respects to them. We should first have asked their permission and have made a sacrifice of food and said our prayers before taking of their waters. That is why they have broken your machines. And, Master, they have not done with you yet.'

He said all this so quietly, without melodrama or any effort at effect, that it was deeply impressive. I saw a look of consternation on the listening black faces.

'What can I do to put it right?' I asked him.

He shook his grey head sadly, saying: 'I do not know. Truly I do not know. They are angry with me, too. You saw how they threw me out of the place of prayer? They tell me they would have killed me if I had tried again.'

'Suppose,' I asked him, 'I wrote a letter to the spirits to beg forgiveness and put it in a bottle and buried it at the foot of the painting of the eland for the spirits to read, would that help, d'you think?'

He did not think long. With a light I had not seen in his eyes since the day after our meeting with the buffalo, he exclaimed: 'Master, it's a very good plan!'

While he stood beside me I sat down at once to write the letter. I wrote quickly, for in some odd way it seemed already written inside myself. At the same time I felt it important to make it as formal and correct as possible. This is how I remember it:

In camp, Sunset,
Thursday,
October -

To The Spirits,
The Tsodilo Hills.

We beg most humbly the pardon of the great spirits of these Slipperty Hills for any disrespect we may have shown them unintentionally and for any disturbance we may have caused in their ancient resting place. At the foot of this great painting, which is such clear evidence of their presence and of their power to make flesh and blood create beyond its immediate self, we bury this letter as an act of profound contrition, hoping they will read it and forgive us. We beg that anyone coming after us, finding this letter and reading it too will be moved by it to show them greater respect than we have done.

'Do you think that all will be well now?' I asked Samutchoso when we stood up.

'Would you like me to find out?' he asked.

'Please,' I requested.

Thereupon he took out his needle and thread again and stood there once more, with bowed head, looking deep into the lifeline in his hand. For some time I watched that grey head in the oldest attitude of communion with a spirit beyond his and my own tight round of knowing, moved as I had seldom been before. Below us the dawn came up fast, its light breaking over the vast plains like wave upon wave of some multitudinous sea incarnadined.

Then Samutchoso looked up quickly to say in a voice trembling with emotion: 'All is well, Master. The spirits ask me to say that henceforth all will be well with you. Only they warn me that when you get to the next place to which you are going you will find one more unhappiness waiting for you. They ask you not to be discouraged by it, because it will be an unhappiness that belongs not to the future but the past.'

We returned in silence to camp. For the first time no bees came to attack us. Our Land-Rovers started up and took us promptly from the presence of the hills without hitch. We took Samutchoso to his home and, when I left him, I was sad to see that, although I might be free of the experience, he had not yet done with it. I knew he felt as near to me as was possible to someone not of his race. He had treated me as a friend and I am certain wished me well. Yet there was a strange compelling note of regret in his voice when, on saying farewell, he remarked: 'The spirits of the hills are not what they were, Master. They are losing their power. Ten years ago they would have killed you all for coming to them in that manner.'

It was a cry straight from his heart and the final utterance of an experience which seemed to me to be an example of the injury the coming of the European had done to the being and spirit of Africa. Samutchoso's gods were dying from a contagion brought by us, and against which he and his kind had not our inborn immunities. Now to whom and to what could he turn? For even he, illiterate and unimpressive in the rags and tatters of our civilization, knew that without his gods life would lose its meaning and inevitably lead towards disaster. His face and his cry rode with me all the hundreds of miles on the hard journey to Maun.

•

When I [returned to the Kalahari thirty-five years later], the ostensible purpose was to help in the making of another television film, 'Testament of the Bushman', which would record how they had fared after my sojourn among them in the central desert more than a generation before. What I saw then was shattering. Whatever I might have hoped to have achieved for their protection and the promotion of their culture had proved utterly vain.

The Tsodilo Hills, which I had discovered, or perhaps rediscovered, for European man, were by now so well known that there were several roads to it and even a landing strip at the hills themselves to make them accessible to the increasing numbers of tourists, induced in the first instance, I fear, by my films and books into wanting to see them. I myself, because of pressures of time, landed there on an airstrip large enough to take sizeable aeroplanes, and found two other planes already drawn up at the side waiting for their cargo of tourists to return from the hills where they had been to look at the most accessible rock-paintings for a few hours on their way to somewhere else.

Only one incident redeemed the visit from the arid platitude it has become for the world of today, to give me back some of the original sense of wonder and special meaning with which those hills had once invested me, and that was a coincidence too remarkable to be misunderstood. As I walked from the plane to the edge of the landing strip I saw two black men coming through the surrounding bush towards us. When they came nearer I thought I knew one of them, but this seemed so unlikely that I dismissed it until one man began to wave his hand at me in an excited manner and suddenly I saw that it was Samutchao who, with his father Samutchoso, had been one of my guides on my first expedition to the hills. At that time he was a young fisherman and breeder of cattle and goats along the Okavango River, but now he had moved out and organised himself and a whole community of Makoba clansmen around water found for them by the government of Botswana, close to the hills – which at the same time had enabled it to dispossess the Bushman of yet more of his vital and shrinking hunting grounds. Samutchao had obviously become the most important person in the area and a person of power, which I was to find had not improved him. However, he went gladly back with me and my companions into the hills.

Together we retraced the journey to the first rock-painting I had discovered, one hot summer's morning, glowing on yellow sandstone above the thorn trees. We climbed up to the ledge underneath the paintings themselves where I had buried in an empty bottle of Plymouth Gin the letter I had written to the spirits of the hills, begging their pardon for the irreverence of our intrusion and our inconsiderate behaviour on our arrival.

The pool of everlasting water we found dry and empty. The tree bearing the fruit of the knowledge of good and evil, of which the book speaks, had gone. I asked Samutchao what had happened to the water, and the question broke through his indifference. His nonchalant body became violent as it were with new life, and he waved both his arms at the pit empty of water and almost shouted: 'All gone, gone, gone! All gone with the spirits back into the earth where they came from.'

And I remembered how already, thirty-five years before, on the morning when we had climbed up to offer our letter of contrition to the spirits and the white-haired Samutchoso – whose name meant 'He who was left after the reaping' – having consulted the spirits in the manner I described, turned to me and, with a voice of unbelievable sadness, remarked even then: 'You know, Moren, the spirits are not what they were. They are losing their power. Even ten years ago they would have killed us for what we have done.'

All the way out of the desert I kept thinking back many years to the moment when I realized that it would be fatal to expose the desert to human husbandry, and that its great contribution to life could be in its preservation as an area stretching from the foothills of the Transvaal, the borders of the Shashi, Limpopo and Zambezi down to the Molopo river, up and across the border of South West Africa to the Namib Hills, north to Mossamedes, taking the Okavango firmly in its sweep, and all the rest where a rich sandveld, turned fertile by millions of years of natural rehabilitation, could be turned into a last keep of the original life of Africa, a keep unlike any other, because it would be enriched as a fortress also of our aboriginal man. The desert, even its Okavango delta, clearly had no contribution that was at all lasting to make to the market economics of our exacting technological day, but it could have a great, spiritually enriching future as a place where man could have access, as it were, to creation's original bureau of standards and from time to time come to measure the values of his being against the master values as they were in the beginning.

Some of us had indeed already started to work for some such dream when the events which now divide Africa so tragically against itself overtook us and, for the moment, as far as the physical world is concerned, the light that was in the dream lies like a lamp shattered in the dust. The hope that remains is the kind of **Promethean** hope which has to create from its own wreck the thing that it contemplates, and it is a hope that is singularly in the keeping of the great memory with which we began.

• UPSTART CITY •

William Plomer (1903–1973)

William Plomer was born in the Transvaal town of Pietersburg, of British parents in 1903. He spent some of his early years in South Africa and some in England, and he lived most of his later years overseas. Nonetheless, though his stay in South Africa was a short one, his experiences in the country produced much of what was best in his prose and certainly, in his poetry. In his early years he collaborated with Roy Campbell (and, to a lesser extent, Laurens van der Post) on the publication of the controversial literary journal, Voorslag.

The extract following appears in **The South African Autobiography,** *published in 1984 but based on earlier autobiographies. William Plomer, his mother and brother returned from a sojourn in England to join Mr Plomer Senior in Johannesburg in August 1911.*

At this period Johannesburg (to quote the brilliant Lewis Mariano Nesbitt, who left in *Gold Fever* a memorable account of it) was 'an ultra-modern city on the American plan, where every vice had its panders, and every kind of licentious orgy is perennial'. Standing more than five thousand feet above sea-level in a limpid, sun-baked, rarefied atmosphere, the city, only twenty-five years old, had been conjured out of the waving grass by greed of gold. Seen from a distance it differed from others by the prevalence of whitish mounds, which seemed to have risen among the very streets. Composed of quartz dust impregnated with cyanide of potassium, these small mountains, the excreta of gold-grubbing, gave the urban landscape unusual perspectives. Beneath them man-made shafts extended for three or four miles vertically into the earth, and in these mines, a single one of which might employ ten thousand men, a large population, mainly black, toiled hard and sometimes dangerously for gold.

The black men had come to the Rand not because they wanted to but because they had to earn money to pay their taxes and could not earn it at home. This economic pressure, or exploitation, would now, I suppose, be called 'colonialism'. This propagandist word had not then been invented: the process of developing, or milking, 'new' countries was still called colonisation. Sensible men knew that, like other human activities, including Christianity and Socialism, colonising sometimes led to horrible abuses but need not necessarily or entirely be an evil thing. Mid-Victorians, like my father, who had been brought up to be obedient and to think and do what they were told, and who were not of a questioning or analytic turn of mind, took it for granted that colonisation was on the whole a good thing, which, properly managed, brought the supposed benefits of civilization to the colonised as well as undoubted profits to European entrepreneurs and prestige to European empire-builders.

In 1911 the streets of Johannesburg were orchestrated with the clanging, hissing, and whining sounds of trams, with the clop-clop of horses' hooves, and occasionally with the crack of a forty-foot wagon-whip. The older residential parts of the town, such as Doornfontein, near which we lived, already had atmosphere. Quick-growing cypress, mimosa, and eucalyptus groves were already tall and shady; they lent an air of age and mystery to villas and small mansions built in the nineties by newly rich German Jews, Scotch engineers, speculators in real estate, successful doctors, or tarts. Often rather German in style, with bizarre turrets of hot red or mustard-yellow brick and with ornamental verandahs trimmed with cast-iron lace and muffled with flowering creepers and grenadilla vines, they already had the glamour of outmoded mannerism (like twenty-year-old fashion magazines) and even a touch of secretive melancholy: even then they looked to me like settings for hidden dramas of family life.

In these surroundings, so adaptable is a child, I felt no less at home than I had in English gardens or drawing-rooms, or in the streets of London. I listened with excitement to the big hailstones drumming on the corrugated-iron roofs in summer thunderstorms, when flashes of lightning, like vast magnesium-flares, made the livid landscape jump. As at Louis Trichardt, swarms of flying ants came out on moist evenings, and the last rays of the sun, as the dark-blue thunder-clouds rumbled away with fainter echoes, picked out the yellow fruit of the dark-leaved loquat trees and the bunches of pink, beadlike fruit on the feathery-leaved pepper trees, while a light steam rose from the fresh-smelling earth. Indoors our Zulu house-boys moved about bare-footed, dressed in loose white blouses and shorts piped with scarlet – active, patient, warm-hearted, warm-blooded beings, handsomely made, and perfect in their goodness to this child.

• JOHANNESBURG •

Herman Charles Bosman (1905–1951)

This commentary on Johannesburg was written by Bosman in the mid-1940s, and appeared in **A Cask of Jerepigo.**[1]

Taken out of its ancient African context, Johannesburg is one of the world's newest cities. I don't know whether any of the old 1886 pioneers survive. Perhaps there are still here and there a few genuine pioneers, who came to Johannesburg with the first gold rush: it won't be at all extraordinary, because they all seem to have been remarkably tough. But there are any number of men and women living in Johannesburg today who were children in Johannesburg's childhood, and have seen the city change and grow and develop as they themselves, leaving childish things behind, have grown to a maturity which is already passing into a dignified or dissolute old age.

Quite recently I spoke to a gentleman who made reference to certain steps chopped into the sides of the railway cutting just off Twist Street. That was before there was a bridge over that part of the line.

'We had gone to school across the open veld, there, for several years,' my informant said, 'and then the Netherlands Company excavated that cutting and laid the tracks, and so we school-boys had to dig steps of our own into the sides of the cutting, in order to continue with our education. I was the youngest of the group and the older boys had to help me up by pulling on my satchel.'

This gentleman also informed me that those old steps, crudely carved by the hands of school-children, had suffered much from erosion during the many years of disuse, and he didn't think they were there any more. But he still had the straps of that satchel in a suitcase, somewhere, he said.

'They didn't issue any certificates in that school,' this gentleman explained, 'so I kept those straps from the satchel to show my prospective

---

1 *A background to the work of Herman Charles Bosman appears on page 9.*

employers that I had had a schooling. And I have still got those straps – just in case.'

You can still come across lots of people who can tell you about the spirit that prevailed here in the early days when Johannesburg was a roaring, wide-open mining camp, in which every citizen was imbued with the one laudable desire of making all the money he could in the shortest possible time. It was an all-in-scramble with no holds barred. The place teemed with short-cuts to a gaudy opulence. And venturers from all parts of the world heard that there was money going in Johannesburg, and they flocked here to get some. And through some of the quaint whimsicalities of the Roman-Dutch law, which was the basis of legislation in the Transvaal Republic, some ways of making money were regarded as being less legitimate than others.

Thus when members of a spirited fraternity, hailing in the main from Australia, alighted at Park Station and started getting busy with their luggage, their activities gave rise to a good deal of unfriendly comment. For the sole luggage that these gentlemen had brought with them were home-constructed sandbags which they wielded on the populace, left and right, with a singular effectiveness.

The members of this fraternity, perhaps not unjustly, resented the discouraging attitude which officialdom adopted towards their industry as an unfair discrimination, based on the fact that they were newly-arrived immigrants who still had to ask passersby the way to the Stock Exchange or the Rand Club, when they wanted to go and look for customers. The point of view of the authorities seemed to be. 'You can see for yourself that we impose no restrictions. You can do anything you like to a man in order to take his money off him. Only you must not hit him with your luggage.'

Even to-day this seems an unreasonable sort of distinction to make. Not allowing a man from foreign shores to contribute his luggage to the building up of a new nation and a new culture.

And talking about culture, I believe that Johannesburg has got all those attributes, mainly in the form of very raw material as yet, which will enable it eventually to occupy a leading place in the world of art and letters.

I would like to put forward my naive views on this subject in such a way as to try and avoid, as far as possible, anything in the way of controversy. But I believe, frankly, that as a source of new cultural inspiration to the world Europe is finished. Europe has got a background of unrivalled magnificence. Almost every town and city of Western Europe is impregnated with ancient splendour. But as far as the spirit of the peoples of Western

Europe is concerned, these are glories that have run to seed.

For this reason it is most depressing to find painters in this country – some of them not without a good measure of creative talent – slavishly following the tricks of technique which contemporary European artists are employing with an ever-increasing complication of subjective subtleties as a substitute for individuality. Nothing can take the place of the raw inspiration of life itself, expressed with all the strength of a creative personality. Nobody knows this fact better than the European artists themselves, who are not glad that their inner force has decayed, but who simply can't help themselves.

It is therefore all the more regrettable that our South African artists, as a whole, should have no clear sense of values in this matter. You can learn all the technique you like from Europe. That's what Europe is there for. But if you don't put your own spirit into what you paint, either because you haven't spirit of your own or because you don't know how to express it, then what you produce cannot be anything more than synthetic rubbish.

But I believe that this is only a passing phase with South African artists. They are not trying to meet Europe on her own ground – which in itself would be an impossible enough task – but they are actually trying to copy Europe on her own ground. And this is pure clownishness.

But this stage will pass. And I believe that after that South Africa, with Johannesburg as its cultural centre, will find itself in an era of inspired creation, sprung forth out of the passion of love for this country, when we shall produce art that will reach heights of real grandeur because the note it strikes is authentic, and whose beauty will endure because it is our own.

We have got everything for it here. What has already been achieved in Afrikaans literature is a fine augury for the future. America has produced Edgar Allan Poe and Mark Twain, two sublime literary figures whose true influence is being felt only today. But Africa has not spoken yet. I believe that it is possible to see Johannesburg as it really is only when we view it as a place of mystery and romance, as a city wrapped in mist. Is there any other city that is less than sixty years old – and the origin of its name already lost in the shadows of Time?

People who were present at the christening of Johannesburg say that the town was named after the second baptismal name of President Kruger. Others with equal authority say it was called Johannesburg after Johan Rissik. Other candidates – and in each case their names are put forward on most excellent authority – include Christiaan Johannes Joubert, Veldkornet Johannes Meyer, Johannes Lindeque, and Willem Gerhardus Christoffel

Pelser (the latter, possibly, because his seemed to be the only set of names that didn't have Johannes in it).

There are at least another dozen claimants. And you need have no hesitation in supporting any one of them. The evidence in each case is indisputable.

With its sky-scrapers, Johannesburg is to-day no mean city. These tall edifices of concrete and steel would look highly imposing anywhere, leave alone just being dumped down in the middle of the veld. But we still bear one or two traces of our mining-camp origin. For instance, there is the Public Library.

• THE CENTRE • OF SOUTH AFRICA

Sarah Gertrude Millin (1889–1968)

At the outbreak of the Second World War, Sarah Gertrude Millin was living with her husband in Johannesburg. The following extract, which describes Johannesburg in 1939, is taken from one of her autobiographies, **The Measure of My Days**, *which was published in 1955.*[1]

When the war began Johannesburg was not yet thirty years old, but it was the centre of South Africa, and so it had been from its birth. When we arrived there were still corrugated-iron buildings in the heart of the city. Yet it was undeniably (if not technically) a city.

At the same time, it was also undeniably a mining town. For right through it, right beneath its streets, ran the gold reef (a hundred miles of it worked today). And the tarnished-silver mine dumps made part of its sky line. And even now that the buildings are so tall, there are ridges – not ten minutes' ride from the centre of the town – from which eighteen or twenty dumps can be seen in one sweep of the eye; and in some places, when the noise of the day is over and the wind blows right, one can hear too a murmur like the breaking of far-away waves; and this murmur is the distant sound of the perpetual rhythmic thunderous crushing of the ore by the battery stamps – the heart-beat of Johannesburg and the Union of South Africa.

The rocky ridges, where people have blasted sites for their houses and gardens, look across many miles of country. Where we live now it took six months of blasting with a rock-drill, and two years of the convict labour one engages, to make a garden; and much of the soil had to be brought. All the year around the sun gives shape, colour and clarity to the things of South

---

1 *The life and writing of Sarah Gertrude Millin is introduced on page 59.*

Africa, but round the south-western coast it rains only in winter, and higher up it rains only in summer. In the winter-time, in the Transvaal, the grass is an ash-blonde colour, and the unwashed trees are dusty.

Autumn and spring are merely names. A dust-storm blows and brings the rain and this is autumn. A dust-storm blows and brings the rain and this is spring. But the autumn rains are followed hard by the winter cold, and the spring rains herald the long, strong summer – eight months of blue skies, sudden blackness, lightning and thunder like bagpipes and tom-toms; passionate discharge of rain; the forgiving return of the sun and the blue; everything new and resurgent, everything alive, everything hurriedly growing. And in Johannesburg, because it is six thousand feet above sea level, and because of this vigorous climate, and because one lives on top of the world's gold, the people, like their city, are new, alive, hurried, growing and perhaps a bit mad. In Johannesburg things happen. Most of the things that happen in South Africa have their origins in Johannesburg.

•

The city part of Johannesburg is not beautiful. Johannesburg is laid out like a gridiron, and the regular strips are close and narrow because in the old days the Government was advised that narrow streets would mean more sites for shops, and frequent crossings more corner sites – to the additional profit of the Government.

To-day the buildings in Johannesburg are eighteen and more storeys high, the streets look narrower and closer than ever and can hardly serve the great traffic; and the city that, with its space, on its hills, in its brilliant air, might have been one of the most beautiful in the world is no more than a place of business, neither attractive nor convenient, and never can be more.

Johannesburg city accompanies its mines from east to west, and, both east and west, it links up with other Reef towns, so that now, for a hundred miles, there flows an almost continuous city. In the centre of Johannesburg are the big retail shops – many of them those cheap cash shops which have done so much to ease and sweeten the lives of poor people; the banks, the offices of mining and professional men, motor-town. South Africa is a highly motorised country. In one of its provinces, indeed, there are three or four motor-cars to each tax-payer.

After the retail shops come the big wholesale shops, the big warehouses, the industrial concerns. The signboards appear with Oriental names; the shops being to dwindle from wholesale to retail; there are native eating-houses, Indian tailor shops, and crazy sheds of discoloured corrugated-iron where the broken-down or the never-risen of all kinds and colours swarm and mingle. These congeries were at their worst when we arrived in Johannesburg. A bishop of Johannesburg told me he had never seen anything like them – not even in Buenos Aires, where, for many years, he had worked among seamen.

Outside the city are native towns, the beneficent work of Johannesburg municipality.

So this, then, is how we live in Johannesburg: the people in the suburbs – from upper to lower middle-class; the white-collar men in the heart of the city; the poor whites, the poor backvelders, the down-and-outs, the would-works, the won't-works, the lower Orientals, the half-castes and various kinds of natives, all confused in the slums; the miners in and around the mines that are in and around the town.

• LIFE IN THE • LOCATIONS

Es'kia Mphahlele (1919–)

Born in the Pietersburg area, Ezekiel (later Es'kia) Mphahlele moved with his family to Marabastad, a 'location' (as townships were then called) on the outskirts of Pretoria in the 1930s and later to Orlando (the township outside Johannesburg formerly known as Sophiatown).

Shortly after he was awarded his Master's degree, he left South Africa for Nigeria because he was in disfavour with the South African authorities. For many years his writings were banned in this country. After a number of years in exile, during which he served among other things as a professor of English at two American universities, he was permitted to return to the country of his birth in 1978, where he became Professor of Comparative and African Literature at the University of Witwatersrand.

He has published a number of novels, short stories and poems and is a noted critic and teacher. The following extracts are from his best-known work, **Down Second Avenue**, *an autobiography published in 1959.*

Marabastad, like most locations, was an organised rubble of tin cans. The streets were straight; but the houses stood cheek by jowl, rusty as ever on the outside, as if they thought they might as well crumble in straight rows if that was to be their fate. Each house, as far as I remember, had a fence of sorts. The wire always hung limp, the standards were always swaying in drunken fashion. A few somewhat pretentious houses could be found here and there. These were, like the rest, of corrugated iron. But they had verandahs paved with concrete, and the pillars were of concrete too. The grim old man down our street who worked for the Portuguese Legation had such a house. There was one in Tenth Avenue, and two in Thirteenth Avenue. The other verandas, where any, were paved with mud, and about four poles supported the roof unevenly.

There was only one house which had a flower garden. This faced Barber Street, and it belonged to a man who boasted a Coloured wife, Gertie, and a large brood of uppity children who were good at insulting their father because of his very dark complexion. In fact, this family was reputed to be the only one that had a coal stove. It was possible, because at Christmas-time long queues of Marabastad residents stood waiting with dishes of dough in front of the Indian-owned ABC Bakery, to have bread or cakes baked at a shilling for a standard dish.

In the morning and afternoons Marabastad was always covered by a blanket of smoke coming from the coal braziers which were put in the yard to burn out before we carried them into the houses in winter, or in the backyard in warm months.

The backyards were always inclined to be dirty, much as the people swept them continually with home-made grass brooms. Most of the houses had a room or two to let out to a family or single persons. So it was not uncommon to find about three braziers blazing away in the same yard.

Ra-Stand, as we called the inevitable white superintendent of the location, was always particular about keeping the streets free of dirty water and dead cats and dogs. But the backyards seemed to be beyond him. The only time we ever saw this personage was when we went to pay our fourteen shillings rent or when he drove up the only tarred road, Barber Street; which was the reason why he was thought of only as the owner of Marabastad stands. Otherwise, the location seemed to be the property of the police. Farther into the location, dirty water and flies and dead cats and dogs and children's stools owned the streets.

Marabastad wasn't fenced in as other locations outside Pretoria were. Nor were Bantule or Cape Location. So one could enter it from various directions. But the only white people we ever saw in Marabastad apart from the location superintendent, and the police, were a white minister of the Methodist church or a white priest of the Anglican church and a school inspector who came and went surreptitiously. Many years later a white woman came to put up a soup kitchen. After a few months she disappeared with the kitchen. It never occurred to us that a white person could ever have cause to be in the location unless he was in charge of something or some people. I never even gave it a thought, and I don't think any other resident ever felt concerned about it.

Saturday night. Darkness. Sounds of snoring from my uncle at the corner. Like the muted lowing of a cow. Tomorrow the other uncle sleeping with him on the floor will complain that he had been roused from his sleep by the snoring. My younger brother doesn't stir beside me. Nor the youngest uncle the other side of him under the same blanket as we. They say I'm a bad sleeper and when sleep descends on me there is going to be tugging and tossing and rolling among the three of us. I know the cold air coming through the hole in the flooring boards will whip us out of sleep as it plays upon bare flesh, else one's leg will rest on my neck and then I shall dream that some fiend is slitting my throat and I shall jump up with a scream. My sister also on the floor is kicking the leg of the table she's sleeping under. Grandmother and three of Aunt Dora's children are lying quiet on the old double bed. The only door and the only window are shut. Hot. With two frayed blankets on us it's good to feel hot. I can't sleep. I can't get up to walk about in the yard because my bones are aching because I was cleaning the house and turning everything up and choking in the dust I was making. Sweating. Blowing off the salt water from my lips. Kneading my nose to ease the tickling sensation inside it. No use. The boxes and some of Grandmother's worthless collections on the boards resting on the rafters will never be free from dust ever. And then the boxes on the floor containing old handbags and hats and trinkets given by some longforgotten missus, had to come down from their high stack. But grandmother said to leave them as I found them.

Music of U-NO-MES band at the Columbia still travels along the night which is what the handbills meant by 'Daybreak Dance'. Still no sleep only things to remember like Saul and Rieta down our Avenue. This morning they woke up to find Rieta had rolled on to their new baby and killed it and they are in the cells this moment. Saul and Rieta. One seldom spoke of Saul without saying Rieta. Drank too much beer, the two, and quarrelled and sometimes Rieta bit one of Saul's fingers and they cried together all which made grandmother say those two were Sodom and Gomorrah and now they went to fetch God's infant from where it had been lying in peace and then killed it. Saul and Rieta, two thin people, thin as Satan's messengers grandmother said, as thin as water-reeds walking for ever as if blown by the wind. The Saturday night buzz has now been muffled. Siki is walking down the street playing his guitar the one he carries about on him, the guitar he plays while he coughs on and on, for he has been coughing ever since I knew him, a long long time. Siki's music comes and goes and comes and goes and I can see him passing on the side of our house, see him as if I were outside, rolling down to the house where he lives with his brother who feeds him and clothes him. Is he with – no, he can't be playing like that if he's with

Katrina, Katrina his girl friend who looked after him often. The music fades and fades and is gone fused with the night.

•

Saturday night [twenty-five years later]. Electric lights! How beautiful they look from a distance. So dull in themselves but, clustered like that, quivering, blinking, little fiery gems set in the fabric of night, they are fascinating. Standing here in a dark little world, viewing them from afar, miles away, you know they are beyond your reach. The more beautiful they look the more distant they appear – or, perhaps, the more distant they are the lovelier they look.

Here, a dark township, Orlando; below there, a seething mass of darkness with the usual Saturday night screams and groanings and drums: that's Shanty Town. Up there, another part of Orlando with lights, not too far to reach, but smiling and blinking at you ironically; then far away, clusters and clusters of them. They might have been bathed in water and emerged bright, clean, with a crystal texture, in the magical context of night. They look as if you might rake them into a container and leave a sieve on the surface of this summer night. They assume at once the man-made form and the unattainable, at any rate for the moment.

A hot, mothy night; there is no sleep. Out of the house into the yard. You take a deep breath and contemplate the beauty of distant electric lights until the children have gone to bed because you use the sitting-dining-room as a study. It has always been like this, since Second Avenue – waiting until the family has gone to bed before you did your studies. Rebecca has been at this sort of game too. It's the final year of her three-year diploma course in social work. She left teaching when Verwoerd, Minister of Native Affairs, made it clear that African teachers were going to be used for training children to be slaves. Day in and day out in the week she comes back from school at five o'clock and begins to cook, and I wash the children and studies begin at nine.

Your mate has gone to bed early tonight and there is a story you want to write – or rather you want to write a story and while you think how to begin you look at electric lights. You might try to place Parktown, or Parkwood, Emmarentia or Westcliff or Northcliff, where those lights can be; but you give it up after a while.

Pictures, fantasies, strivings, wishes, desires, memories and all other creatures of the intellect come to torment your being. Then you think how sordid life is; how ludicrous the very idea of life is; what a fruitless, petty, endless game it may be and mustn't be.

Things close in upon you; you find yourself in a tightly closed-up room. There seems no way out. You once flattered yourself that you had some talent, ability, honest thoughts and longings, and splendid ideals. You even fancied you had what man recognizes as ambition. Perhaps you had a trade or profession, and you wanted to tell the world what you wanted, what you felt and thought in some manner; you wanted to give life something the men would not allow you to – speak when you're spoken to, the world seemed to say. Eventually you didn't give life anything. It resented your efforts. The strivings and desires in you continued to torment you, to tease you out of yourself. But there was no exit from that prison. You knew it was your soul that was imprisoned.

Of course, the easiest way out would be to leave the soul in this cage, and start a new life, resolve to fling ambition to the winds, and just become a thoroughly sensuous animal; leave inspirations, ambition, ideals, planning and aesthetics to the elect. Or you might deny the existence of that in you which cherishes ambition and the rest, and seek no more than food, shelter, clothing. What joy and abundant satisfaction they must derive from who did not wish for anything more than the bare necessities, like an ox!

Or you might booze all these extra-physical stirrings out of your system, as so many, oh so many, educated Africans do.

Those electric lights in the distance continue to blink and tease the spirit of night: little sparkling fires, so unearthly, so inorganic. But of course once you were sensitive to things that are, enough to know that they weren't there and should be, you couldn't go back, could you? And your tribal umbilical cord had long, oh so long, been severed and all the talk about Bantu culture and the Black man developing along his own lines was just so much tommy rot. You just felt the world getting too small for you, over-contracting and shutting you in. A stuffy place, the world could become; as stuffy as the room from which you came out. If you tried to go away somewhere and ceased to care you'd still be in the larger denomination of the world which required man to care; you'd become a more bitter cynic; and while you shrivelled up in the acid of your cynicism the world wouldn't be at all worse off after your exit. No step backwards and so you must move and fight with the rest for a better and greater South Africa. Do it in some way but do it. It's no pastime but a desperate necessity and the knowing it galled you.

Orlando. A glorified Marabastad. Saturday night is the same as it was twenty-five years ago in Marabastad minus the ten-to-ten bell because now the curfew law is only for the city and suburbs to protect a frightened and neurotic white population which keeps revolvers and narcotic drugs under pillows. Yes, it is still the same, the only tarred roads being those leading to white superintendents' offices. The township has been spreading west and south since 1934 in three-roomed units; not east because that's the direction in which Johannesburg lies, twelve miles away; not north because that's where the line of gold mines is. We have been paying a sub-economic rental of fifty shillings a month for four rooms without electric lights or water-borne sewerage, and now the rents have gone up a scale stopping at £50. Near us is one of the biggest electric power stations in the world. As Orlando spreads into Meadowlands, Mofolo, Dube, Jabavu, Moroka, Molapo, Moletsane, holding more than 200,000 souls altogether, it also develops ulcers in the form of shanty towns; like the one just below us. And still the black metropolis grows, meeting other townships of refugees who have been removed from western towns which like Africans only as labourers. Faction fights must be a source of amusement only to some white supreme chief of the Bantu who decided to force people into ethnic compartments and threw thousands of single men into huge dormitories in hostels with high fences around them.

The lights quiver as brightly as ever, looking so clean, so jubilant, so fresh, teasing the primitive springs of life in you which in turn respond to that symbolic call of the lights coming across to you, wrapped in the mystery of night.

• TROPICAL OUTPOST •

William Plomer (1903–1973)

The following extract by William Plomer appears in **The South African Autobiography,** *published in 1984 but based on earlier autobiographies. William Plomer's family settled in Louis Trichardt in 1906 and it is of this region that Plomer writes.*[1]

My father was now appointed to act as resident magistrate at Louis Trichardt, an oulandish and unhealthy spot at the foot of the Zoutpansberg mountains, well inside the tropics and highly malarial. By this time my brother John had enlarged the family. He had been born at Pietersburg in 1907, and in spite of the attentions of a bibulous midwife he burst into the world with all the thrusting health and cheerfulness I had lacked. It was thought that he might take after 'poor Uncle Durham, who was killed in the war.'

It is strange that my father should have arranged to take his wife and two young children with him to such a place. A civil servant goes where he is told, and naturally wants his family with him. He was not yet forty, very active and enterprising, and his roving, open-air life had greatly improved his health, but I doubt if he allowed for the hazards. I cannot think that my mother was enthusiastic, but her sense of loyalty would have persuaded her that her place was with her husband.

Louis Trichardt was about eighty miles from Pietersburg. There was no railway, and there were no made-up roads. This was before the age of the automobile, and the only way to get there was by trundling ox-wagon through the blazing wilderness, like *voortrekkers.* I was nearly four, and can remember something of the journey, which seemed unending.

Louis Trichardt took its name from the commandant of a number of burghers, alleged to have been tiresome, lazy, or importunate men banished

---

1 *The life and work of William Plomer is introduced on page 163.*

by Kruger to found a settlement there. At the time of our arrival the so-called township consisted mostly of a few derelict or ruined houses. Most of the inhabitants had been scattered or eliminated by malaria or by the Magato and South African wars. The surrounding district was romantic in a **Rider Haggardish** way. Diamonds and emeralds, copper and gold were to be found, and although game, with the destructive advance of the white man, was getting scarcer, there were still, besides lions, not a few giraffes and hippopotami, besides wildebeeste, eland, sable, and tsesebe. In the mountains, not easily accessible, was a wonderful lake with weird surroundings and no apparent outlet. It was covered with wild-fowl of many kinds. They were seldom disturbed, because it was shunned by the Africans, who believed it bewitched. It was said to have been formerly the scene of human sacrifices.

African life was not yet completely spoiled. At times there were spectacular primitive dances ***en masse***, carried out with great vigour and sexual posturing, to the vibrant music of drums and giant xylophones. 'Can the white people dance like mine?' a local chief asked of a visiting white official. He received an evasive reply, with an allusion to splendid balls given in the palace of the Great White Queen, whom he was perhaps left imagining in the performance, almost nude, of a frantic and provocative ***pas seul*** in the presence of her loyal and enthusiastic subjects.

The only dwelling available for my father and his family was primitive and barely habitable. It consisted of three rooms with walls of ***pisé de terre*** faced and roofed with corrugated iron. The floors were of stamped clay. There was some sort of wood-burning stove, no bathroom, no water laid on, and an earth-closet at a distance which gave shelter to spiders, hornets and lizards. The previous occupant had fenced off an acre or so from the open veld and had tried to make some sort of a garden, for which the land was well suited, as the soil was fertile and a stream flowed through it. He had planted a few cypresses and indigenous trees, and there was a flourishing banana grove.

Autobiographers who enlarge at length upon their trivial recollections of infancy are to be shunned like lakes bewitched, but the first episode or vision of a man's surroundings to stick in his memory is often a strong clue to his future character. This was true of my father, my mother, and myself (Skip the next page or two, reader, if you are allergic to this sort of thing).

My father's first memory was of a fit of rage. He was playing when very small with his brother Durham in Kensington Gardens, near the water-garden at Lancaster Gate. Durham picked up a bottle that was lying on the grass, threw it at him, and hit him on the nose – whereupon Charles flew at him in a blind fury but somehow caught a front tooth on a button of

Durham's coat, and the tooth was wrenched from its socket.

My mother's first memory was of Cotgrave. No more than four or five years old, she was at luncheon with her governess. Her parents being away from home, the footman who was waiting on them had not troubled to wear his livery. The child instantly noticed this and ordered him to go and put it on. There spoke the being who believed all her life long in custom and ceremony – in which alone, according to Yeats, are innocence and beauty born.

As for me, my first memory of any significance is of a brilliant spring morning at Louis Trichardt. It had rained in the night, but now the sky was cloudless and the world of a celestial freshness and fragrance, exhaled by the sparkling green veld and wafted in the air. I strayed out of the garden, and standing on the bank of the stream suddenly saw on the opposite bank, perhaps twelve feet away, two large birds, a kind of wild duck perhaps. One was resting on the ground; the other stood beside it. Their plumage gleamed like many-coloured enamel in the sun against a background of reeds, their eyes glinted like jewels, and they showed no sign of alarm, but watched me as I watched them. My feeling was partly one of delighted discovery, like that of an ornithologist discovering a new species, partly of pure delight, both heightened into a kind of ecstasy, as of mutual understanding and joy, as if the birds and I knew that we were part of the same life and that life was splendid.

After this there came a rush of sensuous experience of a growing and a shining world which could be touched and heard and smelt and tasted as well as seen – the forms and textures of plants, the rasping leaves of the Cape gooseberry; the clear yellow flowers and hairy swollen pods of a nameless shrub; the long white thorns like steel nails that stuck out everywhere from the thorn trees; the intense perfumes of the small aromatic flowers of the veld; the metallic dinning of the cicadas at midday and the cool colloquies of doves in the afternoon. Then there were insects – the multitudes of flying ants that came fluttering and flickering out after rain, shedding their talc-like wings, which they left thickly littered upon the moist earth; the flexible, hard-shelled, varnished millipedes which curled up when touched; the striped hornets; the tarantulas that waited, motionless as ornaments, on a white-washed wall.

At night one could hear lions roaring far off, or the nearer howling of jackals, more sad and wonderful than frightening, or the loud choruses of frogs never tired of congratulating the full moon on its brilliance and always using the same formula:

First Frog: *Le roi*
Second Frog: *est allé.*
Third Frog: *Et où? et où?*
All: *à Cognac, à Cognac, à Cognac*[1]

When the veld, in a very dry season, caught fire one night, the flames roared and crackled all round the house, mounting higher and higher in raging arabesques, while our servants tried to fend them off with branches: then suddenly a man on horseback, who had come to see if we were all right, burst magically through the curtains of flame.

At night, almost every night, could be heard the far-off singing of Africans, monotonous, melancholy, strangely stirring. With the touch of warm brown skins I was already familiar. Maud Dgami was my first and faithful African nursemaid, and I remember the house-boys, their gentle and easy movements, their white teeth and their clean loose clothes smelling of soap, and cotton, the pink palms of their hands, their horny feet; and how once, when the bridge over the stream had been swept away after a cloud-burst, they helped my father to mend it. I see him now, with the turbulent muddy water swirling round his white thighs and their dark brown thighs, and their naked arms lifting great stones into place, all under a blue-black sky, while on the bank flowering pinks were shaking in the rain-fresh wind.

---

1 Le roi: – *The King*
est allé – *has gone*
Et où? – *And where? Where?*
A Cognac – *To Cognac*

• PIETERMARITZBURG, • THE LOVELY CITY

Alan Paton (1903–1989)

Alan Paton was born and educated in Pietermaritzburg. He was a noted educationist, politician and writer. Initially a science teacher for a few years, he was appointed principal of Diepkloof Reformatory in 1935, which he proceeded to convert from a prison to a school. Paton later became the chairman of the South African Liberal Party. After retiring from active politics, he established a reputation as a balanced liberal political commentator.

Paton made his name as a writer with his world-renowned novel, **Cry, the Beloved Country,** *which was published in 1948. Subsequent to that he published two novels, numerous short stories, many poems and a number of biographies.*

The following extracts are from the first volume of his autobiography entitled **Towards the Mountain** *which was published in 1980.*

Pietermaritzburg, the lovely city. It lies in a basin of hills, in the valley of the Umsindusi River, which enters from the west and leaves in the east, where it will soon join the Umgeni on its journey to the sea.

The hills to the north, though we would not call them mountains, are big ones, and the trains from Durban to Johannesburg have to climb them. In my boyhood this was done with much puffing and whistling, and later with that electric sound which is louder than a hum and more musical than a growl. Above that would be the sound of the sirens which the growing boy at first compared unfavourably with the whistles, but later accepted fully. He would lie awake at night and listen to the sound of the trains in the hills above his city, with feelings of pride and exaltation.

Pietermaritzburg, being a Voortrekker foundation, was a rectangular city of parallel streets crossing other parallel steets at right angles. It confined itself to the rectangle except for the outgrowths of the Town Hill, Mountain Rise, Scottsville, Alexandra Road, and Prestbury. Access to unspoiled nature was immediate. From our house in Pine Street we crossed the road and were at once in the country. A small stream, the Dorp Spruit, ran below the steeply ascending hills, which were covered in summer with waving grass that became brown in winter, and when set alight caused those spectacular nocturnal fires, the memory of which is inseparably bound up with my boyhood.

My reaction to nature was intense.

I cannot describe my early response to the beauty of hill and stream and tree as anything less than an ecstasy. A tree on the horizon, a line of trees, the green blades of the first grass of spring, showing up against the black ashes of the burnt hills, the scarlet of the fire-lilies among the black and the green, the grass birds that whirred up at one's feet, all these things filled me with an emotion beyond describing. And then in the fold of all south-facing hills were patches of indigenous trees and undergrowth, which we called, hardly ever, the forest, but more often the bush, probably under the influence of the Dutch '*bosch*', which later became the Afrikaans '*bos*'. These folds were the kloofs, another word of Afrikaans origin, still retained in American English as 'clove'. As often as not a small stream ran down the kloof, and on its banks grew ferns and the wild begonia whose soft stems we would chew for their acid juice. A rare joy was to find the magnificent orange clivia, now protected, then rapidly disappearing. A glade of clivias in flower, in one of the larger stretches of bush that might be called a forest, is a sight not to be forgotten. The stream would run over black stones, descending rapidly, sometimes with little waterfalls. And one might, though perhaps only once in a lifetime, catch a glimpse of the small mpithi antelope, shy and delicate. If the expanse of bush were large, one might hear the call of the greenspotted wood dove – 'my father is dead, my mother is dead, all my relations are dead' – and its melancholy ending, 'and my heart goes du-du-du-du-du-du.' Or the equally liquid but not melancholy call of the fukwe, also with the refrain, 'du-du-du-du-du-du,' dropping continuously down the scale. And the whippoorwill, the piet-my-vrou, a bird seldom seen but abundantly heard, arriving from the north in October and returning north in March, and calling night and day while it is here. And the purple-crested loerie. When it is in flight, in its colours of red, green, and purple, it is one of the most beautiful sights in nature, and can evoke from the watcher cries of wonder.

I was much older before I responded, and no less intensely, to the beauty of plain and sky and distant lines of mountains. When I first saw the expanse of the Transvaal highveld and the desolate stretches of the Karoo I did not at once acknowledge that they were beautiful. The qualities of harshness, starkness, and seeming endlessness did not seem to me to be compatible with beauty.

Pietermaritzburg, like all South Africa except the Western Cape, has a summer rainfall, although it can every few years experience a winter downpour of ten to twenty inches, which turns the Umsindusi into a mighty river and the Dorp Spruit into a raging torrent. The annual rainfall is in the region of thirty-five inches, which means that the hills surrounding the city are green and luxuriant in summer. Mist often lies on the tops of the hills. Robert Louis Stevenson expressed my deepest feelings in those line from his poem 'To S.R. Crockett':

Be it granted to me to behold you again in dying,
Hills of Home! and to hear again the call;
Hear about the graves of the martyrs the peewees crying,
And hear no more at all.

The peewee, or peewit, is a member of the plover family. So is the titihoya. I do not remember that I ever heard it in the hills of Pietermaritzburg, but I certainly heard it on the top of Natal's Table Mountain in my student years, and in the hills of Ixopo when I was a young schoolmaster. And when one heard it in the mist and rain, the bird itself unseen, it caught at one somewhere – shall we say it plucked the strings of the heart? – as it must have plucked at the heart of Robert Louis Stevenson on some Scottish hill.

The intensity of these experiences I concealed from others. I do not know why. And whether there was some reason for it, whether I had ever revealed too much and been rebuffed, or more likely laughed at, I cannot now remember. One of the effects of this concealment was to create a private world of the self. In that sense I could have been described as a lonely child. But not as an unhappy one. I was too much in love with the world into which I had been born. Of its political and racial realities I knew exactly nothing. I had no idea that before I turned twelve the world would be plunged into the most terrible war of all history, and that the young men of Britain, France, Germany, and Russia would die in the mud for nothing. Nor had I any idea that I lived in a country where almost no child of colour could hope to aspire to the richness of the life that I was going to lead.

No, my world was the world of hills and grass and rain and mist, and of birds seen and unseen, and of the crying of the trains on their way to Johannesburg. Pietermaritzburg was to me the lovely city, and in calling it thus I was not, as one critic has suggested, practising the arts of the beautician. A beautician presumably tries to create, or at least tries to imitate beauty. But my beauty was already created, in that place where I was born.

• DURBAN • BREAKWATER

Roy Campbell (1901–1957)

The following extract is taken from Roy Campbell's second autobiography, **Light on a Dark Horse**, *which was published in 1951.*[1]

In the more secret-looking pubs round the Dockside near the Breakwater or North Pier, in Durban, one can see groups of unkempt conspirators conversing in hushed voices as if they were plotting the overthrow of human society. Each has an ancient-mariner-like expression which could be guaranteed to hypnotise and detain the thirstiest wedding-guest for hours. Fortunately for the community, these strange human amphibians are not interested in weddings, funerals, feasts, and other functions which concern our own common-or-garden existences. They seem entirely pre-occupied with hearing out each other's yarns. But for the unblustering quietness of their voices, you would take them for **Bolsheviks** or **nihilists**: and besides, instead of encouraging each other with the convulsive **southpaw** ataxia of the lifted fist, they are distinguished by a more pleasing and persuasive semaphore. They appear to be accompanying the low musical hum of their voices on invisible accordions, by extending and contracting their palms in continuous rhythm; and occasionally extending their arms so wide that they appear to be trying to stretch outsize imaginary concertinas beyond the limits of their capacity. In this position they remind you of becalmed albatrosses and mollymauks, when they fling their wings wide in the hope of catching a breeze that will enable them to 'take off' from the sea.

It comes upon one as quite a surprise, on overhearing a snatch of their conversation, that this weird semaphore is merely a vast exaggeration of the

---

1 *The life and writing of Roy Campbell is introduced on page 25.*

sign by which the harmless but fanatical freemasonry of anglers (when describing the size of their catches) can be recognized all over the world, from China to Peru. These are none other than the redoubtable Breakwater-fishers of Durban to whom Brian Vesey-Fitzgerald devotes the climax and grand finale of his monumental classic on the 'Big Game Fishes of the World'!

The passion for fishing amounts to insanity in Durban. Where else in the world are 'fish describers' given as birthday presents? These consist of two arms with extended palms, roughly fretsawn out of plywood, and each measuring about five feet long; they are meant to save reminiscent anglers from unnecessary arm-strain when recounting their experiences. Such were the pair presented to my famous Cousin Ethelbert by my brother Archibald. When held our horizontally, for accordion-practice, they give Ethelbert the wingspan of a wandering albatross, or a Spitfire plane, and come in handy for describing some of my cousin's catches when he is in a confidential mood – which is frequent enough. They are feather-light and easy to handle.

Samson Pillay, my Indian servant, was the most pleasant and intelligent fishing companion. He was then about fourteen, and was a ragged urchin I got from Mrs. General Botha, for whose family he was previously the bait-catcher, at Botha House, half a mile or so away. All British ex-Servicemen who were in military hospital either at Howick, Oribi Flats, Springfield, or any other big South African hospitals, will remember Samson as the owner of the 'Fast-Quick-Ready Laundry Services,' which smartened up their battle dresses for jaunts into Durban or Pietermaritzburg. He now owns three cars, and is a highly prosperous man, I am glad to say.

Samson and I were very excited waiting for the migration of 'sardines' to come. I had never seen the phenomenon before, since I had lived only on the Zululand side, North of Durban; and the shoals peter out under the terrific massacre by sea-birds, fishes and porpoises, long before they reach the North Coast. They generally swerve out to sea and disperse twenty miles south of Durban.

It was about half an hour before sunrise when Samson woke me to say the 'sardines' had come. Going on to our verandah, I was astonished at what I took to be the faint foreglow of sunrise on masses of banked white clouds: but when I rubbed the sleep out of my eyes I realized that the clouds were made of birds.

Along the coast they formed a galaxy about forty miles long. According to the press, that one swarm reached from Port Shepstone to Kelso junction, though in an hour or two it had almost entirely dispersed. Far out to sea were other swarms like clouds of smoke against the faintly-lit horizon. Nearer, they looked like swarms of midges or mosquitoes. Nearer still, they were like locusts; but it was only overhead that they were struck by the emerging radiance. The sea was black, but ripped everywhere by phosphorescent splashes made by giant fishes. The density of the pilchards, together with the oil which exuded from their chopped and slaughtered bodies, and lay like a film on the water, had becalmed the sea and entirely stopped the huge lines of breakers from rising and rolling in so that there was no surf at all. Only a faint Mediterranean swell was perceptible, but every time it creamed softly on the shingle it scattered a fringe of glittering silver bodies over the beach.

As soon as the light became clear enough, the first white streak and splash of a ganner was the signal for them all to begin diving. Imagine the Victoria Falls, and that every drop of water in them were the size of a turkey or a goose, and had the velocity of a feathered rocket-shell. In that superb cataract (which makes Niagara look like a village pump!) the more fiercely and steeply the Zambezi plunges downwards into the abyss, so also the higher and more steeply the volumes of vapour and mist spiral up over the crest of the cataract forming myriads of rainbows (that give the surrounding Rainbow Forest its name, almost hiding it from view). It was the same with this living cataract of birds. The falling birds shot sheer from a ceiling of about a hundred and fifty feet high, raising ten-foot plumes of smoke with the percussion of their fall, so that the sea looked as if it were tufted with millions of waving plumes of pampa-grass. The air was scribbled white with a sleet of falling arrows. Yet slowly, like the smoke of a huge cataract, the birds who had already dived, rose spirally between these whizzing shafts, formed in clouds above them, circled, descended again to the 'ceiling', where they hovered for a short time, as if sighting themselves, before they fired their white projectiles once more into the cataract.

I have never seen snow fall thicker than these birds. They all dived from the same height. How or why they never collided is a mystery to me. Yet they were snowing upwards as well as downwards, and no two flakes so much as brushed each other. The full radiance of the rising sun then struck these millions of giddy snowflakes, turning them into showers of coloured confetti; orange, crimson, scarlet, heliotrope, gold, and rose: and I recalled the mystic lines of **Rimbaud** –

> *Where sleep you in that sky of topless silence*
> *(Millions of golden birds) predestined Power?*

When each bird had gorged its fill of a dozen or so of pilchards it simply did the Roman Emperor's trick of vomiting up the repast and returning with new appetite to the feast. Never were more ethereal and seraphic colours lavished on such a spectacle of debauched gluttony and jaw-chopping frenzy, bathing it in all the splendours of the spectrum.

When the sun rose clear the beauty of the scene vanished; the birds also dispersed more widely; but one saw better what was happening on the surface of the sea which was ripped open by huge fishes leaping into the air – sunfishes, swordfishes, sharks, rays, springers, and barracoudas – scattering the pilchards like smithereens of winnowed silver over the surface of the sea.

• ON BEING HERE •

Lionel Abrahams (1928–)

Born in Johannesburg, Lionel Abrahams graduated from the University of the Witwatersrand in 1955. Since his early association with Herman Charles Bosman, he has devoted himself both to creative writing and to promoting literature in South Africa. He has published two collections of poetry and a sequence of short stories, and is a noted critic, editor and publisher. One of his most recent projects has been to edit a number of volumes of Bosman's works.

This extract is an adapted version of the article published in Leadership *magazine in the 1980s.*

If my approach in this article strikes an unusually personal note for *Leadership*, that is apposite to my theme. I want to discuss my style of commitment to being and remaining in South Africa and register my resistance to various kinds of pressure against it. It is a commitment I don't remember consciously formulating, but rather discovered long ago, as if it were one of my inborn traits emerging from latency. Nevertheless, this sort of feeling about one's place is far from being unique to me: I think I speak for many.

A renowned author on literature, language and society (whom I do not name because I want to spring my discussion from something he is reported to have said during a private conversation) recently visited this country to deliver a series of lectures. I was lucky enough to learn of his presence in time to attend the last of them. In his closing remarks he acknowledged that in coming here to contribute to our intellectual life he had chosen to disregard the cultural boycott. I was therefore startled to be told of his advice to a young man who had contrived a brief private interview with him. At the end of their discussion the sage demanded, 'Why haven't you packed your bags?'

The story is worth recording simply because it was told and therefore reflects a line of thinking about our situation: that those who can ought now to be leaving the country. It is not unfamiliar advice, and it comes from a variety of directions, and carries different implications accordingly.

When a young relative of mine who has recently emigrated to America urges the family to follow suit she has it in mind that we are endangered by the tide of violence that is coming in over the land. Her apprehension for us is fed by what she learns from the American media, and is only enhanced by the sinister fact that the South African media tell a less alarming story.

And we have to grant that, even by the light of that less alarming story, something in the shape of the near future is for once plain for everyone to see: there will be more violence, if only because what has been done, said, thought and felt so far about the use of bombs, guns, teargas, stones, etcetera, has established a momentum which cannot immediately, suddenly, be annulled. Moreover, since violence like any envy feeds upon itself, for a while at least the violence to come will probably be grosser than what we have seen so far.

When various others advise us to get out – that is, those of us privileged to enjoy the option – the considerations may range from ease of conscience to 'culture', from personal freedom to a desire not to obstruct revolution, in some cases a desire actively to advance it, from the welfare of one's children to (all of a sudden!) the welfare of one's money.

But when the profound thinker I referred to above advises a young intellectual to join the exodus, what he primarily has in mind must surely not be the risk of material poverty nor the risk of terror, bereavement, injury or death brought about by civil strife. Such a keen and philosophical observer of the modern world must know that everywhere, in greater or lesser measure, violence is constantly a potential and suffering is ineluctable. The concern of such a man must surely be with meaning. 'Go from here,' he is saying to that young man, 'because the conflict that absorbs all meaning in this place does not belong to such as you. In the struggle for political survival between black and white Africans, you have no vital interest. Neither in enduring the conflict nor in the victory of either side can you hope to discover the intensity of meaning by which to fulfil your moral and intellectual potentiality.'

By attributing this point of view to a visitor I have already begun my rebuttal of it. It is an outsider's perception, even when a native professes it. It is a highminded, informed, rational, perhaps even wise judgement, but it lacks warmth and intimacy. It does not recognise the possibility of an emotional commitment to the place, the sort of commitment that would require one not merely to receive or discover meaning in the given social situation but to contribute meaning by the manner of one's being.

Now, there is a usefully evasive empty phrase – 'the manner of one's being'! I have to leave it empty when I give it a general reference, because each of us who is governed by this emotional commitment will find his own way of expressing it. In this it is different from other forms of commitment. The commitment to being here becomes, simply, the commitment to being oneself in the place that is part of oneself. As I set the words down my mind's ear rings with objections on behalf of all those who have no choice but to be here and yet are prevented by poverty, oppression and the disciplines of political struggle from being fully themselves. What can I say? Except that I want that fullness for them as well. Also that precisely such an awareness belongs to the meaning of my being here.

My life's meaning is involved with my being here; I seem to have no choice in the matter. As for my way of expressing the commitment, it is the relatively passive and detached way of a writer, critic, editor and teacher. I spend my time trying to be truthful and trying to serve the makers of literature. If these sound like cosmopolitan endeavours, they are not so. They relate to what is here, what I am familiar with, what I am rooted in. I know that I could not conduct them validly except here.

For others, the commitment will be expressed by a more specific witness, an earthier love, a directed course of action, identification with a collective, some form of struggle to conserve or to remake the country. I know that it is possible, too, to remain here physically and yet to lie low or float aloof, engaged in issues of aesthetic or spiritual exploration or the humbler ones of personal survival and comfort; and nor do I mean to direct scorn toward any who take those ways: to some extent we all have to follow them some of the time – I certainly do.

But it is evidently part of what is called 'the South African way of life' for a substantial number of whites, judging by much of the fare offered by the English radio programmes of the SABC, to try to live, in one's head at least, as though this were another country. In this respect I find myself un-South African: our metropolitan heritage, and particularly its English component, is profoundly precious to me, I don't want attenuate its influences, alienate it, lose touch with it; but on the other hand, I have little patience for the trivia and trash of English popular culture, and especially so when these are displacing indigenous matter to sustain the cosily evasive, half-mad myth that we are somewhere else.

Being here promises to become increasingly uncomfortable for a time, but unless brute circumstance overwhelms my commitment, while I am here I want to be *here*, with the Zulus, the Xhosas, the Tswanas and the rest, with the Afrikaners, white and brown, with the Indians, the Portuguese, the Greeks and the other minorities, with the creators and thinkers of the land – people like Douglas Livingstone, Njabulo Ndebele, Charles van Onselen, Nadina Gordimer, Athol Fugard, Matsemela Manaka, Guy Butler, Modikwe

Dikobe, Ahmed Essop, Barney Simon, Ricky Burnett, David Goldblatt, among dozens I could name – and even with the politicians, from Terre'blanch through the Bothas to Boesak, and the confusion, frustration and danger to which they subject all of us.

•

But let me be ... specific with one ... instance which moves me particularly. It is that of the young woman who, during a year abroad, was urged by revolutionaries in exile whom she happened to encounter in New York to delay her return home by two years. She was compelled, however, to come back as planned, and at first was appalled to the point of paralysis by the bleakness, tension, danger and guilt that home represented to her after a year of unremitting unrest. It took her a few months to re-establish her network of connections and reopen her channels of creative expression. But then, without muffling her awareness of all that troubles our state, she immersed herself in the active living of her Johannesburg life. It is for her a life of awareness, a life that connects her by a score of threads to a whole range of creative and socially significant endeavours, theatrical, educational, literary, artistic and journalistic. According to her testimony, this vital and eloquent participation in a city's inner life was not available to her in New York or London, simply because there the elements of value and meaning in her life had constantly to be re-explained, dissolved in simplifications, in the absence of a great foundation of common knowledge and experience.

She is one of the pragmatically committed young, black and white, who, little by little in the most living of ways, are remaking our society, not directly its laws and power bases but its consciousness and ways of feeling. What they represent is something more substantial than hope. (I leave hope to the politicians, who have to deal in promises and have to reduce each other's promises to prospects of despair). These young live by a spirit of stoic endurance, taking on what is present, both now and here, full of the intense consciousness that revolutionary times have forced upon them, full of the ***élan*** of challenge, giving their days all the meaning they are capable of.

For themselves, and for me, and surely for all who are determined to stay, they make profound sense out of being here.

• NIAGARA FALLS •

Rupert Brooke (1887–1915)

Rupert Brooke is best known for his war poems, which appealed to the widespread spirit of romantic patriotism during World War One, before public feeling swung toward disillusionment. In the two years before the war, Brooke travelled to America and the South Seas. The following passage appears in his **Letters from America**, *which was published posthumously in 1916.*

Samuel Butler has a lot to answer for. But for him, a modern traveller could spend his time peacefully admiring the scenery instead of feeling himself bound to dog the simple and grotesque of the world for the sake of their too-human comments. It is his fault if a peasant's *naiveté* has come to outweigh the beauty of rivers, and the remarks of clergymen are more than mountains. It is very restful to give up all effort at observing human nature and drawing social and political deductions from trifles, and to let oneself relapse into wide-mouthed worship of the wonders of nature. And this is very easy at Niagara. Niagara means nothing. It is not leading anywhere. It does not result from anything. It throws no light on the effects of Protection, nor on the Facility for Divorce in America, nor on Corruption in Public Life, nor on Canadian Character, nor even on the Navy Bill. It is merely a great deal of water falling over some cliffs. But it is very remarkably that. The human race, apt as a child to destroy what it admires, has done its best to surround the Falls with every distraction, incongruity, and vulgarity. Hotels, power-houses, bridges, trams, picture postcards, sham legends, stalls, booths, rifle-galleries, and side-shows frame them about. And there are Touts. Niagara is the central home and breeding-place for all the touts of earth. There are touts insinuating, and touts raucous, greasy touts, brazen touts, and upper-class, refined, gentlemanly, take-you-by-the-arm touts; touts who intimidate and touts who wheedle; professionals, amateurs and ***dilettanti***, male and female; touts who would photograph you with your arm round a young lady against a faked background of the sublimest cataract, touts who would bully you into cars, **char-à-bancs**, elevators, or tunnels or deceive you into a carriage and pair, touts who would sell you picture postcards, moccasins, sham Indian beadwork, blankets, tee-pees, and crockery; and touts, finally, who have no apparent object in the world, but just purely, simply, merely, incessantly, indefatigably, and ineffugibly – to tout. And in the midst of all this, overwhelming it all, are the Falls. He who sees them instantly forgets humanity. They are not very high, but they are overpowering. They are divided by an island into two parts, the Canadian and the American.

Half a mile or so above the Falls, on either side, the water of the great stream begins to run more swiftly and in confusion. It descends with ever-growing speed. It begins chattering and leaping, breaking into a thousand ripples, throwing up joyful fingers of spray. Sometimes it is divided by islands and rocks, sometimes the eye can see nothing but a waste of laughing, springing, foamy waves, turning, crossing, even seeming to stand for an instant erect, but always borne impetuously forward like a crowd of triumphant feasters. Sit down close by it, and you see a fragment of the torrent against the sky, mottled, steely, and foaming, leaping onward in far-flung criss-cross strands of water. Perpetually the eye is on the point of descrying a pattern in this weaving, and perpetually it is cheated by change. In one place part of the flood plunges over a ledge a few feet high and a quarter of a mile or so long, in a uniform and stable curve. It gives an impression of almost military concerted movement, grown suddenly out of confusion. But is swiftly lost again in the multitudinous tossing merriment. Here and there a rock close to the surface is marked by a white wave that faces backwards and seems to be rushing madly upstream, but is really stationary in the headlong charge. But for these signs of reluctance, the waters seem to fling themselves on with some foreknowledge of their fate, in an ever wilder frenzy. But it is no **Maeterlinckian** prescience. They prove, rather, that Greek belief that the great crashes are preceded by a louder merriment and a wilder gaiety. Leaping in the sunlight, careless, entwining, clamorously joyful, the waves riot on towards the verge.

But there they change. As they turn to the sheer descent, the white and blue and slate-colour, in the heart of the Canadian Falls at least, blend and deepen to a rich, wonderful, luminous green. On the edge of disaster the river seems to gather herself, to pause, to lift a head noble in ruin, and then, with a slow grandeur, to plunge into the eternal thunder and white chaos below. Where the stream runs shallower it is a kind of violet colour, but both violet and green fray and frill to white as they fall. The mass of water, striking some ever-hidden base of rock, leaps up the whole two hundred feet again in pinnacles and domes of spray. The spray falls back into the lower river once more; all but a little that fines to foam and white mist, which drifts in layers along the air, graining it, and wanders out on the wind over the trees and gardens and houses, and so vanishes.

The manager of one of the great power-stations on the banks of the river above the Falls told me that the centre of the river-bed at the Canadian Falls is deep and of a saucer shape. So it may be possible to fill this up to a uniform depth, and divert a lot of water for the power-houses. And this, he said, would supply the need for more power, which will certainly soon arise, without taking away from the beauty of Niagara. This is a handsome concession of the utilitarians to ordinary sightseers. Yet, I doubt if we shall be satisfied. The real secret of the beauty and terror of the Falls is not their height or width, but the feeling of colossal power and of unintelligible disaster caused by the plunge of that vast body of water. If that were taken away, there would be little visible change; but the heart would be gone.

The American Falls do not inspire this feeling in the same way as the Canadian. It is because they are less in volume, and because the water does not fall so much into one place. By comparison their beauty is almost delicate and fragile. They are extraordinarily level, one long curtain of lacework and woven foam. Seen from opposite, when the sun is on them, they are blindingly white, and the clouds of spray show dark against them. With both Falls the colour of the water is the ever-altering wonder. Greens and blues, purples and whites, melt into one another, fade, and come again, and change with the changing sun. Sometimes they are as richly diaphanous as a precious stone, and glow from within with a deep, inexplicable light. Sometimes the white intricacies of dropping foam become opaque and creamy. And always there are the rainbows. If you come suddenly upon the Falls from above, a great double rainbow, very vivid, spanning the extent of spray from top to bottom, is the first thing you see. If you wander along the cliffs opposite, a bow springs into being in the American Falls, accompanies you courteously on your walk, dwindles and dies as the mist ends, and awakens again as you reach the Canadian tumult. And the bold traveller who attempts the trip under the American Falls sees, when he dare open his eyes to anything, tiny baby rainbows, some four or five yards in span, leaping from rock to rock among the foam, and gambolling beside him, barely out of hand's reach, as he goes. One I saw in that place was a complete circle, such as I have never seen before, and so near that I could put my foot on it. It is a terrifying journey, beneath and behind the Falls. The senses are battered and bewildered by the thunder of the water and the assault of wind and spray; or rather, the sound is not falling water, but merely of falling; a noise of unspecified ruin. So, if you are close behind the endless clamour, the sight cannot recognize liquid in the masses that hurl past. You are dimly and pitifully aware that sheets of light and darkness are falling in great curves in front of you. Dull omnipresent foam washes the face. Farther away, in the roar and hissing, clouds of spray seem literally to slide down some invisible plane of air.

Beyond the foot of the Falls the river is like a slipping floor of marble, green with veins of dirty white, made by the scum that was foam. It slides very quietly and slowly down for a mile or two, sullenly exhausted. Then it turns to a dull sage green, and hurries more swiftly, smooth and ominous. As the walls of the ravine close in, trouble stirs, and the waters boil and eddy. These are the lower rapids, a sight more terrifying than the Falls, because less intelligible. Close in its bands of rock, the river surges tumultuously forward, writhing and leaping as if inspired by a demon. It is pressed by the straits into a visibly convex form. Great planes of water slide past. Sometimes it is thrown up into a pinnacle of foam higher than a house, or leaps with incredible speed from the crest of one vast wave to another, along the shining curve between, like the spring of a wild beast. Its motion continually suggests muscular action. The power manifest in these rapids moves one with a different sense of awe and terror from that of the Falls. Here the inhuman life and strength are spontaneous, active, almost resolute; masculine vigour compared with the passive, gigantic power, female, helpless and overwhelming, of the Falls. A place to fear.

One is drawn back, strangely, to a contemplation of the Falls, at every hour, and especially by night when the cloud of spray becomes an immense visible ghost, straining and wavering high above the river, white and pathetic and translucent. The Victorian lies very close below the surface in every man. There one can sit and let great cloudy thoughts of destiny and the passage of empires drift through the mind; for such dreams are at home by Niagara. I could not get out of my mind the thought of a friend, who said that the rainbows over the Falls were like the arts and beauty and goodness, with regard to the stream of life – caused by it, thrown upon its spray, but unable to stay or direct or affect it, and ceasing when it ceased. In all comparisons that rise in the heart, the river, with its multitudinous waves and its single current, likens itself to a life, whether of an individual or of a community. A man's life is of many flashing moments, and yet one stream; a nation's flows through all its citizens, and yet is more than they. In such places, one is aware, with an almost insupportable and yet comforting certitude, that both men and nations are hurried onwards to their ruin or ending as inevitably as this dark flood. Some go down to it unreluctant, and meet it, like the river, not without nobility. And, as incessant, as inevitable, and as unavailing as the spray that hangs over the Falls, is the white cloud of human crying .... With some such thoughts does the platitudinous heart win from the confusion and thunder of Niagara a peace that the quietest plains or most stable hills can never give.

• OF STRANGERS AND • BARBARIANS

John Steinbeck (1902–1968)

Born in California, Steinbeck studied science at Stanford University and then worked successively as labourer, pharmacist, caretaker, fruit-picker and surveyor. His most popular novel, **The Grapes of Wrath** *(1939), was awarded a Pullitzer Prize. Other novels of his include* **East of Eden, Of Mice and Men** *and* **The Pearl**, *and he has also published several collections of short stories. Steinbeck was awarded the Nobel Prize for Literature in 1962.*

The following two extracts are taken from the autobiographical **Travels with Charley.** *Published in 1962, it is an account of his journey, together with his French poodle Charley, to rediscover America, and has been described as 'a pungent pot-pourri of places and people'. The first extract describes his feelings about the enormous Sequoia (Redwood) trees, which were at one stage close to extinction. The second extract is an account of what he felt when he returned to his home town, Salinas in California.*

I stayed two days close to the bodies of the giants, and there were no trippers, no chattering troupes with cameras. There's a cathedral hush here. Perhaps the thick soft bark absorbs sound and creates a silence. The trees rise straight up to zenith; there is no horizon. The dawn comes early and remains dawn until the sun is high. Then the green fernlike foliage so far up strains the sunlight to a green gold and distributes it in shafts or rather in stripes of light and shade. After the sun passes zenith it is afternoon and quickly evening with a whispering dusk as long as was the morning.

Thus time and the ordinary divisions of the day are changed. To me dawn and dusk are quiet times, and here in the redwoods nearly the whole of daylight is a quiet time. Birds move in the dim light or flash like sparks through the stripes of sun, but they make little sound. Underfoot is a mattress of needles deposited for over two thousand years. No sound of footsteps can be heard on this thick blanket. To me there's a remote and cloistered feeling here. One holds back speech for fear of disturbing something – what? From my earliest childhood I've felt that something was going on in the groves, something of which I was not a part. And if I had forgotten the feeling I soon got it back.

At night, the darkness is black – only straight up a patch of grey and an occasional star. And there's a breathing in the black, for these huge things that control the day and inhabit the night are living things and have presence, and perhaps feeling, and, somewhere in deep-down perception, perhaps communication. I have had lifelong association with these things. (Odd that the word 'trees' does not apply). I can accept them and their power and their age because I was early exposed to them. On the other hand, people lacking such experience begin to have a feeling of uneasiness here, of danger, of being shut in, enclosed and overwhelmed. It is not only the size of these redwoods but their strangeness that frightens them. And why not? For these are the last remaining members of a race that flourished over four continents as far back in geologic time as the upper Jurassic period. Fossils of these ancients have been found dating from the Cretaceous era while in the Eocene and Miocene they were spread over England and Europe and America. And then the glaciers moved down and wiped the Titans out beyond recovery. And only these few are left – a stunning memory of what the world was like once long ago. Can it be that we do not love to be reminded that we are very young and callow in a world that was old when we came into it? And could there be a strong resistance to the certainty that a living world will continue its stately way when we no longer inhabit it?

•

I find it difficult to write about my native place, northern California. It should be the easiest, because I knew that strip angled against the Pacific better than any place in the world. But I find it not one thing but many – one printed over another until the whole thing blurs. What it is is warped with memory of what it was and that with what happened there to me, the whole bundle wracked until objectiveness is nigh impossible. This four-lane concrete highway slashed with speeding cars I remember as a narrow, twisting mountain road where the wood teams moved, drawn by steady mules. They signalled their coming with the high, sweet jangle of hame bells. This was a little little town, a general store under a tree and a blacksmith's shop and a bench in front on which to sit and listen to the clang of hammer on anvil. Now little houses, each one like the next, particularly since they try to be different, spread for a mile in all directions. That was a woody hill with live oaks dark green against the parched grass where the coyotes sang on moonlit nights. The top is shaved off and a television relay station lunges at the sky and feeds a nervous picture to thousands of tiny houses clustered like aphids beside the roads.

And isn't this the typical complaint? I have never resisted change, even when it has been called progress, and yet I felt resentment towards the strangers swamping what I thought of as my country with noise and clutter and the inevitable rings of junk. And of course these new people will resent the newer people. I remember how when I was a child we responded to the natural dislike of the stranger. We who were born here and our parents also felt a strange superiority over newcomers, barbarians, *forestieri*, and they, the foreigners, resented us and even made a rude poem about us:

The miner came in forty-nine,
The whores in fifty-one.
And when they got together,
They made a Native Son.

And we were an outrage to the Spanish-Mexicans and they in their turn to the Indians. Could that be why the sequoias made folks nervous? Those natives were grown trees when a political execution took place on Golgotha. They were well toward middle age when Caesar destroyed the Roman republic in the process of saving it. To the sequoias everyone is a stranger, a barbarian.

• THE WONDER CITY • OF THE WORLD

Stuart Cloete (1897–1976)

Born in Paris, Stuart Cloete was educated in England, and came to South Africa in 1925, where he worked as a farmhand before purchasing his own dairy farm in the Transvaal. In 1933, he was encouraged to become a writer by Sarah Gertrude Millin and soon afterwards, he sold his farm and left the country for overseas. Years later he returned to South Africa, where he eventually retired to Hermanus.

By the time of his death Cloete had published fourteen novels (most of them based on historical events in South Africa), some verse and a variety of articles. His first novel, **Turning Wheels** *(1937), was translated into ten languages. His most famous novel is probably* **Rags of Glory** *(1963). Cloete described himself as 'a first-class second-class commercial writer' – an estimation, according to the compilers of the* Dictionary of South African Biography, *'not far off the mark'. 'His racy stories of romanticised characters getting in and out of adventurous predicaments,' they maintain, 'made him justly popular.'*

The following description of New York shortly before the outbreak of World War Two, is taken from the second volume of his autobiography entitled **The Gambler: An Autobiography (1920 – 1939)**, *which was published in 1973.*

This was New York where everyone, as we came in, said: 'What a shame it's not a clear day so that you can see the skyline.' Who wanted to see the skyline? I had seen it a hundred times in pictures, in the illustrated papers, in films. I could almost have sketched the New York skyline. What I saw before me was fairyland. Rising out of the pale mist above the cool, green sea were sunlit golden towers, pinnacles, domes – a mythical heavenly city rooted in the clouds. Never has anyone had a more beautiful approach to

New York, the wonder city of the world.

In a few hours I was to see it. To drive down these man-made canyons, made in a few decades, but deeper than a great river could have cut them in ten thousand. And at the bottom, between the high cliffs, ran – not water – but a tide of men and women, no bigger from where I stood looking down on them from the top of my skyscraper than pin-heads, legless spots, that moved this way and that among the chitinous shining cars that crawled insect-like through the thoroughfares.

Accustomed to cities – to London and Paris – I was still enthralled. Never had I dreamed of this immensity, of so many people moving at such speed along the streets, up and down the buildings vertically, swiftly, in silent elevators, and horizontally again – to and fro – at every level. Twenty floors up, thirty, fifty, sixty, and still they moved about their work, calmly, neatly, industriously, like ants. Like swarming ants pressed for time, for here time was a palpable force. I was exposed to such noises as I had never heard before. The scream of sirens, the throbbing of a thousand engines, the inaudible vibrations from hundreds of thousands of others. The people's bodies were pierced by waves of radio music. They were breathing air strong with gasoline, with steam, with sweat. These were supermen. America and Americans, a place and a race apart. The latest thing. The last producer of our age. All this came to me, not on the first day, though I felt it then, but over the years, building up a picture of this might, this colossal power.

What are the things that struck me most? Uniformity. That is the basis of America's greatness. There can, after all, be no efficiency without standardisation. No mass production of the custom-built. This seems strange at first, but it makes sense. For instance, heaven must be uniform. Can one imagine angels of various colours with different coloured wings? No, angels are white, with white swans' wings. Perhaps for a Negro they are black with sable wings. But each of us sees them as uniform. It seems to me that these manifold vibrations and tensions, combined with the astonishing clearness of the atmosphere and savage climatic variations, produce a particular type of man – active, nervous, of an unparalleled energy. They are the people who get things done, and fast.

Impressions. The immediate impressions were first the slim, svelte beauty of the women, their well-dressed neatness, their perfect figures. They had not the chic of the Parisienne, this was something different, crisp, girdled, silken, rayonned, shod in high heels as neat as the hooves of a deer.

In the great boulevards – the rich avenues – was more uniformity. A uniformity of mink, of women superbly dressed, coiffed, with plucked eyebrows and painted lips. Even their mouths were standardised. The latest mouth from *Vogue*, from Elizabeth Arden, from Helena Rubenstein. Never were there so many women at one time so beautiful, so perfumed, and at the same time so odourless – so alike that they might all have been sisters.

I was surprised at the shabbiness of the police. New York's finest, and certainly one of the most courageous, forces in the world, armed and ready to do battle with the underworld of gangsters and hold-up men who roamed the city like wolves, singly and in packs. Later, this was explained. It appeared that the police had to buy their own uniforms. I was also interested in the quality of the police horses. I saw a squadron ride past. They were not of the same class as those of the London mounted police, which are nearly all thoroughbreds, but they were wonderfully matched, as alike as peas in a pod. Uniformity again, all bays with black points. I was surprised to see that they only had leather reins, not chains. In a riot they would be quickly rendered helpless by a few slashes with a razor, but American crowds are motorminded and more nervous of horses than the British.

And Grand Central Station – I think you could put Nôtre Dame into it and still have lots of room left over. I saw, on that first day, men carrying bags of money over their shoulders accompanied by armed guards with drawn guns. There were armed guards in the banks, an armed guard outside jewellers' shops. It was just like the films.

This was not the America of the school books, of the atlas. This was the New World. The land of the silver screen, filmland, fairyland.

One of the things that struck me as very typical was the big red second hand on the clocks in the cafeterias. It swept on round and round. It seemed to force me to watch the seconds pass. Each one gone forever. Hurry up with the sandwiches and coffee. Time is money. There is need for haste – this was the land of haste. No one had the time to pass the time of day. Questions were answered with a monosyllable, as if words cost money. Money and time were synonymous.

•

It is difficult for other nations to understand the richness of America. And even Americans, though they speak of God's own country, seem sometimes not to understand how true this is, and how fortunate they are. In no country in the world is there such opportunity for success. Success on every level, from the highest academic honours to success on the lowest gangster and criminal terms – in his way **Al Capone** was a great success. There is success through brains, through hard work, through luck, through beauty, through strength, through religion. In no country, because of its vastness, is there so much room at the top. I have thought of America as if it were the keyboard of a piano. There are extra notes at both ends of the scale. Unheard of idealism at the one end and unparalleled crime at the other. The range of these extra notes are the key of American culture, of her greatness, of the paradox of immense variety and incredible uniformity – again extremes. America is like its climate – a country of violent change – where life is never dull, and the word 'impossible' without meaning.

• THE CITY OF • DREADFUL NIGHT

Rudyard Kipling (1865–1936)

Born in Bombay, India, this British writer visited and worked periodically in South Africa between 1896 and 1908. Probably most widely known for his children's stories in **The Jungle Books** *and* **Kim,** *he also published numerous short stories on life in India as well as a considerable body of poetry, including a number of poems dealing with the Anglo-Boer War. He received the Nobel Prize for Literature in 1908.*

The following essay, written by Kipling when he was not yet twenty, is a portrait of the Indian City of Lahore in the late 1880s. It was published in Kipling's **Life's Handicap – being stories of mine own people** *in 1899.*

The dense wet heat that hung over the face of land, like a blanket, prevented all hope of sleep in the first instance. The cicadas helped the heat, and the yelling jackals the cicadas. It was impossible to sit still in the dark, empty, echoing house and watch the **punkah** beat the dead air. So, at ten o'clock of the night, I set my walking-stick on end in the middle of the garden, and waited to see how it would fall. It pointed directly down the moonlit road that leads to the City of Dreadful Night. The sound of its fall disturbed a hare. She limped from her form and ran across to a disused Mahomedan burial-ground, where the jawless skulls and rough-butted shank-bones, heartlessly exposed by the July rains, glimmered like mother o'pearl on the rain-channeled soil. The heated air and the heavy earth had driven the very dead upward for coolness' sake. The hare limped on; snuffed curiously at a fragment of a smoke-stained lamp-shard, and died out, in the shadow of a clump of tamarisk trees.

The mat-weaver's hut under the lee of the Hindu temple was full of sleeping men who lay like sheeted corpses. Overhead blazed the unwinking eye of the moon. Darkness gives at least a false impression of coolness. It was hard not to believe that the flood of light from above was warm. Not so hot as the sun, but still sickly warm, and heating the heavy air beyond what was our due. Straight as a bar of polished steel ran the road to the City of Dreadful Night; and on either side of the road lay corpses disposed on beds in fantastic attitudes – one hundred and seventy bodies of men. Some shrouded all in white with bound-up mouths; some naked and black as ebony in the strong light; and one – that lay face upwards with dropped jaw, far away from the others – silvery white and ashen grey.

'A leper asleep; and the remainder wearied coolies, servants, small shop-keepers, and drivers from the hack-stand hard by. The scene – a main approach to Lahore city, and the night a warm one in August.' This was all that there was to be seen; but by no means all that one could see. The witchery of the moonlight was everywhere; and the world was horribly changed. The long line of the naked dead, flanked by the rigid silver statue, was not pleasant to look upon. It was made up of men alone. Were the womenkind, then, forced to sleep in the shelter of the stifling mud-huts as best they might? The fretful wail of a child from a low mud-roof answered the question. Where the children are the mothers must be also to look after them. They need care on these sweltering nights. A black little bullet-head peeped over the coping, and a thin – a painfully thin – brown leg was slid over on to the gutter pipe. There was a sharp clink of glass bracelets; a woman's arm showed for an instant above the parapet, twined itself round the lean little neck, and the child was dragged back, protesting, to the shelter of the bedstead. His thin, high-pitched shriek died out in the thick air almost as soon as it was raised; for even the children of the soil found it too hot to weep.

More corpses; more stretches of moonlit, white road; a string of sleeping camels at rest by the wayside; a vision of scudding jackals; ekka-ponies asleep – the harness still on their backs, and the brass-studded country carts, winking in the moonlight – and again more corpses. Wherever a grain cart atilt, a tree trunk, a sawn log, a couple of bamboos and a few handfuls of thatch cast a shadow, the ground is covered with them. They lie – some face downwards, arms folded in the dust; some with clasped hands flung up above their heads; some curled up dog-wise; some thrown like limp gunny-bags over the side of the grain carts; and some bowed with their brows on their knees in the full glare of the moon. It would be a comfort if they were only given to snoring; but they are not, and the likeness to corpses is unbroken in all respects save one. The lean dogs snuff at them and turn away. Here and there a tiny child lies on his father's bedstead, and a protecting arm is thrown round it in every instance. But, for the most part, the children sleep with their mothers on the house-tops. Yellow-skinned white-toothed pariahs are not to be trusted within reach of brown bodies.

A stifling hot blast from the mouth of the Delhi Gate nearly ends my resolution of entering the City of Dreadful Night at this hour. It is a compound of all evil savours, animal and vegetable, that a walled city can brew in a day and a night. The temperature within the motionless groves of plantain and orange-trees outside the city walls seems chilly by comparison. Heaven help all sick persons and young children within the city to-night! The high house-walls are still radiating heat savagely, and from obscure side gullies fetid breezes eddy that ought to poison a buffalo. But the buffaloes do not heed. A drove of them are parading the vacant main street; stopping now and then to lay their ponderous muzzles against the closed shutters of a grain-dealer's shop, and to blow thereon like grampuses.

Then silence follows – the silence that is full of the night noises of a great city. A stringed instrument of some kind is just, and only just audible. High overhead someone throws open a window, and the rattle of the woodwork echoes down the empty street. On one of the roofs a hookah is in full blast; and the men are talking softly as the pipe gutters. A little farther on the noise of conversation is more distinct. A slit of light shows itself between the sliding shutters of a shop. Inside, a stubble-bearded, weary-eyed trader is balancing his account-books among the bales of cotton prints that surround him. Three sheeted figures bear him company, and throw in a remark from time to time. First he makes an entry, then a remark; then passes the back of his hand across his streaming forehead. The heat in the built-in street is fearful. Inside the shops it must be almost unendurable. But the work goes on steadily; entry, guttural growl, and uplifted hand-stroke succeeding each other with the precision of clock-work.

A policeman – turbanless and fast asleep – lies across the road on the way to the Mosque of Wazir Khan. A bar of moonlight falls across the forehead and eyes of the sleeper, but he never stirs. It is close upon midnight, and the heat seems to be increasing. The open square in front of the Mosque is crowded with corpses; and a man must pick his way carefully for fear of treading on them. The moonlight stripes the Mosque's high front of coloured enamel work in broad diagonal bands; and each separate dreaming pigeon in the niches and corners of the masonry throws a squab little shadow. Sheeted ghosts rise up wearily from their pallets, and flit into the dark depths of the building. Is it possible to climb to the top of the great Minars, and thence to look down on the city? At all events the attempt is worth making, and the chances are that the door of the staircase will be unlocked. Unlocked it is; but a deeply sleeping janitor lies across the threshold, face turned to the moon. A rat dashes out of his turban at the sound of approaching footsteps. The man grunts, opens his eyes for a minute, turns round, and goes to sleep again. All the heat of a decade of fierce Indian summers is stored in the pitch-black, polished walls of the corkscrew staircase. Halfway up there is something alive, warm, and feathery; and it snores. Driven from step to step as it catches the sound of my advance, it flutters to the top and reveals itself as a yellow-eyed, angry kite. Dozens of kites are asleep on this and other minars, and on the domes below. There is the shadow of a cool, or at least a less sultry breeze at this height; and, refreshed thereby, turn to look on the City of Dreadful Night.

Doré might have drawn it! **Zola** could describe it – this spectacle of sleeping thousands in the moonlight and in the shadow of the moon. The roof-tops are crammed with men, women, and children: and the air is full of undistinguishable noises. They are restless in the City of Dreadful Night; and small wonder. The marvel is that they can even breathe. If you gaze intently at the multitude you can see that they are almost as uneasy as a daylight crowd; but the tumult is subdued. Everywhere, in the strong light, you can watch the sleepers turning to and fro; shifting their beds and again resettling them. In the pit-like courtyards of the houses there is the same movement.

The pitiless moon shows it all. Shows, too, the plains outside the city, and here and there a hand's-breadth of the Ravee without the walls. Shows lastly, a splash of glittering silver on a house-top almost directly below the mosque Minar. Some poor soul has risen to throw a jar of water over his fevered body; the tinkle of the falling water strikes faintly on the ear. Two or three other men, in far-off corners of the City of Dreadful Night, follow his example, and the water flashes like heliographic signals. A small cloud passes over the face of the moon, and the city and its inhabitants – clear-drawn in black and white before – fade into masses of black and deeper black. Still the unrestful noise continues, the sigh of a great city overwhelmed with the heat, and of a people seeking in vain for rest. It is only the lower-class women who sleep on the house-tops. What must the torment be in the latticed **zenanas** where a few lamps are still twinkling? There are footfalls in the court below. It is the ***Muezzin*** – faithful minister; but he ought to have been here an hour ago to tell the Faithful that prayer is better than sleep – the sleep that will not come to the city.

The *Muezzin* fumbles for a moment with the door of one of the Minars, disappears awhile, and a bull-like roar – a magnificent bass thunder – tells that he has reached the top of the Minar. They must hear the cry to the banks of the shrunken Ravee itself! Even across the courtyard it is almost overpowering. The cloud drifts by and shows him outlined in black against the sky, hand laid upon his ears, and broad chest heaving with the play of his lungs – 'Allah ho Akbar'; then a pause while another *Muezzin* somewhere in the direction of the Golden Temple takes up the call – '*Allah ho*

Akbar'. Again and again; four times in all; and from the bedsteads a dozen men have risen up already – 'I bear witness that there is no God but God.' What a splendid cry it is, the proclamation of the creed that brings men out of their beds by scores at midnight! Once again he thunders through the same phrase, shaking with the vehemence of his own voice; and then, far and near, the night air rings with 'Mahomed is the Prophet of God.' It is as though he were flinging his defiance to the far-off horizon, where the summer lightning plays and leaps like a bared sword. Every *Muezzin* in the city is in full cry, and some men on the roof-tops are beginning to kneel. A long pause precedes the last cry, *'La ilaha Illallah'*,[2] and the silence closes up on it, as the ram on the head of a cotton-bale.

The *Muezzin* stumbles down the dark stairway grumbling in his beard. He passes the arch of the entrance and disappears. Then the stifling silence settles down over the City of Dreadful Night. The kites on the Minar sleep again, snoring more loudly, the hot breeze comes up in puffs and lazy eddies, and the moon slides down towards the horizon. Seated with both elbows on the parapet of the tower, one can watch and wonder over that heat-tortured hive till the dawn. 'How do they live down there? What do they think of? When will they awake?' More tinkling of sluiced water-pots; faint jarring of wooden bedsteads moved into or out of the shadows; uncouth music of stringed instruments softened by distance into a plaintive wall, and one low grumble of far-off thunder. In the courtyard of the mosque the janitor, who lay across the threshold of the Minar when I came up, starts wildly in his sleep, throws his hands above his head, mutters something, and falls back again. Lulled by the snoring of the kites – they snore like over-gorged humans – I drop off into an uneasy doze, conscious that three o'clock has struck, and that there is a slight – a very slight – coolness in the atmosphere. The city is absolutely quiet now, but for some vagrant dog's love-song. Nothing save dead heavy sleep.

Several weeks of darkness pass after this. For the moon has gone out. The very dogs are still, and I watch for the first light of the dawn before making my way homeward. Again the noise of shuffling feet. The morning call is about to begin, and my night watch is over. *'Allah ho Akbar! Allah ho Akbar'*. The east grows grey, and presently saffron; the dawn wind comes up as though the *Muezzin* had summoned it; and, as one man, the City of Dreadful Night rises from its bed and turns its face towards the dawning

---

1 *Allah ho Akbar – God is the Greatest*

2 *La ilaha Illallah – There is no other god but God*

day. With return of life comes return of sound. First a low whisper, then a deep bass hum; for it must be remembered that the entire city is on the house-tops. My eyelids weighed down with the arrears of long deferred sleep, I escape from the Minar through the courtyard and out into the square beyond, where the sleepers have risen, stowed away the bedsteads, and are discussing the morning **hookah.** The minute's freshness of the air has gone, and it is as hot as at first.

'Will the ***Sahib*** out of his kindness, make room?' What is it? Something borne on men's shoulders comes by in the half-light, and I stand back. A woman's corpse going down to the burning-**ghât**, and a bystander says, 'She died at midnight from the heat.' So the city was of Death as well as Night after all.

• THE LIVING WORLD •

Gerald Durrell (1925–)

Gerald Durrell was born to British parents in India in 1925. When he was three, the family returned to England. Then, to escape the cold of England, the Durrell family moved to the island of Corfu, off the coast of Greece. Perennially interested in animals, Durrell founded the Jersey Zoological Park, of which he remains the director.

He has published numerous books, many of them autobiographical and most of them combining his sensitivity to nature with his sense of the hilarious.

The first of the following extracts comes from his book **Birds, Beasts and Relatives** *and the others from a later book,* **My Family and Other Animals**.

Corfu lies off the Albanian and Greek coast-lines like a long, rust-eroded scimitar. The hilt of the scimitar is the mountain region of the island, for the most part barren and stony with towering rock cliffs haunted by blue-rock thrushes and peregrine falcons. In the valleys in this mountain region, however, where water gushed plentifully from the red and gold rocks, you would get forests of almond and walnut trees, casting shade as cool as a well, thick battalions of spear-like cypress and silver-trunked fig trees with leaves as large as a salver. The blade of the scimitar is made up of rolling greeny-silver eiderdowns of giant olives, some reputedly over five hundred years old and each one unique in its hunched, arthritic shape, its trunk pitted with a hundred holes like pumice stone. Towards the tip of the blade you had Lefkimi with its twinkling, eye-aching sand dunes and great salt marshes, decorated with acres of bamboos that creaked and rustled and whispered to each other surreptitiously.

To go back to Corfu, for me, was to go home. We had first arrived there a year or two before and had quickly settled into a bright crushed-strawberry pink villa with green shutters shaped not unlike a brick. It crouched in a cathedral-like grove of olives that sloped down the hillside to the sea, and was surrounded by a pocket-handkerchief-size garden, the flower beds laid out with a geometrical accuracy so dear to the Victorians, and the whole thing guarded by a tall, thick hedge of fuchsias that rustled mysteriously with birds.

However luxurious our various gardens had been in England they had never provided me with such an assortment of living creatures. I found myself prey to the most curious sensation of unreality. It was rather like being born for the first time. In that brilliant brittle light I could appreciate the true huntsman's red of a lady-bird's wing case, the magnificent chocolate and amber of an earwig and the deep shining agate of the ants. Then I could feast my eyes on a bewildering number of creatures unfamiliar to me. The great furry carpenter bees, which prowled like electric-blue Teddy bears, humming to themselves, from flower to flower, the sulphur-yellow, black-striped swallow tail butterflies, with their elegant cut-away coats, that pirouetted up and down the fuchsia hedge doing complicated minuets with each other and the Humming Bird hawk moths that hung stationary, suspended by a blur of wings in front of the flowers, while they probed each bloom with their long, delicate proboscis.

I was exceedingly ignorant as to even the simplest facts about these creatures and had no books to guide me. All I could do was to watch them as they went about their business in the garden or capture them so that I could study them more carefully at first hand. Very soon my bedroom was filled with a battalion of jam jars and biscuit tins containing the prizes that I had found in our tiny garden. These had to be smuggled surreptitiously into the house for the family, with the possible exception of Mother, viewed the introduction of fauna into the villa with considerable alarm.

•

Spring merged slowly into the long, hot, sun-sharp days of summer sung in by cicadas, shrill and excited, making the island vibrate with their cries. In the fields the maize was starting to fill out, the silken tassels turning from brown to butter-blond; when you tore off the wrapping of leaves and bit into the rows of pearly seeds the juice would spurt into your mouth like milk. On the vines the grapes hung in tiny clusters, freckled and warm. The olives seemed weighed down under the weight of their fruit, smooth drops of green jade among which the choirs of cicadas zithered. In the orange-groves, among the dark and shiny leaves, the fruit was starting to glow redly, like a blush spreading up the green, pitted skins.

Up on the hills, among the dark cypress and the heather, shoals of butterflies danced and twisted like wind-blown confetti, pausing now and then on a leaf to lay a salvo of eggs. The grasshoppers and locusts whirred like clockwork under my feet, and flew drunkenly across the heather, their wings shining in the sun. Among the myrtles the mantids moved, lightly, carefully, swaying slightly, the quintessence of evil. They were lank and green, with chinless faces and monstrous globular eyes, frosty gold, with an expression of intense, predatory madness in them. The crooked arms, with their fringes of sharp teeth, would be raised in mock supplication to the insect world, so humble, so fervent, trembling slightly when a butterfly flew too close.

Towards evening, when it grew cooler, the cicadas stopped singing; their place being taken by the green treefrogs, glued damply to the lemon-tree leaves down by the well. With bulging eyes staring as though hypnotised, their backs as shiny as the leaves they sat amongst, they swelled out their vocal sacs and croaked harshly and with such violence that they seemed in danger of splitting their damp bodies with the effort. When the sun sank there was a brief, apple-green twilight which faded and became mauve, and the air cooled and took on the scents of evening. The toads appeared, putty-coloured with strange, map-like blotches of bottle-green on their skins. They hopped furtively among the long grass clumps in the olive-groves, where the craneflies' unsteady flight seemed to cover the ground with a drifting curtain of gauze. They sat there blinking, and then would suddenly snap at a passing crane-fly; sitting back, looking a trifle embarrassed, they stuffed the trailing ends of wing and leg into their great mouths with the aid of their thumbs. Above them, on the crumbling walls of the sunken garden, the little black scorpions walked solemnly, hand in hand, among the plump mounds of green moss and the groves of tiny toadstools.

The sea was smooth, warm, and as dark as black velvet, not a ripple disturbing the surface. The distant coastline of Albania was dimly outlined by a faint reddish glow in the sky. Gradually, minute by minute, this glow deepened and grew brighter, spreading across the sky. Then suddenly the moon, enormous, wine-red, edged herself over the fretted battlement of mountains, and threw a straight, blood-red path across the dark sea. The owls appeared now, drifting from tree to tree as silently as flakes of soot, hooting in astonishment as the moon rose higher and higher, turning to pink, then gold, and finally riding in a nest of stars, like a silver bubble.

In the summer, when the moon was full, the family took a bathing at night, for during the day the sun was so fierce that the sea became too hot to be refreshing. As soon as the moon had risen we would make our way down through the trees to the creaking wooden jetty, and clamber into the *Sea Cow*.... We would anchor [...] in deep water and then dive over the side to gambol and plunge, and set the moonlight shaking across the waters of the bay. When tired, we swam languidly to the shore and lay on the warm rocks, gazing up into the star-freckled sky. Generally after half an hour or so I would get bored with the conversation, and slip back into the water and swim slowly out across the bay, to lie on my back, cushioned by the warm sea, gazing up at the moon. One night, while I was thus occupied, I discovered that our bay was used by other creatures as well.

Lying spread-eagled in the silky water, gazing into the sky, only moving my hands and feet slightly to keep afloat, I was looking at the Milky Way stretched like a chiffon scarf across the sky and wondering how many stars it contained. I could hear the voices of the others, laughing and talking on the beach, echoing over the water, and by lifting my head I could see their position on the shore by the pulsing lights of their cigarettes. Drifting there, relaxed, and dreamy, I was suddenly startled to hear, quite close to me, a clop and gurgle of water, followed by a long, deep sigh, and a series of gentle ripples rocked me up and down. Hastily I righted myself and trod water, looking to see how far from the beach I had drifted. To my alarm I found that not only was I some considerable distance from the shore, but from the *Sea Cow* as well and I was not at all sure what sort of creature it was swimming around in the dark waters beneath me. I could hear the others laughing on the shore at some joke or other, and I saw someone flip a cigarette-end high into the sky like a red star that curved over and extinguished itself at the rim of the sea. I was feeling more and more uncomfortable, and I was just about to call for assistance when, some twenty feet away from me, the sea seemed to part with a gentle swish and gurgle, a gleaming back appeared, gave a deep, satisfied sigh, and sank below the surface again. I had hardly time to recognize it as a porpoise before I found I was right in the midst of them. They rose all around me, sighing luxuriously, their black backs shining as they humped in the moonlight. There must have been about eight of them, and one rose so close that I could have swum forward three strokes and touched his ebony head. Heaving and sighing heavily, they played across the bay, and I swam with them, watching fascinated as they rose to the surface, crumpling the water, breathed deeply, and then dived beneath the surface again, leaving only an expanding hoop of foam to mark the spot. Presently, as if obeying a signal, they turned and headed out of the bay towards the distant coast of Albania, and I trod water and watched them go, swimming up the white chain of moonlight, backs agleam as they rose and plunged with heavy ecstasy in the water as warm as fresh milk. Behind them they left a trail of great bubbles that rocked and shone briefly like miniature moons before vanishing under the ripples.

•

Winter came to the island gently as a rule. The sky was still clear, the sea blue and calm, and the sun warm. But there would be an uncertainty in the air. The gold and scarlet leaves that littered the countryside in great drifts whispered and chuckled among themselves, or took experimental runs from place to place, rolling like coloured hoops among the trees. It was as if they were practising something, preparing for something, and they would discuss it excitedly in rusty voices as they crowded round the tree-trunks. The birds, too, congregated in little groups, puffing out their feathers, twittering thoughtfully. The whole air was one of expectancy, like a vast audience waiting for the curtian to go up. Then one morning you threw back the shutters and looked down over the olive-trees, across the blue bay to the russet mountains of the mainland and became aware that winter had arrived, for each mountain peak would be wearing a tattered skull-cap of snow. Now the air of expectancy grew almost hourly.

In a few days small white clouds started their winter parade, trooping across the sky, soft and chubby, long, languorous, and unkempt, or small and crisp as feathers, and driving them before it, like an ill-assorted flock of sheep, would come the wind. This was warm at first, and came in gentle gusts, rubbing through the olive-groves so that the leaves trembled and turned silver with excitement, rocking the cypresses so that they undulated gently, and stirring the dead leaves into gay, swirling little dances that died as suddenly as they began. Playfully it ruffled the feathers on the sparrow's backs, so that they shuddered and fluffed themselves; and it leapt without warning at the gulls, so that they were stopped in mid-air and had to curve their white wings against it. Shutters started to bang and doors chattered suddenly in their frames. But still the sun shone, the sea remained placid, and the mountains sat complacently, summer bronzed, wearing their splintered snow hats.

For a week or so the wind played with the island, patting it, humming to itself among the bare branches. Then there was a lull, a few days' strange calm; suddenly, when you least expected it, the wind would be back. But it was a changed wind, a mad, hooting, bellowing wind that leapt down on the island and tried to blow it into the sea. The blue sky vanished as a cloak of fine grey cloud was thrown over the island. The sea turned a deep blue, almost black, and became crusted with foam. The cypress trees were whipped like dark pendulums against the sky, and the olives (so fossilized all summer, so still and witch-like) were infected with the madness of the wind and swayed creaking on their misshapen, sinewy trunks, their leaves hissing as they turned like mother of pearl, from green to silver. This is what the dead leaves had whispered about, this is what they had practised for; exultantly they rose in the air and danced, whirligiging about, dipping, swooping, falling exhausted when the wind tired of them and passed on. Rain followed the wind, but it was a warm rain that you could walk in and enjoy, great fat drops that rattled on the shutters, tapped on the vine leaves like drums, and gurgled musically in the gutters. The rivers up in the Albanian mountains became swollen and showed white teeth in a snarl as they rushed down to the sea, tearing at their banks, grabbing the summer debris of sticks, logs, grass tussocks, and other things, and disgorging them into the day, so that the dark-blue waters became patterned with great coiling veins of mud and other flotsam. Gradually all these veins burst, and the sea changed from blue to yellow-brown; then the wind tore at the surface, piling the water into ponderous waves, like great tawny lions with white manes that stalked and leaped upon the shore.

APPENDIX – IS THE TRAVEL BOOK DEAD?

Kingley Amis

The vogue for the highbrow travel book shows no immediate signs of abating. At any rate, here are two more endeavours in that field. The usual characteristics of such books are, first, a leaning towards the more elaborate and unfashionable graces of prose, rightly unfashionable they seem to me, if I may show my hand thus early – and, secondly, a desire to get away from the exhausted sterilities of western civilisation so feelingly alluded to from time to time by Mr Priestley. In themselves, these two things may be all very well, though I judge it unlikely; in practice, however, the stylistic graces degenerate briskly into an empty and indecent poeticism, apparently based on a desire to get into the next edition of *The Oxford Book of English Prose,* while the escape-motive is only with difficulty to be distinguished from the feeling that the other fellow's grass is greener, that the really good time, or good life, is going on somewhere else. The two tendencies, in these degraded forms, find remarkably unhallowed expression in Mr Laurie Lee's volume.

The experienced reader will know what to do with a book whose blurb announces, as if in recommendation, its author's claim to 'the enchanted eye… of a true poet,' but the reviewer must act differently. His part is to soldier grimly on, trying not to mind too much the absence of a verb in the opening sentence, the incessant din of adjective and poeticality ('the scarred and crumpled valleys,' 'the oil-blue waters'), the full close of the first paragraph, mannered as any Ciceronian ***esse videatur:***

> *And from a steep hillside rose a column of smoke, cool as marble, pungent as pine, which hung like a signal over the landscape, obscure, imperative and motionless.*

The effect is a little marred through having been anticipated, three sentences earlier, by a cadential ('raw, sleeping and savage.') Another item on the list of things to try not to mind too much is the prevalence of lists – cf.

Mr Auden's *Spain*, which Mr Lee has perhaps been cf.-ing too – like 'the bright façades ... the beggars ... the vivid shapely girls ... the tiny delicate-stepping donkeys,' and so on; and yet another one is the 'striking' image – 'fragrant as water' – which at first sight seems to mean almost nothing, and upon reflection and reconsideration is seen to mean almost nothing. One way of summing up this book would be to call it a string of failed poems – failed not-very-good poems too, for whoever said that bad poetry is much more like poetry than good poetry is, was in the right of it there.

This kind of objection, however, though compulsory for the reader of almost any highbrow travel-book, is here purely trifling. The really telling strictures emerge from a mulling-over of what Mr Lee actually reveals to us about Andalusia. The figure of the narrator himself, having terrific fun with a drum in a wedding procession, carrying *two* guitars 'everywhere,' carefully recording every pass made at his wife, drinking like mad at a party in a telephone exchange while the switchboard lights 'twinkled unheeded' (not too good for people who wanted to ring the doctor) – can safely be left on one side. One might even haul to the other side the bull-fighting question, although the author's taste for 'the sharp mystery of blood' will remain unshared in some quarters, where, in addition, the use of the phrase 'the moment of truth' will appear a little worse than ***naïf***, and to upbraid a bull for having no grace or honour or 'vocation for martyrdom' will appear a lot worse; if we enjoined these duties upon a bull, he would not understand us. But the least attractive part of Mr Lee's portrayal of Spain is his portrayal of Spaniards, so far as this can be debarnacled from rhetoric, generalisation and rhapsody. The effect is not what he evidently intends; where he seeks to show us gaiety, mere instability or hooliganism emerges, unselfconsciousness is detectable as coxcombry or self-pity, while the gift attributed to Andalusians of greeting others' misfortune with a shrug or a grin is neither mature nor admirable. I am sure these people are not as bad as all that, just as I am sure that they are not in touch with the 'pure sources of feeling' and the 'real flavours' of life, whatever these entities may be; Coleridge put Wordsworth right on peasants a long time ago. Perhaps too many people in England do watch television, or do they watch it too much of the time? Anyway, *nostalgie de la boue*[1] is not the answer; it is silly to sleep on straw in the inn yard if you can get hold of a bed; and while it is no doubt better to be gay and have sores than to be un-gay and not have sores, it is better still to be fairly gay and not have sores.

---

1 *Nostalgie de la boue – nostalgia of the mud*

GLOSSARY

Al Capone (1899-1947) leader of the Mafia in Chicago in the 1920s
auberge *(French)* an inn
Baedeker a traveller's guide book, named after the first guide-book publisher, Karl Baedeker (1801-1859)
baksheesh *(Arabic)* gratuity
bastinado *(Spanish)* beating with a stick
biniou a Breton bagpipe
bogles people who tend to get bogged down, or who impede the progress of others
bolero a Spanish dance
Bolsheviks supporters of Lenin during the 1917 Russian Revolution; communists; ones who favour revolution
bona fides evidence of acceptibility; credibility
café au lait *(French)* coffee with milk
ceilidhe *(Irish)* an informal gathering for traditional music
chamois *(French)* a type of soft leather
char-à-banc *(French)* motor coaches for carrying tourists
contrabando *(Spanish)* contraband, smuggled goods, prohibited trade
Coptic Egyptian Christian Church
deus ex machina *(Latin idiomatic)* literally, 'a god from the machinery' meaning one who rescues another at the last moment. Derives from ancient theatre, when 'gods' would be lowered on to the stage by means of machinery, usually to save the hero from imminent disaster.
dilettanti people enjoying a light interest in the arts *(derogatory)*
Doré, Gustave (1832-1883) French graphic artist, painter and sculpter with a fantastic imagination and gift for the grotesque.
dragomen Arabic interpreters
Drang nach Osten *(German)* a German Nationalist political term referring to the drive for *lebensraum* ('living space') by military expansion eastwards.
egúngún *(East African)* ancestral masquerade
élan dash, sprint
en masse *(French)* all together; in a mass
ennui *(French)* boredom; mental weariness from lack of stimulation
epicure one who indulges in the pleasures of the table. Cf. Epicurus
Epicurus an ancient Greek philosopher who identified pleasure with virtue
esse videatur *(Latin)* so it seems
faux pas *(French)* blunder, especially verbal
flamenco a Spanish gypsey dance
fritillary a type of butterfly

ghât *(Anglo-Indian)* mountain pass; steps to a river
Gyppos menservants
hookah *(Arabic)* an oriental pipe with a long tube which passes through water to cool the smoke
hors d'oevres *(French)* a first course of a meal; an appetizer
hypothec property belonging to a debtor
khamseen the hot Egyptian wind
kirsch a cherry liqueur, especially German
lieder *(German)* German Romantic songs
Maeterlinck, Morris (1862-1949), Belgian philosopher, poet and symbolist writer who won the Nobel Prize for Literature in 1911.
manzanilla *(Spanish)* a dry sherry
minuet a dance
morris a dance
Muezzin a Muslim crier
nach *(German)* towards, cf. ***Drang nach Osten***
naïf *(French)* naïve, innocent
Nibelungen (from Scandinavian myth) a member of a Scandinavian race of dwarfs, owners of a hoard of gold and magic treasures who were ruled by Nibelung, king of Nibelheim (land of mist).
nihilist proponent of an extreme form of scepticism maintaining that nothing has real existence; anti-establishment
nouveau riche *(French)* one who has acquired wealth recently, especially one who displays this ostentatiously
papier mâché *(French)* paper pulp used for molding, e.g. into boxes
pas seul *(French)* a dance for one person (*pas de deux,* a dance for two)
patio *(Spanish)* a paved garden area; courtyard adjoining a house
pensione *(French)* a boarding house
phalanx a line of soldiers in, or ready for, military combat
Philistinism indifference to culture. Philistine - an inhabitant of ancient Palestine
pisé de terre *(French)* the worst of earth (e.g. dung)
Promethean a hope in the gods for help (ancient Greek)
punkah *(Anglo-Indian)* a large fan
Rhodian ex-student or alumni of Rhodes University in Grahamstown, South Africa
Rider Haggard, Sir Henry (1856-1925) English author of colonial literature and mythical tales of adventure in Africa, among them *King Solomon's Mines*
Rimbaud, Arthur (1854-1891), a French symbolist poet whose verse was fiercely independent of religious, political and literary orthodoxy.
Sahib *(Indian)* master
shamba *(Anglo-African)* farm; smallholding
southpaw left-handed person, especially a boxer
sporran *(Scots)* a kilt pouch
strathspey a Scottish dance
Uhuru political cry for independence from colonisation, espe-

cially in Africa

verboten *(German)* forbidden

zenanas *(Indian)* women's apartments

Zola, Emil (1840-1902), French author whose work focused on vice, human appetites and instincts.

ACKNOWLEDGEMENTS

Oxford University Press (Southern Africa) is grateful for permission to use the following copyright material:

1. Herman Charles Bosman: *Innocents Abroad* from ***A cask of jerepigo*** (1964). Reprinted by permission of Human & Rousseau (Pty) Ltd.
2. Aldous Huxley: *Why not stay at home?* from ***Along the road.*** Reprinted by permission of Mrs Laura Huxley and Chatto and Windus.
3. Laurie Lee: *Spain revisited* from ***A rose for winter.*** Reprinted by permission of The Hogarth Press.
4. J B Priestley: *Lilac in the rain* from ***Self-selected essays.*** Reprinted by permission of Mrs J B Priestley.
5. Roy Campbell: *The Camargue* from ***Light on a dark horse*** (1951). Reprinted by permission of Teresa Campbell, Francisco Campbell Custodio and Ad. Donker (Pty) Ltd.
6. Robert Louis Stevenson: *Travels with a donkey* (Routledge and Kegan Paul), in public domain.
7. G K Chesterton: *The ballad of a strange town* from ***Tremendous trifles*** (Methuen), in public domain.
8. Ernest Hemingway: *Paris* from ***A moveable feast.***
9. G K Chesterton: *On two cities* from ***All things considered*** (Methuen London), in public domain.
10. D H Lawrence: *Dull London* from ***Selected essays*** (Heinemann), in public domain.
11. Herman Charles Bosman: *So this is London* from ***Uncollected essays.*** Reprinted by permission of The Struik Publishing Group.
12. Charles Lamb: *Life Awake* from ***Literary friendships in the age of Wordsworth,*** edited by RC Bald (1932). Reprinted by permission of Octagon Books, a division of Hippocrene Books, Inc.
13. Sarah Gertrude Millin: *The reeling earth* - combined extracts from ***The reeling earth*** and ***World blackout.*** Reprinted by permission of A P Watt Ltd on behalf of The Society to Help Civilian Blind.
14. Virginia Woolf: *The artist and the war.* Extracts from ***The letters of Virginia Woolf,*** vol. 6, edited by Nigel Nicolson and Joanne Trautmann. Reprinted by permission of The Hogarth Press.
15. Kingsley Fairbridge: *Bowled over* from ***The autobiography of Kingsley Fairbridge*** (Oxford University Press), in public domain.
16. Dylan Thomas: *Eisteddfod* from ***Miscellany Two*** (Dent). Reprinted by permission of David Higham Associates Ltd.
17. John Betjeman: *An approach to Oxford* from ***The best of Betjeman*** (Penguin). Reprinted by permission of John Murray (Publishers) Ltd.
18. Richard Rive: *Of eccentrics and eccentricities* from ***Writing black*** (1981). Reprinted by permission of David Philip Publishers, Cape Town.

19. Wole Soyinka: *Strange things*. Extracts from ***Aké***. Reprinted by permission of David Philip Publishers, Cape Town.
20. Guy Butler: *West Africa* from ***A local habitation.*** Reprinted by permission of David Philip Publishers, Cape Town.
21. Evelyn Waugh: *Tinka Tinka* from ***A tourist in Africa*** (Methuen). Reprinted by permission of the Peters Fraser and Dunlop Group Ltd.
22. Shiva Naipaul: *Bright lights*. Extracts from ***North of South*** (1978). Reprinted by permission of Andre Deutsch Ltd.
23. Guy Butler: *Among great ghosts* from ***Bursting world.*** Reprinted by permission of David Philip Publishers, Cape Town.
24. Laurens van der Post: *The ambivalent Cape* from ***Yet being someone other.*** Reprinted by permission of The Hogarth Press.
25. Olive Schreiner: *A glimpse of Cape Town in the 1870s* from ***The silver plume,*** in public domain.
26. Richard Rive: *Life in District Six* from ***'Buckingham Palace', District Six.*** Reprinted by permission of David Philip Publishers, Cape Town.
27. Lawrence Green: *The happy isle* from ***A decent fellow doesn't work: experiences of an easy-going traveller in search of pleasure, interesting people and places inside and outside Southern Africa - with a little wisdom gathered along the way*** (Timmins). Reprinted by permission of The Struik Publishing Group.
28. Herman Charles Bosman: *Home Town* from ***A cask of jerepigo*** (1964). Reprinted by permission of Human and Rousseau (Pty) Ltd.
29. Thomas Pringle: *Landing at Algoa Bay* from ***Narrative of a residence in South Africa.*** Reprinted by permission of The Struik Publishing Group.
30. Olive Schreiner: *A glimpse of Cradock in the 1870s* from ***The silver plume,*** in public domain.
31. Guy Butler: *Waiting for the rains* from ***Karoo morning.*** Reprinted by permission of David Philip Publishers, Cape Town.
32. Francis Carey Slater: *Alice and the Amatolas* from ***Settler's heritage.*** Reprinted by permission of Lovedale Press.
33. Laurens van der Post: *The lost world of the Kalahari*. Extracts from ***The lost world of the Kalahari*** (1958). Reprinted by permission of The Hogarth Press.
34. William Plomer: *Upstart City* from ***William Plomer, The South African autobiography.*** Reprinted by permission of David Philip Publishers, Cape Town.
35. Herman Charles Bosman: *Johannesburg* from ***A cask of jerepigo*** (1964). Reprinted by permission of Human and Rousseau (Pty) Ltd.
36. Sarah Gertrude Millin: *The centre of South Africa* from ***The night is long.*** Reprinted by permission of A P Watt Ltd on behalf of The Society to Help Civilian Blind.
37. Es'kia Mpahlele: *Life in the locations* from ***Down Second Avenue.*** Reprinted by permission of Faber and Faber Ltd.
38. William Plomer: *Tropical outpost* from ***William Plomer: the South African autobiography.*** Reprinted by permission of David Philip Publishers, Cape Town.
39. Alan Paton: *Pietermaritzburg: the lovely city* from ***Towards the mountain.*** Reprinted by permission of David Philip Publishers, Cape Town.

40. Roy Campbell: *Durban Breakwater* from ***Light on a dark horse*** (1951). Reprinted by permission of Teresa Campbell, Francisco Campbell Custodio and Ad. Donker (Pty) Ltd.
41. Lionel Abrahams: *On being here* from ***Lionel Abrahams: a reader.*** Also published in ***Leadership Magazine*** (1985). Reprinted by permission of Ad. Donker and Lionel Abrahams.
42. Rupert Brooke: *Niagara Falls* from ***Letters from America*** (Pan Macmillan), in public domain.
43. John Steinbeck: *Of strangers and barbarians* from ***Travels with Charley*** copyright © 1961, 1962 by the Curtis Publishing Co, Inc. Copyright © 1962 by John Steinbeck, reproduced by permission of Curtis Brown Ltd, London.
44. Stuart Cloete: *The wonder city of the world* from ***The gambler*** (Collins). Reprinted by permission of The International Press Agency (Pty.) Ltd.
45. Rudyard Kipling: *The City of Dreadful Night* from ***Life's handicap - being stories of mine own people*** (A P Watt Ltd), in public domain.
46. Gerald Durrell: *The living world* from ***My family and other animals*** (Harper Collins). Reprinted by permission of Harper Collins Publishers Limited (London).
47. Kingsley Amis: *Is the travel book dead?* Copyright 1955 Kingsley Amis, first published in ***The Spectator***, London. Reprinted by permission of Jonathan Clowes Ltd., London, on behalf of Kingsley Amis.

While every effort has been made to trace and acknowledge copyright holders, this has not always been possible.

Should any infringement have occurred, apologies are tendered and any omissions will be rectified in the event of a reprint.